THE TUTTLE TWINS

and the

PLAY FOR POWER

CONNOR BOYACK

ILLUSTRATIONS BY ELIJAH STANFIELD

Libertas Press
2183 W Main Street, A102
Lehi, UT 84043

The Tuttle Twins and the Play for Power

Edited by Chris Jones

ISBN-13 978-1-943521-67-8 (paperback)

10 9 8 7 6 5 4 3

For bulk orders, send inquires to info@libertas.org.

LIBERTAS
INSTITUTE

Other titles by the author:

Skip College: Launch Your Career Without Debt, Distractions, or a Degree

Lessons from a Lemonade Stand: An Unconventional Guide to Government

Feardom: How Politicians Exploit Your Emotions and What You Can Do to Stop Them

The Tuttle Twins children's book series

Ethan Tuttle rested his chin on his palm, watching the passing scenery out the car window. No, not watching. His eyes simply slid over the trees, parked cars, greening lawns, and sprinklers watering dead patches of spring grass. He ticked the window down just a couple of inches, which let a thin stream of cool breeze wash over his face. It smelled of roses, green growing things, and an infinite afternoon of boredom.

At least his sister Emily was roped into the same afternoon he was. She sat against the far window, looking out in much the same way Ethan did. She, however, had her phone, and checked it periodically for texts, Instagram, and Twitter. Ethan should have had his and been ears-deep in music or a TED talk or *something*, but he didn't have his phone, and he didn't want to think about why not. Despite the riot of spring outside the car, Ethan's personal weather system was stuck on midwinter, and it was looking to be cold, and gray, and everlasting.

At least Emily wouldn't be carsick this time. Long, flat freeways were her best friend.

He sighed. His breath fogged the window for a fleeting second, then the breeze dried it, leaving nothing behind.

"Don't act as if I'm taking you to be served as a human sacrifice," Mom said from the driver's seat. She tilted her head up and got an eye on him through the rearview mirror. Her eyebrow crooked upward.

"They probably wouldn't take us anyway," Emily said. "We're supposed to be pure if we're going to appease the gods."

Ethan closed his eyes. The collar of his shirt dug into his neck. He reached up and adjusted it, but it still itched. It was bad enough that he had to put on a suit—his one, Sunday church-going suit—on an otherwise perfectly good Friday afternoon—the first one with any real warmth in it this whole year—to go to the funeral of someone he didn't even know.

He opened his mouth to say something he knew he would later regret, when his father said, "Uh, Ethan? Better not." Dad looked back from the passenger seat to catch Ethan's eye.

"What?" Ethan said, aggrieved. "I didn't even say anything!"

"That's right!" Dad said, brightly. "And it would be so good for everyone if that stayed true, don't you think? You're close to earning that new phone you want. I'd hate for you to have to start over."

"I know this isn't what you most want to do today," Mom said, "but it will mean a lot to me and your father, and it will mean a lot to the Fordes."

"This funeral is important," Dad said, ignoring Ethan sighing hugely behind him. "Dennis Forde was one of the best things ever to happen to this state. It's a privilege to be able to go and pay our respects to a truly great man."

"So sad," Mom said, changing lanes with care as she pulled onto the interstate. "He was only getting started, really. You should have heard the things your Aunt Cathy was telling me they were going to do."

"What happened to him?" Emily said. She paused a moment to take a selfie, her fingers in a peace sign. Ethan always thought it was funny when she did that, as if she were one of those kids that had to be "relevant" all the time online.

"I knew he was sick, I think," Ethan said.

"Brain cancer," Dad said.

Ethan thought that sounded like no fun at all. Perhaps his life wasn't as bleak and hopeless as he had been feeling. "Is that who Aunt Cathy worked for?"

Dad nodded. "That's right. She loved Dennis. Heck, I did too. I used to do business with him when he was an attorney. Most attorneys are, ahem, the sorts of people you want to watch pretty closely, but Dennis was as honest as George Washington."

"I'd have trusted Dennis with my children," Mom said, very quietly.

"We did. That's why we voted for him."

The speed of the car made it hard to hear with the whistling wind. Ethan rolled his window up. "What was so good about him?" he said.

Mom looked at Dad. Dad looked back, as if saying, "You go first."

"Dennis Forde never wanted to be a politician. He just liked helping people," Dad said.

Mom quoted, "Anyone who is capable of getting themselves made president should on no account be allowed to do the job. Douglas Adams. The only people I trust to do a good job in government are the people that don't want a job in government."

"Precisely. When the Secretary of State position came open five years ago, a group of us had to practically lock him in a hotel room and threaten him with house arrest if he didn't run. He had enough money to make a good campaign of it. Everyone liked him."

"Not *everyone*," Dad said with a significant glance.

"Okay, not everyone. But he was honest to a fault. You always knew where you stood with him. He tolerated no funny business, and in his position, he could have been a real scoundrel. He treated his staff like family. Us too."

"Do you remember going waterskiing with their family that one time?" Dad said. "You were maybe six or seven."

"Wait, was his boat a bright yellow?" Emily said. She put her phone away and leaned forward between the front seats.

"That's the one. The *Eternal Sunshine*," Dad said.

"I remember that," Ethan said. "That was him? I thought he was cool."

"He was," Dad said. "But he was more than cool. He was generous, kind, and good. He always had time for kids, business, his family... Heaven knows how he managed it all."

"He was our friend," Mom said, with a catch in her voice. There didn't seem to be anything more to say.

Ethan turned back to the window as the silence stretched. Helena wasn't far from their home in Spoonerville, and they pulled off the exit to downtown within a few minutes. The traffic was awful. Everyone in town was trying to get out for the weekend, and a thin line of cars was headed for the Capitol, where Dennis Forde lay with full state honors under the cupola. Ethan had never liked the building—too cold and empty.

It loomed up in the front window as the car climbed the hill. Already he could tell it was going to be neither cold nor empty this time. A long string of dark-clad mourners streamed up the grounds to join a line that snaked out the door, down the marble steps onto the walkways through the grass, and toward the parking lot.

Great, Ethan thought sarcastically. *This afternoon wasn't going to go quickly, was it?*

But part of Ethan was curious about what sort of person could be so popular he'd have thousands of people come to his funeral on a beautiful Friday.

They stood in line for an hour before even getting into the Capitol, where the line circled the rotunda before even approaching the flag-draped coffin. Thirty more minutes before they got to the coffin itself. All around them bubbled the low murmur of whispered, half-voiced conversation, and Ethan had to agree the surroundings were perfect for such a solemn occasion. It was like a church, tall and echoey, with the smell of incense. The murmur of voices lent the impression that there were thousands more souls arrayed in the space, not just along the ground, but in the air above as well.

When they were finally next at the coffin, Ethan saw there was another line, just after the box. Two women

stood there—he knew one of them well enough—and three children, all of them around the twins' age.

"Hello, Aunt Cathy," Emily said, and stepped up to hug her. Next to Emily's aunt, a dark-eyed woman with chocolate-brown skin smiled a little sadly and glanced at the children, who were obviously hers. Ethan found himself next to the body. The casket was open, the body laid out inside a shiny wooden shell. He didn't look much like a dead man, Ethan decided. Mr. Forde looked like he might wake up at any moment, wink at Ethan, and say, "How did I get here?" That made Ethan smile, just a little to himself, thinking about it.

He was a good-looking man too, with just a hint of gray at the temples. Not very old—not much older than Mom and Dad. Ethan looked up as Mom embraced her sister and imagined what it would be like to be one of the kids standing there, watching people file past his own father.

And then he was in front of his aunt, with an awkward two feet of space between them. Shake her hand? Hug her?

Invite her for dinner?

If you think Ethan should invite Aunt Cathy for dinner on his own initiative, turn to page 167.

If you think Ethan should probably clear it with Mom first, turn to page 300.

"Remember, team, rule number 14 dash B paragraph 12 sub-paragraph 9: It's much easier to kick someone in the butt when your friends are holding them steady." Emily beetled her brows and lowered her voice, as if she were a back-room dealmaker. Kohn's mouth twitched.

"I know you think we did this for principle, and we did. But the most important principle of all is that winning is the only thing. Vince Lombardi said that. We may not get all of what we want by playing ball with these people. But if we don't win, we get *none* of what we want, plus a whole lot of other people don't get what they want. Your parents. Your children. The president. Ultimately the United States of America. It's worth a little flexibility to gain a whole lot more power. So I expect you all to do what has to be done—within the rules, of course—to win. And when we're back in D.C., we'll be able to make some changes to the system. We'll never be able to do that from Helena."

She turned to Kohn. "How did I do?"

His eyes were hooded, but he gave a brief nod. "Pretty well. I think maybe you should be the one sitting in that chair instead of me."

"You have to be thirty to run for senate. Maybe in a couple of decades."

"I'm not committing," Kohn said, "but you made a good argument, and it's hard to think of refutations that would make any difference. They're powerful people."

"George Washington didn't want us to have political parties," Ethan said.

"If only he were here," Kohn said. He shook himself, like a man waking up. "You two have someplace to be, I believe."

"Right," Ethan said. "We should get going. I imagine we'll see each other later tonight."

"You will. And thank you. I know people probably think you're too young to be doing these jobs, but I get so tired of being surrounded by people who do this for a living. It's refreshing to get a point of view that isn't tainted by thirty years of political fighting."

"Anytime, sir," Emily said. "We'll be hard to miss."

Kohn thanked them again, and all three of them went out into the hallway. Two staffers from fundraising stood by the bathroom, talking baseball. At the other end, by the receptionist's desk, the three RNC people were waiting with a woman the twins didn't remember seeing before. With some kind of Jedi-like foreknowledge, Pascoe emerged from an office the moment the twins got even with the door.

"This is Melissa," he said, introducing Emily and Ethan to the woman. "Emily and Ethan Tuttle." He turned to the twins. "She's the point person on the advance team today. You take orders from her. Because I certainly do."

"Is there a rule for that?" Emily said.

He blinked. "Forty-three." Then he went back inside.

"Informative," Ethan said.

Melissa smiled. "It's my favorite, actually: Promptly report your action to the one who requested it. You'd be surprised how often that rule is applicable. Let's get going."

There was room in the truck for the three from the RNC, but they said they'd drive on their own. They sniffed at the twins but didn't say anything. Ed appeared from out of nowhere and handed the truck keys to Melissa, and the twins followed her out to the vehicle. They climbed in and pulled out of the parking lot, the RNC people following them.

Melissa introduced herself as Ed's daughter, a campaign veteran and occasional body or advance-team person. "I heard a lot about you the last few weeks. Pappy was very impressed with you both."

"Ed's an interesting fellow to work with," Emily said.

"He said the same about you."

Melissa was tall and willowy, like a river reed, with long hair so blonde it was nearly silver. Her oval face was forbidding, and she had a nose like the business end of a knife, but her green eyes were kind and her voice soft and welcoming. A study in contrast, this woman.

She might have had a soft voice, but she handled the truck like a NASCAR driver.

"Remember we've got people following us," Ethan said.

"Following is the operative word. They're from D.C. I'm sure they'll keep up."

Ethan wasn't so sure they'd even be able to, but they did make record time out to the venue. There was a lot to do. Every horizontal surface needed a covering of cloth or campaign materials—especially the ones with the donation envelopes stapled to the back—and every vertical surface got either a poster or some red, white, and blue bunting. The truck held endless rolls of the stuff.

Ethan was sure the RNC people would just hang about getting in the way, but they didn't. Right from their arrival they pitched in and added muscle and good ideas to the typed-up plan brandished by Melissa. By three in the afternoon, they had the place looking as good as it could.

"You've got clothes?" Melissa said.

"Backpacks, in the cab," Emily said.

"Suit up, then. I've got food for us here someplace. Or at least the caterer is supposed to. You can eat after you get changed."

It was a good thing the cab was roomy. There was plenty of space for the twins to shed their work clothes and get into Sunday best for the event.

Buttoning his shirt, Ethan said, "Do you think Kohn is going to take your advice? It was a good speech, by the way. I almost believed it."

"I think he was going to do that anyway," Emily said, sliding on her shoes, "which is part of the reason I gave the speech I did. But I think taking that road is legitimate. It might look to other people like selling out, but there are very big issues here. It's not simple. I'm not sure I would do it the way I said in my speech, but I can understand someone who would."

Ethan laid his suit coat in his lap. "I think you can't make that decision when you're two months into a campaign for the Senate. You either make that decision way before that, or you kind of lose the choice, don't you?"

The two of them sat for a minute, staring out the window. The light was just about how it had been yesterday when they'd been there. Macintyre came out of the building, the phone to her ear, talking fast. They couldn't hear what she was saying, but she didn't look happy.

"It's a weird job, working for the party instead of a particular candidate," Emily said.

"Remind me not to take it if they offer," Ethan said. And they opened the door and got out.

Three hundred forty people is a huge crowd. It filled the parking lot and spilled onto the surrounding streets. Emily's finger got tired from pressing the button to shoot photos, and Ethan never wanted to send another tweet in his life, but the crowd roared over Kohn's speech. Pascoe, after a short conversation with Melissa, gave them both a thumbs-up.

By ten, most of the people were winding up and the people were strolling out the door to their cars. Emily and Ethan thanked everyone for coming, one at a time. Several stopped and thanked them for their work.

"We'll send photos to the Rotary clubs," Ethan said to one of the attendees, "I hope we got a good one of you."

"I don't take good photos," the man said, laughing, "So if it's a good one, it's not of me!" His group laughed as if he'd made a fearsome joke, and they moved off under the streetlamps.

"Well, for a group that hasn't had anything to drink, they sure are happy people," Emily said.

"Did you hear some of the stuff they said at the beginning of their meeting?" Ethan said, waving goodbye to another couple. "Rotarians are serious about their cheerfulness. And any group that's worked so hard in so many countries to provide clean water and education to children is okay by me."

It took until almost eleven for everyone to leave, but they were finally able to start taking down the signs and the bunting and collecting the campaign materials for re-use.

Emily went and found Pascoe. She handed him the camera. "Rule number 43 obeyed," she said.

"Well done," Pascoe said. "You two were terrific. Thank you."

"How did the campaign do this evening?"

"Hard to know with Rotarians because there ain't a more positive group of people on God's earth. But I'd say we did pretty well. How did the social media stuff go?"

Ethan tapped open an app. "We didn't trend, but there are a lot of retweets. We got some publicity. The news people all left early, but their reportage sounded positive. The channel 8 woman said we'd make the late news tonight."

"That's good. Dunno what more we could have asked for from it," Pascoe said. "Other than big, fat checks, of course."

"Did we get big, fat checks?" Emily said.

"Some, sure. Lots of other ways to donate, too. People can do it from their phones now. Won't know for a few days. And there are those who want to meet with the body before they dip in the wallet." Pascoe tugged some bunting down and stuffed it into a rolling garbage can.

"All in all, coulda been worse," he said. Some of the starch seemed to have gone out of him. It was late, after all, and he didn't look like a guy who slept all that much.

Melissa came over and gave him a quick hug. "I'm going to get these two home to bed. They're way past curfew. You okay? Looks like most everything is done."

"I suppose. The rest can prob'ly be done by the venue people." He stretched as if his back were a pipe cleaner in need of straightening.

"Rule number 27," Melissa said.

"Good one. I need to remember that."

"There's no rest for the wicked?" Emily guessed.

"Remember it's a long ball game," Pascoe said. "Get out of here. Noon tomorrow, at the office."

"We'll be there," Ethan said.

The next couple of months was more of the same, a practically endless round of meetings, events, discussions, social media campaigns, photography, and fundraising. Through it all, Kohn's lead in the polls continued to grow steadily. The RNC people put their money where their threats were. Ads with other Republican leaders talking about how they needed Randall Kohl in the Senate and how he would be an effective Senator were pumped into the state.

For all the hype about how glamorous political campaigns were, the twins began to see that they were just jobs—interesting sometimes, but often long and dull and not much different than any other kind. They did get to see people and talk about government and what they thought the country needed to do, which they guessed they probably wouldn't have done at a fast-food job.

Pascoe kept up a running education with his assignments as well as his rules. Some they came to know by heart—like 14 (Remember the other side has troubles too) and 12 (Keep your eye on the main chance, and don't stop to kick every barking dog), but probably their favorite was 45: Pray as if it all depends on God; work as if it all depends on you.

And they did. They were footsore and as weary as a cart-horse on market day, but they showed up and did their jobs, always reporting their actions to the ones who requested them (Rule number 43). They were treated more and more like equals by the staff and given more and more responsibility, though that responsibility didn't come with raises, unfortunately. Still, Emily was able to save up a few thousand that, together with her other savings, would get her a decent car.

Homeschooling allowed them to keep working right through to election day too, which delighted Pascoe. He said he didn't know how he could get along without them.

Election day itself arrived. Macintyre returned with her two companions, bringing the best wishes from the president and the success party. Emily was on body duty that night at one of Helena's swankiest downtown hotels. The polls closed at 8, and a few minutes before, Pascoe sent her up to get Kohn from his hotel room and bring him down to the ballroom, where hundreds of well-wishers had gathered to party.

"And bring him down the freight elevator. Press will be camped out at the elevator bank, and we wanna get him into the party without having to get fancy with his statements."

"Are you sure?" Emily said. "What about Rule number 15?"

"The press are not good guys. Rule number 15 does not apply. We don't have to remember to treat good guys better than bad guys where the press is concerned. Skedaddle. He has to be down here in twelve minutes. On your honor now."

"On my honor. Already gone."

Emily rode up to the seventeenth floor and knocked on 1714. The door opened and there stood the stunning Mrs. Kohn, Daniela. "Emily. Come in. He's nearly ready."

She walked into a suite the size of a baseball diamond. Sounds of banging came from the doorway to the left. Daniela went through the one on the right, saying over her shoulder, "I'm just getting my wrap, and then I'm ready. He'd already be finished if he hadn't had a call with CNN just a minute ago."

Emily was going to be sorry not to see Daniela as often any more. Being her assistant at barbecues, standing at the back of the room during her husband's speeches—Emily was going to miss all of that. She'd come to see Daniela as a friend.

"Emily! Is that you?" Kohn said through the doorway.

"It is. Yes, sir."

"Sit down somewhere. I'll be right out."

She wanted to sit—the overstuffed loveseat by the window looked soft enough to sandwich between graham crackers and chocolate—but her legs jumped and pinged, and her heart thudded in her chest. No matter how she told herself the win was in the bag, she couldn't get her heart to believe it. Not all the way.

Kohn came out, tying his red tie to his crisp white shirt above navy-blue pants with a delicate pinstripe. "You look great," he said.

Emily smoothed her dark burgundy dress and smiled.

"You nervous?"

"Terrified," she said. "Aren't you?"

"I'll never admit it, but I haven't been this nervous since the night I proposed to Daniela. How do I look?"

"Underdressed. Get a jacket."

He laughed and put another swish on the knot in his tie. He pulled the knot tight and touched the bottom to make sure it bisected his belt buckle. Perfect. He paused a moment.

"Can I ask you something?" he said.

"You employ me. I serve at your sufferance. You can ask me anything you like."

"And you'll tell me the truth because you always do. It's your defining characteristic. It's why you're in the position you're in. You know that an ounce of loyalty is worth a pound of cleverness."

She smiled. "Rule number 21."

"You're far too smart for your own good." He paused again, and she sensed that he was nervous—not campaign nervous. This was something else.

"Did I do the right thing?" he said abruptly.

"Running for the Senate?"

"Saying yes to the party. The RNC."

"They did come through. They did all they said they would."

"Would I have won without it?"

Emily shifted sideways. Her right hand rubbed her left arm. "Aslan says you never get to know what would have happened."

He chuckled. "No point in arguing with Aslan. But seriously. Suppose I win—"

"You're going to."

"—will the win be worth it? Will I be able to do what I set out to do?"

"More than if you lose."

He ran a hand through his hair. Was it a little more gray than it had been when she'd first seen it?

"Yeah. Well, I suppose that will have to be enough." He went into his room, his spit-shined shoes making no noise on the thick green carpet.

Daniela came out, her cream wrap around her tanned shoulders. Her eyes followed her husband's trail as if she could see the warmth lingering in the air.

"He ask you whether it was worth it?" she said softly.

Emily nodded. She never quite knew what to say to this glamorous, powerful woman. She intimidated her far more than her husband did.

"And what did you tell him?"

Emily swallowed. "I didn't."

Daniela put a hand on her shoulder, her eyes still on the lit oblong of Kohn's doorway. "You can't, anyway. It's not either going to 'be worth it' or 'not be worth it.' We'll *make* it worth it, or we won't. It's not a thing the universe bestows on us. We decide with every breath we take."

"That really should be rule number 1," Emily said.

Daniela's laugh was the ringing of a crystal glass. "Ah, I see Will has filled your head with Morton Blackwell's Rules."

"I had originally thought they belonged to Pascoe and Randall. They quote them all the time."

She shook her head. "Nope. Morton's the founder of the Leadership Institute where those guys trained. Morton was handing them out long before those guys got hold of them. He'll be pleased that they are filtering down to the rising generation."

"I'm serious about the rule thing," Emily said.

"I know, dear girl. But there are things too important to be encapsulated in an eight-word rule. This might be one of them." She tugged a stray fringe of her shawl back over her shoulder. "Regardless, we've done what we've done. All we can do is make the best of it."

"If we win," Emily said.

"Oh, no, Emily. If we win, surely," she said, striding across the carpet to her husband's door, "but even more if we *lose*."

They made it to the ballroom without being accosted by the gangs of press assembled to write and broadcast their reports about the newly-minted US Senator. Kohn mounted the dais to thunderous cheers and called for his campaign staff to join him and his wife.

"I know it won't be long now," he said. "I just want to thank all of you now, when we don't know the results, so that you know I'm truly grateful, win or lose. You are the reason I did this crazy thing in the first place."

This brought cheering loud enough to strip wallpaper. Then the news anchors came on, and all eyes swiveled to the huge TV screens on either side of the stage.

A voice in Emily's ear. "Do we want him out in public when the returns come in?" Ethan said.

"Not our job now," she said. "He's gone where we can't help."

In front of them, just behind the candidate, Ed and Pascoe shook hands and leaned in to hug one another. Pascoe whispered something.

"What rule do you suppose he was quoting there?" Ethan said.

"Has to be one of them," she said.

The announcer pressed her earpiece and said in a voice amplified by megawatt equipment, "We are ready to report the first results from Montana. It appears we have a clear leader in the swing state."

The room erupted in cheers. It didn't take long for the suspense—such as it was—to be over. News organizations from coast to coast waited only half an hour or so to call the race for Randall Kohn, the new junior senator from the state of Montana.

Kohn took the dais one more time to give his acceptance speech. He waved to the jubilant crowd, surging over the floor like the heaving sea. Flashes from cameras went off as if it were the Fourth of July. Kohn and his wife went from one end of the dais to the other, waving and pointing, holding their clasped hands above their heads, the champions of the evening.

Finally the crowd began to chant, "Speech!"

Kohn moved toward the podium, wading through the crowd of staff and friends, a huge smile on his face.

It only wavered once, when he was nearing the microphone. Just before he got there, Macintyre stepped forward and leaned toward him to whisper in his ear. His face flashed from joy to some other, less-happy emotion, but he nodded and stepped to the mic.

"So it begins," Emily said.

"Yeah," Ethan said. "But what is 'it'?"

THE END

Ethan put his hand over the phone. "It's Posey Sandborn. Sandborn Electric. Can you take the call?"

From across the room, a thin, tough woman—the Cathy Harmon Campaign's fundraising director—got up from her battered, second-hand desk and limped across the floor, her hand outstretched. "Angela Hernandez," she said, taking the phone.

For a few minutes, all she said was "uh huh," and "that's right." Down the narrow, dimly-lit hallway, someone made microwave popcorn. The smell made Ethan's stomach rumble.

Then there was a long pause, and Angela said, "How long have you been in business?" She saw the look on Ethan's face and clicked over to the speakerphone so he could hear.

"Twenty-eight years," Sandborn said.

"That's a long time. You started the business from scratch?"

"Well, my father had a small handyman business. Just three or four guys. He brought me along on all his jobs, and taught me to do what he was doing. Pretty soon it was me running the company, and we took off from there."

"How old were you when your father started taking you along?"

"Six. Seven."

"So," Angela said, "is it fair to say that if you hadn't been able to go with your father on those jobs, that he wouldn't have taught you those things?"

"Probably."

"And if you hadn't learned those things from your father, would you have gone to school to become a journeyman electrician?"

"Heck, no. I hated going with him. I only learned what he was doing because it was that or die of boredom."

"Do you regret it?"

She laughed, harsh and unpleasant over the tinny speaker. "No. It was good for me. I wouldn't be here if it weren't for that."

"So what would you say if I told you there's legislation right now to make it so nobody ever gets to go to work with their father on projects like this?"

"I'd say it was nuts."

"And I'd say you were right, except you just spent time telling me that Louis Sulla was the fella that was going to look out for your interests. Who do you think is behind that legislation?"

A silence fell.

"Don't get me wrong. He's not sponsoring it. And it doesn't have a title like 'Stop Young Kids From Learning Useful Skills Act.'"

Ethan cobbled the acronym together in his head and decided SYKFLUSA was probably not a good nickname for a bill.

"It's all about safety," Angela said. "Keep kids safe. Keep them off the worksite. Keep them away from things that could hurt them. If they do get to come watch Mom or Dad work, they have to wear all kinds of safety gear."

"Wait though, that sounds reasonable," Sandborn said.

"It always does. But think it through. What would have happened if your father had to outfit you in non-conductive thick rubber gloves, special aprons, goggles, hard hat, all that gear? Would he have done it so he could take you along?"

Another silence, somewhat briefer. Then Sandborn said, "No. He wouldn't have." Ethan could tell from her voice that she had realized something. He realized the same thing—there could have been a law that prevented him from tagging along with his parents too. And what then? Bad for business, sure—but bad for *everyone*.

"So you'd be an accountant now, and my house would still have unsafe wiring because Sandborn Electric—the only people who cared about my crappy house in my crappy part of town—wouldn't have come out and done the work on my promise to pay over time. You think Behemoth Electric and Plumbing would have given me terms?"

"Not on your life."

"Not on my life. So you think about it, Posey. You look at this kind of bill, and you decide who it's really protecting. Is it because Louis Sulla and Behemoth Electric and their lackey Tad Middleton in the legislature are lying awake at night worried about kids getting hurt working with their folks on the job, or is it because they see smaller businesses coming up in the rearview and they wonder who else is out there making real competition for them? Who could they stop, right now, by making it just a little more difficult to get started? Isn't this how Behemoth stays at the top of the food chain? Not by being the best, but by eliminating their competition?"

No response. But Ethan knew they all knew the answer. He's seen it himself, up close, in what the papers called the "Food Truck Fiasco." They'd won that battle, but very often big business likes to use the power of government to impose regulations that are an annoyance for themselves, but crippling for their competition. Angela had nailed it.

Angela winked at Ethan. "You think about that for a couple of hours, then I'm going to call you back, and you're going to write Cathy Harmon a check." And Angela hung up.

Ethan sat back in his flimsy plastic chair. It groaned underneath him as if it had a personal protest. "That was… pretty good," he said.

"Well, I'm pretty good," Angela said, handing the phone back to Ethan.

"I can't believe you talked to one of the richest women in Montana like that."

Angela laughed, a sound like a car trying to start. "She's a person. The only difference between rich people and me is they have more money. But Posey's hardscrabble, like me. She wasn't always rich. I know how to talk to people like that. Remind them who they were—who they still are, when they think about it."

"You came up from nothing?" Ethan said, putting his head on his hand, leaning on the card table he used for a desk.

"Haven't really come up yet, but that's a story for another time. Quit stalling and dial the phone. Who's next on the list?"

For the first time in a month, Ethan had the day off. Sort of. Dentist appointment in the morning, but that would only take a half hour or so if he didn't have any cavities, and he wasn't going to have any cavities because he brushed and flossed twice a day to keep Mom happy. And also because having your teeth drilled is terrible.

The main thing he wanted to do was go see his friend Gary. Summer was usually a time when he and Gary spent all their time together, but Gary was on a framing crew and worked when it was cool—mornings and evenings—while Ethan worked during the day. The office was a dump, but it had A/C. Loud, inefficient A/C, but A/C nonetheless. So as soon as he finished eating breakfast, Ethan texted Gary to find out if he was around.

"Sure," the message came back immediately. Both of those things were a surprise. Ethan usually had to wait several minutes to a couple of hours for Gary to hit him back, and he should have been on the job today, not waiting around at his house for his friend to text. But, good fortune was good fortune, and Ethan jumped on his bike and rode over.

Gary was sitting on his front porch, looking out over the riot of flowers in the garden, and looking like he'd been hit by a dump truck.

"Gar—what's the matter, man?" Ethan said, dumping his bike in the yard and jogging to the steps.

"Hey, Ethan." Gary didn't move, other than his jaw.

"What's up? You're usually at work. Day off?"

"Lots of them. I got laid off."

Ethan sat down next to his friend. He had to admit, the garden smelled great. That wasn't, apparently, helping Gary feel any better, though. "What happened? I thought you guys had all the work you could do."

"We did. We do. I mean *they* do. But now we have a new round of safety regulations, and it's costing a half-million dollars, so some people have to get laid off,

and the work is getting pushed back. The company has to save money."

"What kind of safety regulations?" Ethan asked, remembering yesterday's conversation with Posey Sandborn.

"Knee pads. Masks. Climbing gear. Ropes. Training. We have, I mean, *they* have, sixteen hours of 'safe work' certification they have to do before they can work on a house again. It all costs money. And because it costs money, it costs people too."

Ethan couldn't see how that could be. "Why not just charge people more? Then they could keep you on."

Gary turned his body a bit and lay down on the wooden slats of the porch. He stared up at the ceiling and sighed. "They probably will. Which will make everyone's houses cost more too, so that's nice right there, but in the meantime they can't take on more work, and they price guaranteed every job they're working right now. So no money for me."

"Just you?"

Gary shrugged. "Me and some other guys."

This was exactly what the phone call with Sandborn Electric had been about. Safety was important, Ethan thought—didn't everyone want to be safe?—but regulations weren't just wave-your-hand-and-presto kinds of things. They cost money. They cost time. And if they were expensive enough, they cost people their jobs. Was it worth it? Who was really counting the cost of the tradeoffs? Was this something people could take care of more easily and cheaply by themselves?

"What about the big contractors? They must be hurting too. Eventually, everyone should get their jobs back."

Gary closed his eyes. "Yeah, see, this is what people outside the industry think. This is what politicians think." Gary opened one eye and looked sourly at Ethan. "The big contractors have margins built into their pricing. They can get away with it because a lot of people are too lazy to check around, or they figure the big guys are better."

"Like when people buy new sound equipment at SuperSonic instead of online, where the same stuff is half the price."

"Yeah, that's a lot the same, I guess. Anyway, they've got the money to comply with all the regulations. But it's worse than that. My boss showed me how it worked. Here. Check this out." He tossed Ethan a plastic-and-fabric knee pad. It was scuffed and worn, clearly not new, but the fabric straps were sturdy and the plastic was as good as any catcher's shin guards.

"What am I looking at?" Ethan said, turning the thing over in his hands.

"Those are my knee pads."

"I thought you said you had to get new knee pads."

"I do. Or, I would."

"Why? These look fine."

"Those *are* fine. They're only a couple of weeks old. But I can't use them on the job anymore."

"Why on earth not?" Ethan said. He couldn't see anything wrong with them at all, except they were an offensive shade of blue.

"Because they don't meet the new regulations. They specify the kinds of knee pads that are allowed. These don't meet the specifications."

That could make sense, Ethan thought, if the new regulations were meant to upgrade the equipment and make it safer. "What's wrong with them?"

"They're not yellow."

"*What?*"

"Yep. And they're not made by the right company, and they don't have ventilation holes below the knee. But other than that, yeah, they're exactly the same."

"Who wrote that regulation? That's insane."

"One of the government safety agencies. They hired consultants from the big companies—of course—to help them write the regulations. You want to guess what kind of knee pads those guys have?"

"Don't tell me," Ethan said, his gut sinking. "They have little ventilation holes, and they're yellow."

"Bingo."

"Anyone on your crew ever have problems with their knees? Some kind of thing that would have been prevented by knee pads being yellow instead of blue?"

Gary opened the other eye. "Science proves yellow knee pads are three times as effective in preventing injury."

Ethan laughed. But then he stopped. "Seriously?"

"Come on. Of course the color doesn't matter. The yellow is just so the pads don't blend in with blue jeans so the inspectors can tell by driving by if they have them on."

Ethan gaped at him. So a legislator or a regulator—either would do—was interested in "safety." He thought tighter safety regulations would be a good idea and make him look good in the papers. He started on the rule, but he didn't know enough about the industry to make it applicable. He needed advice. So he got someone to advise him, and who did he know other than the big companies? Instead of blocking the legislation or the rule, which could be expensive and possibly illegal, they simply loaned their people to the regulator and wrote the legislation so that it appeared to increase safety—good for the government—while conforming to what the big companies were already doing, or could easily afford to do. That worked for them. Everyone won.

Except the company Gary had worked for. And Gary.

"That's terrible," Ethan said. "I can't believe that's what's going on."

"Believe it," Gary said. "I did get two weeks of pay out of the deal, so I have cash and a whole day to blow. Movies? Pizza? Ice cream?"

Ethan said, "I'm still employed, and I'm paying. And you haven't said anything yet that I didn't think was a good idea. Let's treat ourselves to all three!"

Ethan went back to the office the next day full of fire to right what he thought of as a huge injustice and, instead, got trapped in a meeting. But the meeting was part of his job, so he put up with it, and, as so often happens, it turned out to be a good thing.

Because it was a donor meeting, the attendees were the usual suspects: Aunt Cathy; Miss Finn, the campaign director; Angela, the fundraising director; and Emily, who was working as a sort of woman-about-town anywhere she was needed. The guests of honor today were a pair of executive types—an older gentleman in a tailored suit with his silver hair slicked back and a woman of slightly lesser age in a formal business suit, cobalt blue, with a cream-colored blouse and pearls. Her hair was a light shade of blonde, streaked and frosted. Both of them were very tan, as if they'd just come from vacation or something.

They were already deep in conversation with Aunt Cathy and Miss Finn before the twins arrived.

"I hope you don't mind," Cathy said. "This is my niece and nephew, and they're an integral part of the campaign staff here. I'd like them to sit in on our discussion."

"Of course, of course," the man said with a smile, revealing gleaming teeth, all the whiter against the dark tan of his skin. The woman sat primly with a tiny smile on her face that didn't come anywhere near her blue eyes.

"This is Julius Shearer, CEO of Springfield Power, and Harriet Kavner, who runs a media conglomerate, including KBBL and a couple of other TV and radio stations," Cathy said. The twins nodded to the guests, exchanged greetings with Miss Finn and Angela, and took up positions on the loveseat.

Cathy said, "We were just talking about fundraising. You know, I guess, that the campaign is proving to be more expensive than we thought, and Mr. Shearer and Ms. Kavner have some ideas about how to go about collecting additional funds."

"We could easily put a steering committee together with several well-known businesspeople. Parland Construction, for instance. Hemsath Real Estate. A few others. They'd bring a lot of money to the campaign," Shearer said.

"We're not bound by the same campaign contribution limits that federal candidates are," Kavner said, her voice smooth like poured honey. "We can drum up a lot more money in a lot less time."

Ethan didn't like the sound of any of this and tried catching Angela's eye. She pointedly ignored him and kept her gaze on the guests.

"We know you're a good person," Kavner went on. "Everyone says that Cathy Harmon was the key reason Dennis Forde was so successful as Secretary of State. You could be a real force for good if you could get the job."

Cathy held up a finger. "Thanks, but that's bull. Dennis Forde was successful because of who he was. I was privileged just to be a small part of it. Dial back the schmooze and just give it to me straight."

Shearer gave a little laugh and swallowed, but nodded. "Okay. Fair enough. I think Ms. Kavner's point is still valid, though. Sadly, we know Louis Sulla's people too, and he's got bankers and hedge fund managers crawling all over his campaign. I think it's fair to say it's no level playing field when it comes to resources," Shearer said, his eyes darting over the office, its shabby carpeting, second-hand desk, older loveseat, and couch. Just then, as if on cue, the local train went by. The look on Shearer's face said he didn't really have to make his point any clearer.

"What's in it for you?" Cathy said. "It's very nice of you to offer to help, but I can't help thinking there's some reason for you to be here other than fair play."

"Of course there is. Business and government have to work together for things to get done. We're eager to work with you—with all of you," Shearer said, indicating the whole group, "to make our community and our state a place that works for everyone."

Ethan raised his hand. He wasn't sure who was in charge of the meeting, so he looked back and forth from Aunt Cathy to the guests.

They didn't seem terribly sure, either. But finally, the corner of Aunt Cathy's mouth turned up, and she said, "Yes, Ethan? You have a question?"

"I do. Does this 'works for everyone' idea mean my friend Gary?"

Blank looks from the room. He knew there would be. That was sort of the point.

Cathy said, "I'm not sure..."

"Who Gary is? I know. He's not a big shot. He's just a friend of mine who lost his job."

"Times are hard," Kavner said, her face full of a sympathy that Ethan was pretty sure was false.

"He was in construction. Half the state has orange barrels on it."

"Quality employees are hard to find."

"He wasn't fired. He was laid off because his company had to spend a half-million dollars on new safety equipment and training when the company had never had an on-the-job injury in their eight years in business."

Kavner said, "I fail to see how that applies to our discussion here."

Ethan stopped talking to the businesspeople and focused on Aunt Cathy instead. Out of the corner of his eye, he could see Angela. He had her attention now, and he could have sworn she looked amused by his little outburst.

"It's about power, Aunt Cathy. All of this. The power to change the rules so the competition can't catch the bigger companies. Angela and I had this same conversation two days ago with a small electrician's outfit being squeezed by Behemoth Electrical. Which—I think I'm right about this—is a wholly-owned subsidiary of Springfield Power and Light." Now he turned to look at Shearer, and just for a moment he could tell he'd punctured the civilized image.

"Uh, we do own many different enterprises, yes, but at heart we're a small business still. I started Springfield Power myself, with nothing more than a small bank loan."

"Could you get that same loan today? Could I get it?" Angela said. "Did you support the banking regulation that increased collateral requirements for startup businesses? Surely you know the regulation I mean. Passed a couple of years back? There was significant lobbying about it. I think we're all curious as to which side of that argument you were on."

Both the businesspeople looked for a moment as if something in the office smelled very bad.

"Ms. Kavner, Mr. Shearer," Aunt Cathy said, "could I ask you to give us a moment? Clearly we need to have an internal discussion. I doubt it will take more than a couple of minutes. Emily, can I have you escort our guests to the lobby and see if they'd like a cup of coffee or some juice?"

Emily's face said she'd rather cuddle a scorpion, but she got up with a passable imitation of a smile and opened the door with a gesture inviting the guests to follow her. Angela got up and closed the door behind her.

"Now," Aunt Cathy said, "let me understand what the two of you are on about, and make it fast. Those people were about to write me a very fat check, out of which your payroll was going to come."

Angela and Ethan looked at each other for a moment. Then Ethan told Cathy and Miss Finn and Angela about his friend Gary, and about the phone call they'd had with Posey Sandborn.

"I don't think they got up in the morning and said to themselves, 'how can we use the government to block our competition so we don't have to work so hard,' but that's what they actually *do*. They're just covering their bases in case Louis Sulla doesn't win. They want their hooks in here," Ethan said.

"Not terribly eloquent," Angela said, "but essentially that's my feeling as well. Not all companies do it, but most of them, and especially the big ones, use their lobbying and financial power to stop their competition. It's very hard to do in the open marketplace, where customers are almost always looking for a better deal or better service, but government can close off those attack avenues in ways private businesses never could. It's classic protectionism."

Cathy pursed her lips. "I know this argument. I've seen similar things, of course, and Dennis was especially good at ferreting them out and stopping them. It was one of his favorite things to do, dismantling regulations that looked like they were supporting the public but were really there only to keep competition down."

"Yes, exactly," Ethan said. He was suddenly struck again by the wish that he'd been able to know Aunt Cathy's friend and mentor better before he was gone.

"Not so fast," Miss Finn said. "Despite that—every word Cathy has said is true—Dennis worked very closely with a lot of large companies, and they donated to and advised his campaign. You probably weren't aware of that."

Ethan hadn't been, but he didn't need to say it.

Cathy's voice was sympathetic, but direct. "We need funds to run the campaign. We won't get into a position to stop any of this if we don't win. And we're not going to win if we don't have money." She turned a hard gaze on Angela. "That's your department, so I'm going to lay this out simply, and then you can tell me what to do, and I'll do it."

"We have enough money to run the campaign for another month," she continued. "We can't do any advertising, so we're not going to be closing the gap, and maybe all we're doing is kidding ourselves. To be awarded the nomination, we have to win the primary, and that is coming up in a month. We have to make our move right now."

"I don't want to promise anyone anything that compromises this campaign or my principles," Cathy said. "On the other hand, my principles won't pay rent and salaries, and they won't snag votes if no one knows about them. So here's the deal, and please understand I'm putting twenty people's livelihoods on the line here—if you tell me that without these people we can raise the money to really make a fight of the race, I'll believe you and tell them to pound sand."

Miss Finn made a little sound in her throat.

"Okay," Cathy said, "I'll work on my phrasing. But in essence, that's what I'll say—but only if you promise me on your honor you can do this. We've worked together for years, Angela. You've never overpromised. And you don't need to do it this time, either. We can let these people back in here, and they can smile and simper and write a check, and we can use that money to go after bigger fish. There are much bigger fish out there, I don't have to tell you. We can use these people the same way they think they're using us."

Angela stood by the door, that enigmatic smile on her face. "You're something else, Cathy, you know that? It's probably why I keep following you from hopeless endeavor to doomed enterprise and back."

"I love you back. But now is the time. What's it going to be?"

If you think Angela should tell Cathy to take their money, turn to page 326.

If you think Angela and Ethan can raise the money other ways, turn to page 349.

"We have to tell all of it," Emily said. "We knew we were going to have to. It doesn't really matter which party is which, or which one is in power, if they're both doing the kinds of things that shouldn't be part of our politics in the first place."

"The ends don't justify the means," Ethan said. "They never do. And yeah, I know that means I'm probably in for some serious trouble for snooping." He cast a worried glance over at Mom.

She snipped on, unperturbed. "I'm sure your father and I will discuss it. There are dubious legalities here as well, but I don't think anyone is going to put you in jail over it."

Aunt Cathy said, "I think it's best that I point people in the right direction, rather than that we have you two in front of the cameras. I'll try to keep your names out of it when I connect you to the people who can get the story in front of people. But it may not be possible. The people I know are fairly aggressive, but if they can't come up with the information through a surprise audit, Ethan's photos might be crucial to establishing guilt or innocence."

"You can have the pictures," Ethan said. "I'll send them to you."

"They'll come back to you," Aunt Cathy said, "if we have to use them as evidence. We'll have to show where they came from."

Ethan nodded glumly. "I knew this job was too good to last."

Aunt Cathy knew the state auditor, a man named Doug Johnson, who had a reputation as something of a bulldog when it came to finding discrepancies in the books. His department wasn't directly involved in campaign finance, but he was in touch with the people who were. They passed it up the chain themselves, one link at a time. When they got to the right guy it was actually a woman, Ellie Ness, at the Federal Election Commission. And she was very interested indeed.

Unusual, they said, for a report to reach them of two opposing campaigns committing fraud in the same way at the same time. Not that campaigns were clean—no, she made no such assumptions—but usually the reporting was asymmetric, or the kind of thing they were doing to escape the finance laws was different. In this case though, with a pair of successful businessmen duking it out, it made a certain sense.

They descended without warning, a whole team of them, hitting both campaigns at the same 8:37am on a Tuesday morning when nobody at the office was prepared for the Feds to arrive and there was no time to cover things up. Ness and her team were in the accounts before the accountants got there, and it didn't take them very long to crack the code on the ledger Ethan had "found." It should have been good news. And it would have been—except for what was found on the ledger.

The twins had just gotten home from a school play when there was a knock at the door. Ethan heard the mutter of conversation in the front hall, then Mom's head popped through the door, accompanied by a look Ethan knew he'd never seen before.

"You need to come to the front room," Mom said, her voice very quiet and deadly serious.

"What's up?" Ethan said, but Mom just shook her head.

That was a kind of bad Ethan couldn't even comprehend. What on earth could this be, that Mom wouldn't even talk about it?

He found out when he got there. On one couch was Emily, white as a linen sheet, and on the other were two black-suited people, a man and a woman, with white shirts and sunglasses in their pockets. They looked like every movie version of FBI agents Ethan had ever seen.

They stood when he came in the room. Ethan didn't know what to do with that, so he took a seat next to Emily, right on the edge of the couch, as if he were going to make a run for it.

Mom settled in the loveseat—none too comfortably, Ethan thought—and the two agents—they had to be agents—sat as well, with their center of gravity over their feet, the better to get up quickly and shoot people. Or, you know, whatever they did.

"I'm Deputy Marshal Jones," the woman said, "and this is Deputy Marshal Smith. We're with the US Marshal's office."

Ethan looked at Mom. She said, "Yes, Ethan, I checked their ID."

"No, it isn't that," he said, turning his gaze back to the Deputies. "I thought Marshals were, I don't know, from the old west or something." Emily grabbed his arm. Her skin was cold, like a wax version of a hand.

Deputy Smith let a thin smile onto his weathered face. "Lots of people think that. It helps to keep a low profile."

Deputy Jones said, "I'm afraid that what I have to tell you isn't going to be terribly pleasant. You probably thought you were doing a good thing by digging up the campaign finance violations of the Bauer campaign. I can't fault you for that. But you also uncovered something that's going to create quite a mess."

"You clean up messes though, right?" Ethan said. "I mean, this isn't something you can't handle."

"We can handle it," Deputy Jones said, "but you can't."

"That's okay," Ethan said, puzzled. "We aren't supposed to handle it."

"You'll have to if your lives are in danger."

"Are they?" He couldn't wrap his head around this. It was like something from a movie.

Deputy Smith said, "Yes."

The twins glanced over at Mom, who was composed and serious, in the efficient mode the twins knew meant she was thinking fast and making plans without looking back and regretting. After a moment, Mom said, "This isn't a warning, is it?"

"Not really," Deputy Jones went on. "The fact is, we're not going to give you any choice. The people whose names were on that ledger are not the sort of people who forgive or forget. They can't take chances that someone like you knows who they are. They have a reputation for being thorough."

"But we don't know anything," Ethan said.

"That won't be what they're told when word gets out that the ledger has leaked."

"We have to leave," Mom said.

"In a manner of speaking," Deputy Jones said.

"We'll have to arrange your departure," Deputy Smith said. "It will need to be… convincing."

Mom pursed her lips. "Not just getting on a plane then."

"No."

"This is nuts," Ethan said. "We're a couple of teenagers. We saw some ledgers. That's it."

Emily spoke up. "And we didn't even really know what we were seeing. It just looked funny."

The Deputies looked at one another. Deputy Smith turned back to the twins and spread his massive hands. "You know that. And I know that. But the bad guys, they don't know that. What they see is a pair of politically-active troublemakers who have been in and out of the news for years, then they go to work for one Senate candidate, and a couple of weeks later they're 'volunteers' at another campaign, where they just happen to be in the right place to take photographs of a ledger that shows money coming into the campaign from places it shouldn't. A couple of days later, that information is in the hands of the first campaign."

"Uh," Ethan said. "I mean, when you put it like that..."

"What you certainly did *not* know," Deputy Jones broke in, "is that the first campaign *also* had money from that same place coming in. That's what your friend overheard."

"You know about that?" Emily said.

The deputies turned their steely eyes on her for just a moment. They didn't have to say anything.

"So both campaigns were dirty," Ethan said. His voice was very sad.

"Yes, although we think the first campaign—yours—was not aware of it at the top levels. It seems it was just one guy. Unfortunately, that's where the serious problems come from."

"Can you tell us what was actually going on?" Mother said.

"We'd rather not," Deputy Jones said.

“Which we realize is unfair. You made yourselves targets and you won’t ever truly know why.” Deputy Smith shifted his bulk on the couch, but it didn’t appear to make him any more comfortable. “Unfortunately, the bad guys don’t know what you don’t know. They’ll be looking to make you stay quiet.”

Ethan’s eyes bugged out. “We’ll never say a word. Never. To anyone.” He glanced at Emily for backup.

She was only too happy to comply. “Absolutely. We won’t even talk about it to each other.”

Deputy Jones shook her head sadly. “That won’t work. These guys will want to make sure you don’t talk. They have ways of making… certain.”

The twins went pale. Mother, however, seemed as if she’d expected this. “Tell us what we have to do,” she said.

“Your husband, too,” Deputy Smith said. “He’ll have to be part of it. I’m sorry.”

Mother nodded, all cool efficiency. “I realize that. He’ll be here in a couple of minutes. I’ve already called him. How long do we have to get ready?”

The Deputies seemed to confer for a moment. They said nothing, but the look that passed between them was eloquent. “A couple of days,” Deputy Jones finally said. “At most. If we can do this before the end of the week, there’s a pretty good chance you’ll survive.”

“Pretty good?” Ethan said.

“Things happen, kid,” Deputy Smith said. “Tomorrow is promised to no one.”

"But *I* can promise," said Deputy Jones, "that tomorrow is going to be very busy for you."

Ethan got out of the family car. The sun shone brightly, the kind of sun that you could only see in western Montana in the midsummer. It was so white it blinded.

But Ethan didn't need to see. And he wasn't sure he could have, anyway, with the tears in his eyes. He knew he shouldn't have started thinking about his friends again.

He grunted, taking control of himself. It wouldn't do to show emotion. That would be suspicious.

Six steps from the car, he pushed through the glass front doors of the campaign. The receptionist desk was empty. The computer monitor was on though, so Bekah was here someplace. She came back from the hallway to the left, carrying some papers. When she saw Ethan, she smiled. "Hey, Ethan. You're here early."

"I just had my family bring me by," he said, and stepped sideways, his hand out toward the parking lot. As he hoped, she looked out and saw the car there with three people in it.

"We're going to the park this morning," Ethan said, in his best approximation of his usual jocular tone. "Just came by to pick something up from the sign room. Anyone back there?"

She thought for a moment. "I don't think so. I'll have Pascoe walk you back."

That saved Ethan trouble. He smiled brightly. "Cool. I'll see you tomorrow then."

Bekah waved him away and sat down at her desk. She punched a button. Pascoe stuck his head out of the office. "'Sup?" he said.

"Ethan needs something from the sign room."

Pascoe made a sour face. "Isn't Kincaid in yet?"

"Nope. It's just us. Go unlock it for him."

For a moment Ethan thought Pascoe might tell her to do it herself, but he didn't. He disappeared into his office for a second and came back out rattling keys. Without waiting for Ethan, he set off into the bowels of the office. Ethan saw the car drive away. Going around back.

Pascoe unlocked the big wooden door to the sign room. "There. Have at it."

"Could you help me? I just need to put a few propane tanks on the dock. Then Dad and I can get them into the car. They're, um, for the cookout later."

Pascoe didn't like this any better. But he walked over to the big metal door and rolled it up. Sunlight blasted in, ricocheting off the polished concrete. Pascoe winced and shaded his eyes. Ethan took a heavy white propane tank and carried it out to the dock. "This one's pretty rusty," Ethan said. "Should I exchange it for a new one?"

"Sure, kid. Great idea." Pascoe got one of his own and put it beside Ethan's. Around the corner came a silver-blue Kia, a man driving, a woman in the front seat, and the shadow of another girl in the back.

"There's my family," Ethan said. "Do you want to say hi?"

Pascoe looked at Ethan like he'd thrown up on his shoes. "I have stuff to do."

"Great. See you tomorrow," Ethan said. He grabbed the handle of the rusty tank. "Should I roll down the door?"

"Please," Pascoe said. He heard the car's trunk latch pop, echoing off the concrete of the loading dock. He turned his back and headed across the floor to the door back to the office proper. Behind him, the metal door rolled down and locked in place.

Pascoe had just reached the hallway when the car blew up.

"No, I swear, I had no idea... I mean, he was *right there*, just, you know, cheerful and eager and all that and then I heard the explosion." Pascoe was sitting on a box in the alley behind campaign HQ, still staring down at the smoldering car. It had been blue, he remembered. A Kia. There was no way to tell what color it had been, not now. He couldn't see the bodies, not with a dozen emergency personnel there.

A big man in a black suit stood next to him, writing Pascoe's statement on a pad. He had identified himself as Deputy Marshal Smith. "Just in the area," he had said. "Lucky for you."

Pascoe couldn't stop words from pouring out of his mouth. "It just blew up. Boom. I was already in the office. It couldn't... that's... that doesn't *happen*."

"You'd be surprised, the things we see," Deputy Smith said. "Are you absolutely certain it was the Tuttles?"

Pascoe's natural cussedness reared its head even through his shock. "Who else could it have been? I was

right there on the dock with the kid. The car came up. It was their car; I've seen it enough times. Dad was driving and the girl was in the back."

"And then the boy..." he consulted a note a page earlier in his book, "... Ethan, put the tanks into it?"

"Yeah."

"Carried them down from the dock and put them in the trunk?"

"They didn't levitate there. Yeah, he took them."

"You sure?"

"Yes, I'm sure. Why would I lie about that?"

"Just asking questions. In a case like this, we have to be certain."

From over by the smoking husk of the car, one of the firefighters called out, "Deputy? Come look at this."

He stuffed the pad into the interior pocket of his jacket and strode over. He left a little gap between himself and the thing the firefighter was showing him. Enough that someone curious could probably see it pretty well from behind.

"What you got?" Deputy Smith said.

"Propane tank. Three or four of them. And look here," he said, pointing with a metal rod. "Hole in one of them. Looks like it corroded and blew up."

There was no way at all that story could hold up to a serious forensic examination. Fortunately, the evidence was hustled into an unmarked black sedan by Deputy Smith and the firefighter, who bore a significant resemblance to an agent called Jones. And Pascoe, who prided himself on having his ears and eyes always open, already remembered seeing everything very clearly, and understanding to the full exactly what had happened. He was telling a bystander the tale, just as he was led to believe it, before the Deputies even drove away.

Deputy Jones sat at the airport table sipping her coffee. Across from her was the girl, Emily. Deputy Smith had the boy, and they were already gone on the 3:10 to London. She checked her watch. Ten minutes before pre-boarding.

Emily fidgeted. "What I can't figure out is how Pas—uh, the man at the office—could have been fooled like that. He's no dummy."

"We believe what we're told to believe."

"That's not true. I don't."

"But you do, whether you like it or not. And especially if you aren't told you're being told. Think about it."

A few passengers queued up at the coffee stand nearby, but the terminal wasn't busy, and they were talking low enough that nobody would be able to overhear them.

Besides, the girl across the table was already dead. Nobody was looking for her—not anymore.

Emily was a smart girl. Instead of arguing with him, she creased her brow and seriously thought about it.

"The sun was bright. I know that dock—you can't see much looking out that door in the morning."

Jones grunted noncommittally.

"He would have expected to see our car. He would have expected Dad to be driving, and me and Mom in our usual places."

"Lighter inside the car or outside?" Jones said.

"Outside. By a lot."

"Easy to see from dark to light, through glass. Not so easy to see from light to dark."

"It makes a mirror," Emily said, nodding. "So he thought he saw us, but he didn't. He just saw some people in a car."

"Good. What else?"

"He told Smith he saw Ethan put the tanks in the back. But he never saw that—he couldn't have, because Ethan never put them in the car. He just thought he did because that was what was going to happen. He assumed it. The door was already down before anything happened."

"Why did he think he saw it, then?"

"People tell themselves stories. I've seen that often enough. And then… Smith interviewed him. He had to tell him what happened."

Jones gave the barest of smiles. "Even though he didn't know, he told it as if he did. Then once he told it—"

"It became true," Emily said in wonder. "He has to stick to it. He'll even believe it. Smith got him to create the memory right there in the interview. So he did. And now *he really remembers it.*"

Jones crumpled her coffee cup and tossed it into the can behind her. "People think memory is like a recorder.

You put stuff in, and out it comes when you need it. But it's nothing like that. You remember all kinds of things that never really happened."

The airport PA bonged and the announcer gave the gate and departure time for their flight. Copenhagen. Split the family, split the destinations, don't travel solo. Standard. Effective. Invisible.

Emily stood and stretched. She looked around as if she hadn't seen the place before. Now she was never going to see it again.

"How often... uh, how well does..." she began. She looked sheepish. "You know. What you do. What we're doing. Does it really work?"

"Nineteen thousand people into the program since 1970," Deputy Jones said. "Never lost a single one."

"That's what the Internet told me," Emily said, slinging her carryon over her shoulder. "But I thought I'd go to the source, you know?"

Jones laughed a little. "Not *everything* on the Internet is false."

Nine months had passed since Randall Kohn's Senate victory, and the pace of the work hadn't let up for a minute. Cathy sometimes wondered if she'd have had less to do if she'd run for the seat herself.

Still, Kohn had been generous, and kind, and the work had given her something to do instead of sit in her house and mourn her sister and brother-in-law. She had, right from the first minute she'd heard of their deaths, blamed herself for their being gone. She had been the one who connected them to the Fordes, and the Fordes had connected them to the campaign, and the campaign had been the thing that got them killed. Carrying propane canisters for a campaign event. Could happen to anyone.

But that's not what Cathy felt like.

The campaign had reached out to her, given her a job—one of their mid-level staffers had simply vanished and left quite a hole—a purpose, and a win, and over the months since her sister died, Cathy had decided life was worth living again.

Now she was on a plane, fulfilling what seemed like the dying wish of her sister—to go to Malmo, in Sweden, and visit the grave of their great-great-grandfather Andersson.

It seemed very odd to Cathy—certainly her sister had never mentioned family history work to her—but cleaning out Susan's room, there wasn't much doubt. Cathy had found, in her sister's own handbag, a map of Sweden and a photograph of the gravesite, with a little paper-clipped note attached— "Have to take Cathy here someday!"

Someday, it turned out, was today.

Customs in Copenhagen was swift and efficient, and Cathy was out with her rented Opal in no time at all, her luggage stowed and the GPS directing her to take the E20 across the Skagerrak to Sweden. No customs there, just a wide plaza with lanes, like a set of toll booths.

An hour later, she pulled smoothly to a stop outside the wrought iron gates of what the GPS called the Malmo Old Cemetery. She wished she'd brought some flowers. Her sister would've thought of that. But she hadn't, and part of her just wanted to get it over with. Unfinished business.

She walked along the rock-covered path, underneath a statue of a long, curving spike with a man reaching for the sky. On a nearby bench sat an old, bent woman, tossing bread crumbs to the pigeons.

Cathy found the gravestone without too much trouble. It was unremarkable, birth and death dates underneath a name. She thought she might feel something there, a pull from the past, or something. But no. The day was warm, sunny, with a couple of meandering clouds. Still chilled though, and in the shade of some of the obelisks there was still patchy snow.

Suddenly she didn't know why she'd come at all.

"Sorry," she said to the stone. "I wish I knew why I thought this was a good idea."

"Oh, it was a good idea, all right," said the obelisk behind her. She turned, and from around the stone came the old woman, leaning on a cane, the fringes of her crocheted shawl obscuring her face. "My name is Emma. My brother Emil and I have been waiting for you."

From the other side of the obelisk, a boy stepped into the sunshine. She knew this boy.

Then the woman straightened and tossed off her shawl. Cathy knew her too, and she wasn't old at all. They were teenagers, in fact. Only they were dead. That was the confusing part.

"Hi, Aunt Cathy," Emily said, with a bright, free smile. "I suppose we'd better explain."

THE END

Kohn
Republican for U.S. Senate
Kohn
Republican for U.S. Senate
Kohn
Republican for U.S. Senate

"Alannah is my friend. It's always better to work one of these jobs with a friend," Emily said. "We'll take the job working in vote hunting."

Kohn nodded and finished chewing his celery. "Excellent," he said. "We make calls all day, and you can make them from anywhere, but there's something magical about being here at the HQ if you can make it down here."

"Great," Ethan said. "We don't have an air-hockey table at home."

They got the introduction from Alannah, but before she was finished the shift leader came to have a word with them. He was tall, balding, and his face had so many lines on it Emily couldn't believe it was capable of expression. He carried a tablet with the gaudiest red case she'd ever seen. He bowed instead of shaking hands, stopping a couple of feet from them as they sat at one of the phone tables.

"I'm Ed," he said.

Ethan stood up and bowed back, tilting at about the same angle. "Ethan Tuttle. This is my sister Emily." Behind him, Emily also stood. She didn't bow. She wasn't sure if she even remembered how to curtsey. If that was the thing to do.

"Where do you two live?" he said.

"Spoonerville."

He nodded. "Good. We don't have anyone in that district yet. We were figuring we'd be able to pick up someone down the road. It's good territory for us." He went over to the maps and ran a finger across them. Turning back to the twins, he said, "Do you think your parents will be voting for Randall?"

The twins looked at each other. "I think we can safely promise that. I don't think they'd drive us to work for someone they didn't approve of," Emily said. Ed reached into one of the buckets of pins and pulled out a red one.

"Address?" he said. They told him, and he stuck a pin in the map on their street. It was lonely. He swung up the tablet, tapped it a couple of times, and grunted.

"How long you two lived there?" he said. That was the first of a long series of questions. By the time Ed was finished, he had a fistful of data punched into the machine, and he stabbed it one more time. A printer whined over by the far wall. Ed pointed at it.

"Over there, you'll get a list of names and phone numbers. Alannah will tell you what to do when you call them."

"Couldn't we just send email?" Emily said.

He shook his head. "Not a chance. People ignore email. They take phone calls from local numbers, or if they let them go to voicemail, we have a system for that too."

"You know," Emily said, "they make robots that can make all these calls. I read about it in *Time* magazine."

"That's hilarious. Nobody reads *Time* magazine. Also, we can let the robots dial, but it needs to be your voice on the line because if it isn't, then the *other* robots detect it and send us straight to voicemail, or block the call. There's no substitute for humans on this one."

"What about the do-not-call list?"

Ed shook his head. "Doesn't apply to political campaigns. We're exempt. Any more questions? Not that I'm not being entertained by this little chat."

The twins looked at each other. Ethan shrugged. "Nope. We're good."

And they were put to work.

The Cool Room was every bit as cool as it sounded. Mounds of chips, vending machines that vended whether you had money or not, fridges filled with drinks, plus air hockey and ping-pong tables—everything a growing teenager needed.

On the main office floor, Ethan was set at a table over by the maps, and Emily got one in the back corner, about as far away as she could possibly be. Ethan's long folding table had four laptops on it, open to an app that looked like a phone with multiple lines. The thing was lit up like the Fourth of July. When he clicked on his handset, his own line was the little green one down on the bottom of the right column, and all the amber ones were other people calling out. If those lines started blinking, that meant someone was on hold. That didn't happen a lot, but sometimes someone would raise his hand and wave, and Ed would walk over to them, have a short conversation, and sometimes take the headset and the call himself. To Ethan, that looked like a failure. He resolved not to have it happen to him. He was smart. He could handle whatever people might dish out.

The screen was divided in two, with names and phone numbers down the left and the phone menu on the right. Down at the bottom was a green button that said, "Ready?" In front of him on the table, he had a paper that gave the script for the call, along with some frequently asked questions. He read it through three or four times, until he felt like he had a good handle on the patter, and then he put his headset on and clicked the ready button.

One of the names on the list lit up and the sounds of a phone dialing sounded in his ear. Thomas Marsh, the name read. A window opened on the screen with a number of check-boxes to be clicked, depending on how things went. The call was answered on the second ring.

"Hello?"

A man's voice. "Mr. Marsh?" Ethan said, pitching his voice low, the way they told him to.

"Speaking."

"Mr. Marsh, my name is Ethan Tuttle, and I'm calling from the headquarters of Randall Kohn for Senate. Do you have just a minute?" Even to Ethan, this sounded authoritative and adult. His chest puffed out a half inch.

"I do. What's this about?"

"Mr. Kohn asked me to call you and let you know that he is running for the Senate seat in Montana, and he would appreciate your support."

"Lovely. What kind of support is Mr. Kohn interested in?"

"Well, there are several levels of support, depending on how committed you are to helping out." Ethan followed the script word-for-word. "For instance, we could use many more volunteers to make phone calls to voters. We have thousands of yard signs, free to a good home. But Mr. Kohn's campaign would most benefit from a financial contribution. As I'm sure you know, running for the US Senate is expensive."

"I'm aware of that, yes. I'm also aware of Mr. Kohn's resources, which are a lot greater than mine. I don't think I'd be interested."

"That's fine, sir. I'll pass that on to Mr. Kohn. Could we deliver a sign to you though? And would you be willing to make a few phone calls on his behalf?"

A pause. What sounded like a sigh. "I'd be willing to take a sign, yes. I like Randall."

"That's wonderful, sir!" Ethan said, clicking the relevant box in the window. "I can have it to you later this week. Is there a good time for you?"

They negotiated a moment, Ethan clicked that information into the window, and the call terminated. One for one. Nothing to it at all.

Next to him, one of the other phone workers, a girl about Ethan's age, was having a more difficult time. "I'm convinced Mr. Kohn will listen closely to what his constituents have to say," she said, with a tone in her voice that said she'd rather be doing something else at the moment.

"No, sir, that's not the way I see it. Citizen input is critical to Mr. Kohn. He'll try very hard to find out what the people of the state want before he casts a vote." Pause.

"Sir, I'm... That's... Okay, sir. I'm sorry you feel that way. Have a good evening." She clicked a button, jerked off her headset and tossed it on the desk.

With the headset on, Ethan had thought she was much older, but as she wiped her hand over her face, he saw that she wasn't much older than he was. A year or so, maybe. Strawberry blond, with a round face and a dimple when she smiled, which she did right then, seeing him staring at her.

"You don't win them all," she said. "At least he wasn't rude."

"What was his problem?" Ethan said.

"He wanted to know how Randall was going to make decisions about how to vote on stuff in the Senate."

"What were the options? Rolling dice? A Ouija board?"

She laughed, low and in her throat, and Ethan liked the sound of it. "Maybe I should have said that. It might have gone better."

"I heard what you told him. That sounded pretty good. But apparently it wasn't what he wanted to hear."

She shook her head, a shower of rose gold. "He said that's not how a senator should make decisions."

"How did he want Kohn to do it?"

"He wanted him to take a position and stick to it, and if we don't like that position, we shouldn't vote for him."

Ethan looked at the young woman, and she looked back at him. Finally, Ethan said, "Uh, that sounds pretty good too."

"It had occurred to me."

"I'm Ethan," he said.

"Dara," she said.

"Which of those two do you think is the right way?"

"I thought my way was. But then he said his way, and now I don't know."

"Don't know what?" Ed said, jogging by.

Dara told him about her conversation. Ed laughed. "People have been trying to figure out those things since the concept of voting was put together."

"If you had that kind of power, would you support legislation based on your beliefs, or based on the beliefs of the people you represent??" Ethan said.

"I think there are people at home right now with money to donate to this campaign, and the longer we talk to each other about this the less of that money we're getting."

Ethan and Dara put their headsets on and clicked the green buttons.

It was a couple of weeks later, as the summer was drawing to a close, when Ed stepped in front of Ethan's computer and waved at him. Ethan held up a finger—he was on a call—and talked a woman into making a $25 donation to the campaign and accepting a yard sign.

"Excellent," Ethan said. "You won't regret this, Mrs. McGillicutty. Mr. Kohn is a good man, and he's going to do great things for Montana and the country. You take care now."

He clicked off the button and looked up.

Ed said, "Boss wants to see you."

"I didn't do it. Nobody saw me do it. You can't prove anything," Ethan said. "Besides, it was all Dara's idea."

Dara paused in the middle of dialing. "It's true. My best ideas are all completely illegal."

Ed didn't dignify any of this with a response, just hefted his clipboard and sailed away across the floor in search of other people to browbeat.

"What do you suppose it is?" Dara said.

"I don't know," Ethan said, "but I'll bet you five bucks whatever it is, I'm not interested."

He went around the long table and out toward the front of the HQ. When he got to the door to the good part of the office, Emily was waiting there for him.

"Hey, stranger," Ethan said.

"Hey yourself," Emily said. "You making the campaign any money or just flirting with your girlfriend?"

"I made the campaign $25 just a minute ago. And she isn't my girlfriend. I couldn't have a girlfriend that was better than me at fundraising. What would the other kids say?"

Emily closed the door behind him, and they walked together toward the boardroom. "What's this all about?" Ethan said.

"Beats me," Emily said. "I got called off my sign job same as you did."

"Different job."

"Same difference."

Only one person was in the conference room—Randall Kohn himself. He was in what the twins had taken to calling his "work clothes": button-down shirt—usually white, like today—jeans, and semi-serious black boots with not too much polish. His hair was slicked back, and his face showed he'd been outside a fair amount. He looked like a million bucks. He was worth a lot more than that, of course.

"Ah, the Tuttles. Sit, please. I'm sorry to take you from your duties, but I think we can spare you for a minute."

They took chairs together along the far side of the table. Six or seven empty chairs swiveled gently behind them, toward the back of the room. Behind Kohn, the whiteboard had been extensively scribbled on in what looked like, but probably was not, Klingon. Ethan hoped that meant something about what they were going to discuss, but he thought it unlikely.

"How do you like working at the campaign?" Kohn said.

Ethan and Emily eyed each other for a moment. She shrugged. "I like it fine. It's work. You pay me. That's good enough."

"It helps that you pay pretty well, that the work is fairly easy, and there is this vague sense that I'm doing something to make the world a better place one $25 donation at a time," Ethan said.

Kohn smiled a little. "No complaints, then? You don't feel like your talents are being wasted?"

"I feel like hers are," Ethan said, "as long as we're being completely honest. I know a brother isn't supposed to say nice things about his sister, but she's capable of a lot more than finding places to put signs up."

Emily's mouth dropped open. "Wow. I mean... Wow."

Kohn said, "I'll take that as an unimpeachable testimonial, considering the source."

"Don't let Ethan fool you," Emily said, recovering. "He's a snot and knows more than anyone in the room, all the time—just ask him—but he's also very clever, and he comes up with terrific ideas. I'm sure he's doing well on the phones, but I'm also sure he'd do other things well, things that might be more valuable to the campaign."

"So the admiration society *is* mutual. I wondered," Kohn said. "You'll be happy to know that's the reason I've invited you both for this little chat."

The twins kept their mouths shut and ears open. Kohn fiddled for a second with his cell phone, put it down with a clatter, and smiled at them. "I find myself in need of a couple more brains."

"You can't have mine," Emily said. "I don't know where it is."

"Hilarious. Ed tells me you're a jokester. But the truth is, you're both excellent workers, and you think clearly and speak clearly. I don't know if that's the homeschooling or whether you're just naturally bright."

"Combination of both," Ethan said. "At least that's what Dad says."

"It's not terribly relevant, all things considered. What I want is the benefit of those brains, however you got them. I'm looking for a pair of new people for the advance team and body team. Do you know what those are?"

"Not really," Ethan said.

"I'm probably not the best person to explain this. Campaigns have different teams for different purposes. Most of them don't work directly with the candidate, but some do, and the advance team is one of those. The body team works most closely with the candidate since their job is to manage me personally, get me where I'm going, and make sure I have water and food and other necessities."

"You have people on these teams already," Emily said.

"Yes, I do, but we've had a couple of openings recently. Redistribution of staff."

"And you want us for the job?"

"I do. Despite your youth and your penchant for witty repartee, Ed says you work very hard and you get excellent results. I know from other sources that you have awareness of the value of social media marketing and that you're creative and bullheaded."

"Most people don't believe that to be a positive quality," Ethan said.

"I'm not most people. I'm a candidate for the US Senate. What do you say? Will you accept reassignment? You don't have to. You can go right back to doing what you were doing before, if you like."

"What about one each way," Ethan said. "I stay in the phone squad, and Emily moves to the body team, or whatever."

"No, I don't think that will work," Kohn said, twirling the phone on the table surface. "It's sometimes a question of propriety—being alone with someone is potentially compromising. You understand, I think. So I'd much rather have you both or neither of you."

The twins looked at one another. "Can we take a minute to talk?" Emily said.

"Sure," Kohn said. "I'll be in the hallway." He got up and went out.

"What do you think?" Ethan said.

"I think phone calling is fine, but it gets boring sometimes. This sounds like fun."

Ethan pursed his lips. "It does. But I'm doing really well on my job, and there's… another consideration."

"Dara," Emily said, "and don't bother denying it. She's cool. I like her, too. You wouldn't see her nearly as much."

"You said your goal here was to get a job so you could buy a car. We don't have to do anything more to achieve that. And what about Alannah? You two seem to be getting along really well. You wouldn't see *her* nearly as much."

"It's true," Emily said, scratching her shoulder. "So which way should we go?"

If you think they should take the job, turn to page 84.

If you think they should stick with the job they have, turn to page 188.

"It's not simple," Ethan said. "If it were, this wouldn't be such a tough decision."

He turned to Alannah. "You said you know what your father would do."

Alannah nodded. Then she rocked her head back and forth, as if she were weighing something. "I think so, anyway. You were never quite sure with Dad. He thought about a lot of things in a way most people don't." She looked straight at Aunt Cathy, who gazed steadily back. Nothing showed on her face. "I think he'd tell all of it. But I don't know if that's the right call."

Emily frowned. "On the face of it, it's just about telling the truth. But that truth can have massive repercussions for other people. We all agree, I think, that Evelyn Craddock doesn't deserve to be fired. She didn't do anything wrong. If anything, it was Ethan who did the wrong thing."

"Hey," Ethan said. "That cut still bleeds."

"Let me pour some lemon juice on it then. But seriously. She's a worker. She's a true believer, but she's not involved in the money side of things. Nothing on that ledger is her fault."

Alannah's mouth was tight, like a line drawn on the sidewalk. "Not to mention, all three of us could lose our jobs. You guys actually lose *two,* one with each campaign. That's got to be some kind of record at your age."

"We're not getting paid for one of them," Emily said, "so that's no great loss."

"Still. Even though what Ethan did probably isn't prosecutable, it's not going to look good. There's trouble there if it can't be kept quiet." Alannah seemed to be asking Aunt Cathy a question, but still Aunt Cathy's face gave nothing away.

"Okay, guys," Ethan finally said. "Here's what it comes down to for me. Right now we're possibly the only people that know that both campaigns are dirty. But that's just it: we know *both* campaigns are dirty. That money was going to get to them anyway. If they didn't do it this way, they'd find a different way for the money to get there, maybe a way that's truly illegal instead of just a violation of some rules most people don't know about and care even less about. I'm not sure it's even wrong. I mean, why shouldn't people be able to give whatever they want?" He blew out a breath. "So my vote is to let them both slug it out. I'm done with oppo research anyway. I want to go back to Craddock and tell her we're leaving. Thanks for the experience and all, but we're done. Then we can go stuff envelopes for Kohn and keep our heads down until the whole thing is done. Say nothing, play the game straight, and let the big people do what they do."

Alannah's face showed she wasn't sure that was a good idea. "I think my father would want me to tell, if it were just me. But I don't really know anything. I overheard a conversation is all."

Emily laid a hand on Alannah's arm. "Maybe we're thinking about this wrong. We already told Kohn about Bauer's ledger. What if the right way to go is to talk to them again, only this time, about their own dirty laundry."

Aunt Cathy's face twitched. Emily couldn't tell what that meant, but she kept going.

"Maybe instead of telling the world, we should tell the people involved," Emily said.

"A meeting where we tell them what we know, and ask them to explain, and to stop. Rather than destroying the campaign, we ask it to go straight," Alannah said.

"It does have the virtue of simplicity," Ethan said. "And I can stop working both sides of the street like I want to."

Aunt Cathy finally smiled. "See, I knew you could do it."

The meeting was not a comfortable one. Kohn's face was thunderous, and Maria Norton looked like she had been struck with a plague. In short, about what they'd expected.

"You can't blame Alannah for having ears," Ethan said.

"It's really your fault for employing goons who, one, cheat and, two, aren't smart enough to keep their mouths shut when there are other employees around who might overhear," Emily said.

"Those 'other employees' are supposed to be loyal," Kohn said. He hadn't sat down for the better part of an hour.

"Those employees *are* loyal," Emily said. "Else we'd be having this conversation with the *Times-Intelligencer* instead of with you."

Norton and Kohn locked eyes for a moment.

"So what is it you want?" Kohn said, finally.

Alannah said, "Go straight. That's all. This isn't a blackmail session. It's just... My father wouldn't have worked for anyone who bent the rules. He was aggressive, sure, but he never played the game in the gray area. He wouldn't want his daughter working for anyone who did, I'm sure of it. Anyway, that's how I think of it."

"Dennis was a friend of mine," Kohn said, running a hand through his flowing black hair. "And you're right, he wouldn't have cheated. I don't want to cheat either, no matter what it does for me. I didn't think we really were cheating. But then I saw those ledgers you found, and I realized that when they do it, I think they're guilty as sin, and when we do it, I think we're just taking advantage of loopholes."

Norton said, "The paper trail is clean. But it's your call how you want to play this. If we have to give back the money, there's going to be an almighty scandal."

"No way to hide it?"

She shook her head. "No way. But there might be a way to spin it. I'll have to think about that."

The three teens got up to leave.

"What's your plan?" Kohn said.

They all looked at each other. Ethan finally spoke. "My plan is to go have this same meeting with Evelyn Craddock at the Bauer campaign then go into witness protection."

Kohn tried to stop himself, but he couldn't. He laughed out loud. "You are one interesting kid, you know that?"

"Can I be interesting in your mailroom or someplace where I just do my job and don't have to play James Bond?"

"I bet you can't really just do a boring job, but okay, you talked me into it. You have a job in the mailroom when you want it."

Emily said, "I was thinking my friend Alannah has way more to do than she can actually get done, and she might enjoy having someone help her with the filing and copying and ordering and all. Would that be acceptable?"

"Depends," Kohn said. "Ears open or closed?"

"I've always been a fan of a high-quality pair of headphones, myself," Emily said.

"But neither of us is deaf," Alannah said.

"Understood. Wish granted. Now get out of my boardroom before I remember I should just fire the lot of you and be done with it."

Maybe the campaign went straight. Maybe it didn't. But it didn't use the Bauer material, and there were repeated requests to the staff to keep costs down, so perhaps they did go straight after all. They gave back some $160,000 in as public a manner as possible, and held a press conference to explain that they'd taken the money improperly and that was why they were returning it.

"I cannot stand in the metaphorical shadow of Dennis Forde and be less of an honest man than he was," Kohn said, in a phrase Emily and Alannah agreed was generous, if a little bit over the top.

Ethan and Emily took Evelyn Craddock to lunch and showed her the photographs. Blood drained from her face.

"I snooped. I shouldn't have. I wanted you to know that I am sorry. I'm deleting the photos, and we're quitting the campaign."

Craddock handed the phone back. "I'm surprised you didn't try to sell those to the Kohn campaign. They'd pay you a mint for them."

"Actually, they're doing the same thing. Or they were," Emily said.

Craddock's mouth dropped open. "How... Who are you?"

"We're kids who got mixed up in something we shouldn't have. Anyway, you don't deserve to lose your job just because you trusted a couple of teenagers you don't know anything about," Ethan said.

"I don't know which is worse, that you two conned me or that you're not going to work the D-Day memorial picnic on Thursday."

"Neither do we," Ethan said. "Although if I never see another picnic in my life, it will be too soon."

"You're a good woman," Emily said. "And you made a terrible job almost bearable. Tell your people to keep their noses clean."

"I will. They won't listen because they're up against a juggernaut in Kohn, but I'll tell them. And if you guys ever want a job, call me."

November 5 did actually come, after thousands of pieces of mail, hundreds of hours of arguments, and six formal debates. Bauer's campaign seemed perpetually short of money, and while Kohn could always get more from the candidate himself, the papers were full of congratulations to the two campaigns for not breaking the bank, as had happened so often in the past.

The twins and Alannah spent most of the day blowing up balloons for the party that night. "You know, if we lose, this is going to be a colossal waste of time," Emily said.

People began trickling in about 5pm, well before the polls closed. At 9, when the results began to come in, campaign headquarters was packed to the metal rafters. All the Tuttles were there, Alannah's mother and brothers came, and Aunt Cathy even dropped by.

"For the cookies," she said.

Fanfare. The television reporter turned to the camera and a hush fell over the crowd.

"Good evening, Montana," the anchorwoman said. "We have the first results of the US Senate race, and I think a lot of people out there are in for a shock."

THE END

Emily went over to the blinds and flicked them open to see out. Kohn was in the hallway, chatting on his cell. She waved to him, and he nodded and pointed at the phone.

"He'll be in in a second," Emily said.

It was a couple of minutes, but he did come back in, shoving his phone in his pocket. "What did you two decide?"

Ethan said, "We're going to take your offer, if you pay us more money."

Emily narrowed her eyes at him. "Is that what we decided?"

"Absolutely," Ethan said. "It wasn't that long ago. I'd have thought you'd remember."

"I can do that," Kohn said. "You'll probably be working a bit more too, so that seems fair. What if I gave you each another $1.50 an hour?"

"Great," Emily said, kicking Ethan under the table. "When do we start?"

Immediately, it turned out. Kohn had a scheduled appearance at the Montana District Rotary Convention in front of 340 potential donors at a formal dinner two days later. Someone needed to go out there and scope the place out.

"We don't have a car," Emily said to Kohn, and he said, "I know, we have that taken care of." He walked them through to a different part of the campaign offices, where there were various people in suits and business clothing doing everything from accounting to holding strategy meetings to writing campaign literature. He stopped by the desk of a man Ethan thought must be a hundred and twelve. The man was on the phone, though all he kept saying was, "Uh huh. Uh huh. Great. Uh huh." He held up a finger and rolled his eyes.

Kohn said, "This is Will Pascoe. He's the advance director. You'll be working with him."

Pascoe finally terminated the call and stood up. At least Ethan thought he stood up. It didn't make much difference to the level of his balding gray head.

"Pleased to meetcha," Pascoe said, extending a gnarled hand.

Emily took it. He might look old, but his grip hadn't lost any of its power. Her hand stung.

"Emily Tuttle," she said. "And this is my brother Ethan."

"Replacements for Nolan and Marge." Kohn slapped Pascoe on the back. "He's the best in the business. You can learn a lot from him."

"Right now," Pascoe said, "we have to get out to Springfield. You two opposed to a lengthy car trip?"

"Not as long as we're back by dinner. Mom worries," Ethan said.

Pascoe collected his phone and a huge bunch of keys from his desk, and marched them out the back door to the parking lot. It was like watching a gnome walk through a garden, following him. He punched a button on his key and a car chirped.

And what a car. Purple. A wild, shocking, stare-at-me purple sports car. Pascoe hit another button and the top of the car slid back, upwards, and down into the trunk like a raft sinking.

"It's a convertible!" Ethan said.

"Nothin' gets by this fella, does it?" Pascoe said. "The lady rides up front, unless you got objections."

They didn't. The only other convertible they'd ridden in was their Uncle Ben's, but that one wasn't tricked out like this. Pascoe could have told them they were riding in the trunk, and it would have been okay.

The trip out was marvelous. The day was warm, with a few clouds to give periodic shade, and the convertible had a number of buttons for adjusting the flow of the air. Pascoe fiddled with them until he got what he wanted and said, "You hear me okay back there, Ethan?"

"Yeah," Ethan said, surprised. "I can hear you fine. That's weird. There's hardly any wind."

"Aerodynamics are funny," Pascoe said. "So tell me about yourselves."

"You go first, Ethan," Emily said. "I'm always curious as to how honest we're going to be."

Ethan summed up things pretty quickly—the twins were sixteen; he was older (Emily rolled her eyes—*by six lousy minutes*); they had had quite a few adventures.

Pascoe frowned. "Like?"

"Oh, boy," Emily said. "Here we go."

Ethan held up a finger. "We organized the biggest food truck rally in the state and got regulations repealed allowing them to operate freely." A second finger went up. "We hiked through South America during the worst earthquake there in a century." A third finger. "We put together a coalition to rescue the businesses at Surfdom Beach when a bypass cut off all their traffic." A bunch more fingers. "We opened and ran our own business. We've studied international cartels, hyperinflation, currency manipulation, global trade networks, eminent domain—"

"And we were clowns in the circus," Emily said. "Don't forget that one."

Pascoe's eyes got a little glassy. "How did you pack all that into sixteen years? Some people I know would never get that into sixty."

"We were lucky," Emily said. "Plus I can hit a baseball. Very far. Too far."

"That was awesome though," Ethan said.

"No doubt y'all got a story 'bout that, too," Pascoe said. "Maybe it would be quicker if I got the book version."

"What about you?" Emily said. "How did we get you for a teammate?"

Pascoe snorted. “Y’all are just lucky, I guess. I been around a bit. Done a few things. Never been a clown though. Leastways, not in the circus. ‘Less you count this monkey show.”

“Why are you working on the Kohn campaign? Money?”

“Some. Yeah. I’m good, I get paid. That’s how things work. But I won’t work for just anyone. I’m a winner, and I like winning. Most people in politics are losers. I don’t like working for those people.”

“What about principle?” Ethan said.

“What about it? I won’t work for someone that wants to put a red star on everything, or who thinks 80% tax rates are a good idea, but beyond that? I’m no policy hack. I don’t write papers. I make people look good enough that they win campaigns.” He cast a glance at Emily, on the seat to his right. “You’re thinking that’s a terrible reason and I defile the sacred realm of politics.”

“Actually,” Emily said, “I was thinking it sounded like fun.”

He coughed. “Fun? Well, some. Not all the time, ‘course. But some, yeah. Winning is fun.”

“You win a lot, then?” Ethan said.

“Half. Maybe a little more. It’s hard work. Most people can’t do it. Those who can, we have a shelf life, like. Lose too much, and nobody hires you. You’re a Jonah. Even if you win, there’s always somebody better than you are, so the only way to keep winning is to outwork 'em. Hope you two like being tired."

"It's our favorite."

"Good. This is our exit. Time to get to work."

Pascoe pulled the car up in front of a large building with ivy climbing its outside walls. A door stood open into a dark interior. A sign said "Historic Simpson Hall—Receptions, Events" and had a phone number. "We're meeting the fella who runs the place. Looks like he's already here. Good." Pascoe looked up at the sun and off to the west. He got out of the car, popped the trunk, and went back to rummage. The twins jumped out as well and stood gazing about at the tall trees, the gray stone of the building, the parking lot—empty, but spacious enough for two or three hundred cars. But they really didn't know what they were looking at.

Pascoe hauled a box from the trunk and set it on the sidewalk in front of the purple car. He drew a camera, bulky and black, from inside it and held it out to Emily. "You take pictures?" he said.

She showed him her phone. "With this, mostly."

He humphed and wiggled the camera. "Take this. Strap around your neck. Take off the lens cap." She followed his instructions. "Now go stand over there and point it at us as we come along the walk toward the building."

Emily moved over to stand on the grassy area to the left of the walkway and pointed her camera at Pascoe and Ethan. They walked from the car toward her, Pascoe smiling and waving, Ethan with a look on his face like he hoped someone would explain things to him at some point. They turned right and passed in front of her, moving toward the building. When they reached the doorway, Pascoe marched over to Emily instead of going inside.

"What did you see?"

"Two guys walking into a building," she said.

"What's the light like? You got shadows?"

Emily thought for a second. "Some. The trees shade you pretty well, but there were some moving shadows on your faces."

He considered the trees behind them. "It's only two o'clock. Those trees will completely block the sun by five, which is when a lot of the people will get here."

"When do we get here?"

"Two of us—probably the two of you—will be here tomorrow at noon, unpacking gear, setting up, prepping the venue. One of us—me, most likely—will stick with the body until he gets here at seven."

"The body?"

"Kohn. The body is campaign shorthand for the candidate."

Emily thought for a second. "You want the cameras here?"

Pascoe nodded. "It works."

"Why are we doing all this? Why not call the news stations and have them take the photos?" Ethan said.

Pascoe regarded him with one eye. "You tell me."

Ethan looked at the building, back at the car, and over toward the parking lot. "If you have good cameras here, you can capture people walking into the event. It's a… formal?" Pascoe nodded, a little smile starting on his face. Ethan went on, "So people will be in good clothes, and everyone will be dressed as nice as they can. Photos will be good. People will want them. So they have to be good—no shadows and weird stuff on their faces."

"Good," Pascoe said. "You're not totally hopeless. What else?"

"The body," Emily said, holding up the camera, then crouching down as if she were taking a low-angle shot, "has to look perfect. There will be people here. They'll come from the parking lot and out of the building, so this position will give us a clear shot. His face will be in soft shadow—good enough without our setting up lights—and we can get some good snaps of him talking to people, striding into the building, being greeted by community members. Perfect stuff for commercials."

"And?"

Emily stood up. She looked at Ethan, who shrugged.

Pascoe gave a real smile, this time. His teeth were small and pointed. "The event is critical. Lots of people, big possible donors. These people are connected. That means their friends will read about it. Gonna be 340 people here tomorrow. But the news will hit a hundred times that many people. Our photos gotta be the ones they see. Newspeople are lazy. They'll take their own photos, of course, but if we have a press area, they'll shoot our angles. Plus we'll send them our photos, which some of them will use either because they didn't send anyone themselves or because our people are better than their people. If you make a journalist's life easy, that comes back to help you a hundred times over."

"Social media, too. What if we have a hashtag and post to the campaign Instagram account?" Emily said. "That beats the news cycle. Nothing's faster."

"Twitter maybe," Ethan said, seeing where Emily was going. "We get ours out as he walks in. Front of the news cycle."

Pascoe's smile faded into something like astonishment. "Huh. That's good stuff. Not that I have any of those, so I don't get them at all. But it's publicity. It's all publicity. And that's the same regardless of the medium. You either feed it and have some kinda control over what comes out, or you hand that control to your opponents with a bow on it. They're always waiting to blow a minor slip into a huge kerfuffle. Don't matter that it's nothing—it means what the news says it means, for most people. Maybe not so much for young people."

"*More* for young people, except instead of Brian Williams telling us what to think, it's a Kardashian, and instead of CNN, it's Twitter or Instagram or pick the new app everyone's using today. Those things are supposed to reflect what the public thinks, but really they're telling the public what *to* think."

"Which means we better tell them first," Pascoe said. "All the more reason for us to be here and be ready."

"Young people aren't Rotarians. We'll be the only ones putting out stuff about it," Emily said. "Clean reportage. Our story is the only story."

"Quotes from the event as it happens," Ethan said.

Pascoe was silent. Then he said, "Rule number 9. Political technology determines political success."

The twins gave him blank looks. He sighed. "It means the campaign that uses the latest technology has the best chance of winning. But you two definitely get the idea even if you don't understand my reference." He took the camera back from Emily. "Maybe," he said, "maybe having two kids in diapers wasn't such a bad idea after all." He stalked off toward the building.

"I think he likes us," Emily said.

"Oh, sure," Ethan said. "If he liked us any more, he'd be making us walk back to Spoonerville."

But he did like them, and it slowly became obvious over the course of the day. He bossed them about unmercifully, of course. They carried and fetched until their feet were sore, but every time they did, he took a moment to explain why he was asking for this flag, or that wooden box, or moving this curtain to *here*. Everything had to be looked at. Every moment the candidate was in public was a moment that could either help the campaign or hurt it. It was just like when they worked in the theater—every line, every piece of set, every gesture all put in place on purpose. Was a campaign really any different than a play? And if it wasn't, how could anyone trust the campaigners? What about the things that happened *offstage*? Or, worse still, what if there wasn't any offstage at all—everyone simply acting, all the time?

Pascoe was meticulous. He asked the representative from the Simpson House about the food. Then he quizzed the Rotary representative: Who would be greeting the candidate? Would he have time to eat? What was on the menu? Who was at his table? When, exactly, would he be speaking? Anyone before him? Anyone after him?

Pascoe dug out every single detail, from blocking off a parking space close to the venue—no long walk for Kohn—to the liquid refreshment at the table—lemonade and water—to the color of the tablecloth—dark brown.

"We put the body in his white coat, then," Pascoe said to the twins. "Stands out at the table and against the tablecloth. We want anyone who looks at that table to see him first."

He bullied the venue people almost to tears, but in the end he got everything he wanted.

"Rule number 1: Never give a bureaucrat a chance to say no," Pascoe said to the twins at one point, out of earshot of the others.

"You're making these up," Emily said.

"Am I?"

Early on, thinking ahead, Emily put her phone on record and got as much of the conversations as possible. When they'd asked absolutely everything right down to the probable color of socks the emcee would be wearing, Pascoe and the twins shook hands with the venue people and the Rotary representative and got back into the car. They roared off, the car thundering through the empty lot.

"You gotta timer?" he said to Ethan.

Ethan set one on his phone.

"Clock this," Pascoe said. He pulled onto the street, down the block, and made his way very sedately—far slower than he had coming in—to the highway. Magnolia trees lined the street. It smelled heavenly. Nice town, Springfield, Emily thought.

When the car hit the highway, Pascoe said, "Time."

"Six minutes, four seconds," Ethan said.

"Okay. We hit this point seven minutes before zero hour. Even with bad lights, we can make that easy. Your gizmos got service along here?"

They did. "Great," Pascoe said. "Get ready to send some emails."

Pascoe had a prodigious memory, too. He rattled off places, times, logistics, arrangements, all sorts of things and had them send those to Nanette, Kohn's personal secretary. There was one point where he could not remember the sixth person that would be at Kohn's table though. "Curses. I hate getting old," he said. "Well, we'll have to call back and ask."

"No, we won't," Emily said. She held up a finger, dug her earphones from her pocket, and plugged them in. "One minute." She jumped around until she got that part of the conversation and said, "It's Hank Bethelsmann."

Pascoe swiveled to look back at her. "You recorded all that? All day?"

She smiled.

His laugh boomed out over the freeway. "Oh, we're gonna be dangerous, Tuttles. *So* dangerous."

They got back to campaign headquarters quite late. It was after 7, and Mom had already texted several times to find out when they'd be coming back.

Dad was parked outside, engine off, reading a book. He rolled down the window as they came across the parking lot. "Evening, offspring. You ready to come home?"

"Very," Emily said.

Pascoe shouldered forward and shook Dad's hand. "Will Pascoe. You raise these two?"

"Not yet," Dad said. "It's a sort of work in progress."

"Goin' well so far, lemme tell you," Pascoe said. "These two know stuff it took me twenty years to learn."

"Thank you. I like them fairly well."

"Have them back here 8 a.m. though. We got some Washington folk coming in. Body'll want them here for that." He turned to the twins. "Then we'll send you out in the truck with some people to do the setup. But you're in charge. Don't let them give you crap about being young."

"We'll try," Emily said.

"Rule number 4:. Effort is admirable. Achievement is valuable."

"Should I be writing these down?"

Pascoe laughed and went into campaign HQ. He never answered the question.

They climbed in the car and drove off.

It seemed like they'd hardly been home when it was time to go back, and Dad pulled up sharply in front of campaign HQ. "Working you pretty hard, aren't they?" Dad said.

"I suppose you could say we asked for it," Emily said. "Not that we knew it at the time."

"Enjoying it, though?"

Emily thought about it for a second. "Yes. Enjoying it."

"You hesitated."

Dad always noticed these things. "Yeah, well, I was wondering about the staging of it all. We do an event, and it looks like a bunch of regular folks getting together while the candidate lays out his vision as if he just thought of it all. But really, it's more scripted than a Globe Theater production of Macbeth. Every single thing anyone says, every photo we take, every seat in the hall, it's all part of an elaborate plan to create a certain image."

"And this bothers you?"

"Not... I mean, yes, in one way, but in another way I wonder what I thought was really going on. Just like the theater, they make it look so effortless, and you never see the thousands of hours and dozens of people behind it all."

"Shouldn't it take at least as long as a play? It is the fate of the nation, after all."

Emily sat for a moment. Then Ethan spoke up. He'd been thinking about the same things. "But the camera angle isn't the thing to focus on. It's the ideas. The principles. That's what matters. Are we focusing on those things?"

"You probably aren't. But do you think the candidate is?"

The twins looked at each other. Ethan shrugged. "I don't know."

"What do you think, talking to him?"

Emily said, "I like him."

"That's what you think?" Dad said, his face showing some surprise.

"Instantly. He does it to everyone, I think. I'm not sure he can help it."

"Is this bad?"

"No," she said. "Definitely not. But it's... distracting. Because I like him, maybe I'm not paying attention to what he really is. Maybe I give him a pass instead of listening closely. That's what bugs me."

Dad scooched over so he could see them both at once. "Are you giving him a pass? Think carefully."

They did. It was a long couple of minutes before Ethan spoke. "I'm not. I mean, he's charming. I like him, too, Em. But I really listened to what he had to say when we met him, and I like what I heard. I think he was genuine."

"I thought so too. I'm just afraid of making a mistake. I don't want to find after all this that I'm working for someone I can't really believe in." She watched a couple get out of their car and go into the front office. "We need to go," she said.

"And so you will, but listen for just a minute," Dad said. He laid a hand on Emily's. "We trust you. We know you very well—better than you know yourselves. You know when you're doing right and when you have the feeling you're going wrong. Talk to each other. Be vigilant. But don't be so sure that dressing something up fancy means it's not real. Nor should you believe it's real just *because* it's dressed up fancy. Even if—especially if—you're doing the dressing. Don't read your own press clippings." He winked at Ethan. "And when you get home, I have a couple of books for you to read.

There are some really good insider accounts of political campaigns I think you'll identify with."

Emily blew out a breath. "That works. I hope I can keep my head straight."

"Ethan, how about you?"

"Today's our first event, so ask us again tonight," Ethan said, getting out. "Thanks for listening."

"You know I always will."

They walked through the door to find that they had company. A woman and two men in suits stood inside at the receptionist's desk, chatting idly. They glanced over as the twins came in.

"Good morning," Ethan said. "Has someone helped you?"

"We've been helped, yes," the woman said. She was older, with streaks of gray in her dark red hair. Her eyes glittered, sharp, possibly suspicious. The twins stepped past them and into the main office. Pascoe was there, examining a paper with Ed.

Pascoe looked up when they came in. "There you are."

"Right on time," Emily said, holding up her phone.

"We have company."

"Saw that. Who are they?"

"Big shots from the RNC."

Ethan frowned and lifted his phone. "Jeeves," he said. "What is the—"

"Oh, stuff it," Pascoe said. "RNC—the Republican National Committee. They spend most of the money in these kinds of campaigns. They're here to investigate how we're running things and decide how much money they want to put into this campaign. Winning this Senate seat would be huge for the Republicans.

"Best behavior, then," Emily said, smoothing her skirt. "What do we do?"

"Same thing you were going to do before. Don't be too smart, don't be dumb, and don't talk politics."

"Oh, the irony," Ethan said.

The twins had thought they'd be going right out to the venue, but apparently there was a meeting first with campaign staff and these people from Washington, D.C. Twenty or so people crowded into the boardroom in a long line like a lumpy snake. Ethan and Emily hung back, but Pascoe came to find them. "You'll have to stand, but there's room for you."

"We didn't know we were invited," Emily said.

"You aren't. But you should go anyway. Rule number 22: Never miss a meeting if you think there's the slightest chance you'll wish you'd been there." He disappeared inside, following Bekah, the receptionist, who had arrived with a small mountain of donuts and a jug of milk.

"Where does he get all these rules?" Ethan asked.

Everyone they knew from the front office was there, along with ten or so others, some in suits, but most in jeans or other casual wear. Kohn took a place near, but not at, the head of the table, as if he were deferring to the guests, and maybe he was. Emily saw Pascoe motion to him to scoot over into the head chair, which was still unoccupied as the RNC folk gladhanded their way around the room. Kohn shrugged and slid over.

Pascoe never missed a thing, did he? His game was always on, thinking about perfect placement, staging, presentation. He put his candidate in the right spot, always making him look good.

Pascoe's new placement of Kohn split the trio of big shots, but they didn't seem to mind. The two young men sat to the candidate's right, and the woman to the left. They looked at him expectantly while the donuts were passed around the room. By the time they reached Ethan, all that was left was an apple fritter and a pink frosted cake donut with weird sprinkles. But still, donut, so Ethan took it and handed the fritter to Emily.

"Thanks for coming on short notice," Kohn said. "Let me introduce our guests—they're going to be with us for a few days." He indicated his left. "This is Merriam Macintyre, and these two gentlemen are Ernie Franks and Henefer Eastman. They're from the RNC, here to take a look at what we're doing."

"Just keep going as normal," Macintyre said, clearly the one in charge. "We're here to help, not to muck things up. As a peace offering, we brought these," she said as she tossed a three-gallon bag of chocolate-coated cinnamon bears into the middle of the table.

A chorus of yums ran round the table. Except for Ethan, who scowled and said, "I'd rather be eaten by bears than have to eat them." But he said it low under his breath, where only Emily could hear him.

"Good. More for me. I get your share," she said.

"You three want to explain a bit more about why you're here?" Ed said. He had taken up a chair at the far end of the table, bookending it with Kohn.

Macintyre shared a look with Franks and Eastman, and it was the latter who finally spoke up. "Our function at the RNC is to make sure that good Republican candidates get elected. As you know, there are serious challenges in a number of races—Mississippi and North Carolina come to mind—and we need Montana if we're going to maintain a majority in the Senate in the fall."

Franks took up the thread. "It looks good here. You have a slight lead in the polls in a state we should expect to win. You have a great candidate, and what we can see of your staff is top-notch."

Some smiles at the compliment. Maybe it was sincere, and maybe it wasn't, but it seemed to work just fine either way.

Ed's hand went up.

"You don't really need to raise your hand," Macintyre said.

Ed ignored that. "Are you the ones who decide what resources are going to be committed to the state?"

There was a murmur at this, as if Ed had asked an embarrassing question. Macintyre's smile got a fraction more brittle. Pascoe, who had sidled up to the twins to stand next to them at the back of the room, said under his breath, "Rule number 18: You can't save the world if you can't pay the rent."

"For all intents and purposes, yes, we are. And that's why we're here, since we all seem to be willing to dispense with the bull. We do like what we see from the race and from the candidate. Randall Kohn has decent name ID, few overt negatives, and he's rich enough to buy the election if the electorate would be fine with his doing it. We think they won't, so some outside resources will likely be needed. We don't have unlimited funds, and we aren't going to waste money on a loser if we can help it." She turned slightly to Kohn. "No offense."

"Should there have been? I thought you were just saying you think I'm a winner."

"We do. But there have been some poor decisions made on that score in the past, and we think it's best to get boots on the ground, see for ourselves what's up. This isn't an investigation. We're on your side, whatever happens. We just have a lot of battleground to fight on. If you need us, and we can make a difference, we'll be here. If you don't, or it won't, then we have other fish to fry. Clear?"

"Crystal," Ed said.

Ethan wondered whether "being on your side" meant that the party would be willing to shade the truth, or even subvert it altogether, if that meant Kohn would win. Not for Kohn, obviously—they made it pretty clear this wasn't about him as a person or a candidate—but just because he would put another tally on their side of the board. At what point was it okay to do the wrong thing to get the right thing to happen? Was it *ever* okay? And were the twins the only ones in the room thinking about this, or was it all just part of how politics worked?

Kohn tapped a fingernail on the table. "Anything else you think we ought to know?"

Franks chuckled and said, "Everyone in the other party stinks."

"Oh, we know that already," Kohn said. "Everybody got a donut? Great. Then let's get to work."

The personnel streamed out of the room and split off to their various offices and workspaces. The twins were left in an eddy of the river of people, back in the corner, as everyone else left. When the line petered out, they made a move to leave, but Pascoe put his hand out to stop them.

"Boss," he said, "you want me to stick around for the next bit?"

"Wouldn't have you anywhere else," Kohn said.

"You two stay, then," Pascoe said to them. "You're part of the team. You're in all the way."

"Yes, Tuttles, you hang around. You're Assistants to the Campaign Director, aren't you?"

"Assistants to the *Vice* Campaign Director, I think," Ethan said.

"Rule number 6: Give 'em a title and get 'em involved," Pascoe said. "Take a seat and take all the notes you want, but you, Miss Tuttle, keep the recorder off this time."

And that was how the twins found out what the RNC people were *really* doing in Montana.

Eight people were left in the room. Ethan, Emily, Kohn, the three RNC people, Ed, and Pascoe.

The empty donut box had been quietly removed, though the scent still faintly lingered, and Ethan's stomach growled just a little. Nobody heard, he was sure.

Everyone looked at everyone else, as if it were their idea to have this meeting. The RNC folk took a long look at the twins and decided not to say anything. Not their business who was in the meeting.

It wasn't, actually, Emily thought.

The two men were just what she would have expected from Washington-level political operatives. Late twenties, early thirties, with good but not top-level dark suits, white shirts, and conservative ties. Franks's hair was fractionally lighter than Eastman's. Both had short cuts—Eastman's was longer, but didn't touch his collar—and faces that would be hard to remember. Eastman's nose suggested some kind of middle-eastern heritage somewhere in his past. Skin that had seen the sun, but not recently.

Macintyre, though, was a whole different kettle of fish. Her red hair was neatly cut, but straight as an arrow before curving just under her chin. It was streaked with gray, almost as a statement, and her face had real lines on it. She was likely forty or so, thin, with dark blue eyes that seemed to see everything at once. Light makeup, no attempt at a tan, and a spatter of freckles on her cheeks.

She's the one making the decisions, Emily thought. She could tell by how they positioned themselves, as if the center of gravity was in Macintyre's chair. No matter what the other two did, they orbited it, like planets.

Kohn himself was no lightweight. He'd been in boardrooms with big shots before, and having many millions of dollars made him hard to intimidate. But Emily could see little signs of his nervousness, the way he tapped the table, oriented his chair, kept track of where his people were. Emily realized that with her and Ethan in the room, Kohn had a numerical advantage. Was that why Pascoe had asked them to stay?

"Now," Ed said. "Suppose you tell us exactly why you're here. Not that the other stuff wasn't important and delivered with a high degree of believability. But you already know we're going to win, or you wouldn't be here."

"We don't know it." Sure enough, it was Macintyre who spoke. "Though you're not entirely off base. We strongly suspect Randall Kohn will be the next US senator from the state of Montana. Probably 60-40 chance, at worst."

Franks smiled thinly. "Some of us think that's low."

"Regardless," Macintyre went on smoothly, "the chances are good but not certain. You might win, and you might not. An infusion of cash, an endorsement by a couple of key national figures, some media, those things could be very important."

Ed and Pascoe took turns leaning back in their chairs.

"They could," Ed said. "We wouldn't say no to those things."

"But there are quid pro quos, provisos, addenda, as the Genie would say?" Pascoe said, from the opposite side of the table.

"There are," Macintyre said. "The first one should be obvious: there must be no skeletons in the closet. We need to know our man here is clean. Not just relatively, but Boy Scout clean. We've had our fill of scandals over the last few years. We aren't eager to take on any more. So before a thin dime of RNC money is disbursed, we'll have crawled through everything in this campaign as if we were the *New York Times*. If you don't squeak, we'll find somewhere else to send our hard-donated cash."

Kohn steepled his fingers and kept them locked on Macintyre. He wasn't fidgeting now. The nervousness was gone. "Expected. I'd do the same. What are the other conditions?"

It was Eastman's turn. He leaned forward and let his eyes sweep over Pascoe and the twins on the other side of the table. "We really will check out the campaign. We've all had relevant experience. I know we did some of this when you were back in Washington, but now that the campaign has fleshed out, we'll be doing it again.

We don't require the same level of political cleanliness from the staff that we do from the candidate, but there's still a standard. Some, uh, redistribution, might be required." He clearly didn't want his gaze to linger on Emily or Ethan, but there was the slightest pause there nonetheless.

Pascoe spoke up. "They aren't the ones you should worry about." He had noticed the look, then.

"No offense," Eastman said.

"You guys say that a lot," Emily said. "I do not think it means what you think it means."

"Is that like the Mid-Atlantic version of 'bless your heart'?" Ethan said.

Eastman's eyes widened. Silence, cold and frosty, descended like a hammer to an anvil.

Then Macintyre couldn't hold it in any longer. She burst out laughing like a balloon pricked with a pin. At first no one joined her, but then both Franks and Eastman failed to keep smiles off their faces, and Kohn was chuckling and shaking his head, and then the whole room was laughing their heads off. Emily and Ethan sat there, lone rocks in a heaving sea of hilarity.

"I told you," Ed finally choked out, waving at Pascoe. "You cannot tell what is going to come out of these kids' mouths."

Macintyre leaned forward to look around Pascoe, who was wiping his eyes. "Nobody warned *us*, though. Who are you?"

Ethan went through the introductions.

"That didn't help," Macintyre said. "Why are you here in this meeting? To pump out the hot air when it gets too thick?"

"Rule number 22," Ethan said.

"Never miss a meeting if you think there's the slightest chance you'll wish you'd been there," Emily said.

Macintyre's eyes bugged. "You're going to sit there and quote Morton Blackwell at me? What planet are you two from?"

"That's my fault," Pascoe said. "They probably think I was the one that came up with them."

"Well, I'm completely floored. I take it we can skip these two when it comes to investigation. Or maybe we should spend all our time on them. If we can figure out how to make more of them, we could take over the world."

"Now that we've gotten that out of the way," Kohn said, "you want to tell us if there are any other reasons for your visit?"

"There are a couple other private matters," Macintyre said. "I don't know that they're appropriate for a full staff meeting."

"I asked them here. You can't have anything to say to me that you wouldn't say in front of them," Kohn said.

"There are many things I would say only to you," Macintyre said. "But if you want me to say them anyway, I will, on your strictest confidence and a realization that it would be highly inappropriate for any of this to leave this room."

Kohn shrugged.

Ed said, "Not my first rodeo. I have a pretty good idea what you're going to say."

Ethan thought this might be a great time to get up and leave, but he didn't say so, and Pascoe made no move to dismiss them.

Macintyre said, "All the senate candidates are expected to do certain work for the party both during the campaign and afterward. Especially afterward. This work ensures the future health of the party and the maintenance of our ability to intervene to help get our candidates elected."

"Fundraising," Kohn said.

Macintyre nodded. "For you, certainly. You have a number of very influential people on your board, and you're connected to many more. Most of them we already have hooks in, but it never hurts to have some more. But you'll have quotas. We have a dollar figure in mind. You'll be expected to raise that money between now and election day. Afterward, there will be regular assessments. Additionally, you'll be expected at campaign events for other candidates in places where your presence could tip votes."

"I'll be campaigning for other people even before I've won a seat myself?" Kohn said, brow furrowed.

"Yes. Where we think it will help. And after you win, much more, of course."

"There may be some packaging," Franks cut in. "The 'new Republican wave,' or something like that, where your personal popularity helps a block of candidates including, say, MacDonald in Illinois."

Kohn looked hard at Ed. "I'm not sure I like MacDonald."

"That's not relevant, I'm sorry to say," Macintyre said. "He probably doesn't like you either. But we all have to get along for the party to succeed."

"His positions on trade make no sense. I can't support those."

"No one is asking you to support specific policies. It's more about Republicans sticking together," Eastman said.

That's it, Ethan thought. That's the truth of it. The party before all. The party *above* all. Never mind truth, never mind principle. Power or nothing. And the party was about power.

Which was greater, the power the party wanted to give to the candidate, or the power the party wanted for *itself*?

"Why do I get the feeling there's more of this coming?" Kohn said.

"Come on, Randall," Macintyre said. "You know how the game is played. We're just the best at playing it."

A different kind of silence grew then, sitting among them, bulbous and stinking. Kohn spun a pen around his fingers, thinking. The three RNC people sat very still, not looking at one another, all their attention fixed on Kohn. They said nothing, and it seemed they were prepared to wait all day if they had to.

Kohn finally said, "I won't sell my vote."

"No one ever does," Macintyre said. "And we would never ask it. There are certain issues, however, where it's best to go along with the party because when you do, the issues you care about get the same treatment."

"Treatment?"

"You're familiar with the rules of the Senate, I think. What comes up for vote is a result of negotiation between the GOP and the Democrats. Right now, we're in power, and we aim to remain there, which means we have the last word in what bills do and do not make it to the floor, and what the rules are for debate on those bills. You're going to be very popular in the senate, I think, so there's a good chance that your face on the right kinds of legislation could make it a lot easier for those bills to pass. Then we'll have the right kind of leverage to get your bills to the floor for action."

"Log-rolling. I scratch your back, you scratch mine." Kohn made a face as if he'd eaten something that disagreed with him.

"It's the way of the world. Especially in politics."

"What happens if there's a bill I can't support?"

Macintyre frowned but kept her voice low, urgent. "We can put any hypothetical out there you like. I'd love to promise you you'll never be in that situation, but we both know how this works. You give a little, others give a little back. This is how bills get passed. Compromise. Cooperation. You can put yourself out there in right field like Senator Brand from Kentucky, and where would that get you? You think someone like that has influence? I mean, think about Senator Anders. Guy's been elected nine times. But he's a nutball, and in fifty years he's never had a single bill pass the chamber. Not one. You want that to be your legacy? Having to run for president with that around your neck?"

"President?" Kohn said, his eyebrow cocked.

"Why not? You're young. You're charismatic. You're rich. You're from a swing state. Play ball, and all sorts of possibilities open up." She leaned back then and exhaled, as if she'd spent all the energy she had making that speech. "Besides, you've got a talent for recruiting, that's obvious." She indicated the twins down the table. "Staff like this can take you anywhere there is to go."

As if on some cue, Eastman pushed back from the table and stretched. "I'm sorry, folks, I have to find the facilities."

"I'll show you," Ed said. They moved toward the door.

Macintyre checked her watch. "Oh, crud. I apologize; I have a call with Florida in ten minutes. Do you have a quiet room someplace Ernie and Hen and I could use?"

"I think so," Kohn said. "Pascoe? Can you hook these people up?"

The three of them exited. Ethan and Emily started to get up when Kohn said, "No, hang on a second, Emily, Ethan. I want to ask you something."

They settled back down, more awkward than ever. Kohn didn't seem his cheerful self. He fidgeted, as if he were trying on some new clothes that didn't fit very well.

The door shut behind the others, and the last three sat there for a long moment, Kohn playing with his pen again.

"I really do have some odd ideas," he said. "I don't know if you've had much chance to read my policy position papers."

"Uh, they're on my nightstand," Emily said. "I'll get to them, plus a Nobel Prize treatise on macroeconomics, right after *Oathbringer*."

Kohn laughed short, just once, as if that were all he could manage at the moment. "I won't hold my breath. That book is thick enough to hold up your car while you change the oil. And I'd rather be reading Brandon Sanderson myself. But the RNC is right. No one is going to give my ideas a hearing if I don't do some of the work for the party."

"That sounds like a rule," Ethan said.

Another short laugh. "Number 6,212 or something. I can't ever remember the numbers. But it says 'A stable movement requires a flow of IOUs. Don't keep careful track of them.'"

"What about principle?" Emily said. "Doesn't that come into it?"

Kohn sighed. "Of course it does. But there's another rule that says 'Don't make the perfect the enemy of the good.' This might be time to keep that one in mind. I won't get all of what I want, and I didn't really expect to. But I won't get *any* of what I want if I cut these people off at the knees."

"You'll win without them," Ethan said. Even he could hear the uncertainty in his voice.

"Maybe. Likely, even. But then what? I have one vote in the Senate. With the party behind me, I might have more than fifty votes behind me. That kind of muscle can get things done."

"Their things."

"My things, too."

"What did you want to ask us?" Emily said.

His head came up and his dark eyes laid on them for a moment. "I wanted to ask you to sit in my chair. And then I want to ask you to tell me what you'd do if it were you running."

Emily got up like she'd sat on a pinecone.

Kohn shook his head. "Was I ever sixteen?" he said, but he levered himself out of his chair and moved to the one Macintyre had sat in.

Emily sat heavily in the head chair and looked about at the table as if she were a queen examining her court.

"Okay, gang," she said. "Here's what we're going to do."

If you think they should go along with the party, turn to page 8.

If you think they should tell them to stick it, turn to page 252.

“We can hear you, you know,” Mom called from the dining room.

“No, you can’t,” Emily said. “All you can hear is our fake conversation we use to fool the surveillance equipment. Then we have our real discussion by twin mind meld. Telepathically.”

They came back into the dining room with the dessert. Ethan took the big carton of vanilla ice cream and tugged the top off it. Emily laid the still-hot casserole dish of peach crisp on the table. “Pass your plates, ladies and gents.”

Emily scooped crisp, and Ethan covered it with balls of creamy frozen goodness. For a long moment, there wasn’t any conversation. The silence was punctuated only by satisfied groans from the table.

Cathy was the first one to finish. “Okay, you’ve kept me in suspense long enough. Which is it?”

“Isn’t it obvious?” Ethan said.

“You forget she doesn’t have the twin telepathy we do, Ethan,” Emily said. “Although she is Mom’s sister. I was hoping for some kind of magic there.”

Dad said, “Please forgive my children. They get the sarcasm from my side of the family.”

Mom said, “As convincing as Miss Finn’s argument was, the truth is that while the issues I care about seem to be decided on the federal level, the ones that affect my daily life are far more local.”

Miss Finn opened her mouth to speak, but instead took another bite of crisp.

"Education is one of the biggest concerns in our family. Lots of people think the Department of Education controls education policy, but it doesn't. Most of the decisions that matter on how much money will be spent, what our schools teach, even whether or not it's okay for me to homeschool—those decisions are made right here, in our districts and by our state. Yes, while the federal government delivers a ton of money to the states, and they can use that money as a whip to get what they want, but the debate that really matters on education is the one in Helena."

"More than that," Dad said, "we can't influence the federal government in any meaningful way. Even with a dear sister as one of a hundred senators, we wouldn't have near the influence over policy that we would if that same sister were Secretary of State. What you could accomplish here, as a part of the local government, would outweigh anything you could do as a senator."

"And one more thing. There are going to be good candidates for federal office. But Dennis Forde's replacement in the state government is a choice between you and Louis Sulla. I'd almost rather have Pol Pot than Louis Sulla," Dad said. "Not really, of course."

"I've heard he's not the best," Emily said. "But that bad?"

"We've had business dealings. I wouldn't trust him with the petty cash envelope, let alone as the overseer of several billion dollars of state money. No. He cannot be allowed to take that seat for any length of time. Macrinus in the Governor's mansion isn't my favorite, but he isn't a monster, unless he has encouragement. Sulla will absolutely encourage Macrinus's worst tendencies to graft, cronyism, and corruption."

Cathy pursed her lips. "Okay, that's the two of you. What about you?" she said to the twins.

"We're with these fellers," Ethan said. "You have to take Dennis Forde's place. It was made for you. His ghost demands it."

Mr. Soffits, through this whole exchange, had said nothing. Now he laid his spoon in his bowl and said, "I think that's a fair assessment." He leaned over to catch Miss Finn's eye. "No hard feelings. I feel like I may have had supernatural help."

"I won't pretend I'm not frustrated," she said. "Taking a shot at the Senate would have been a truly noble contest."

"David and Goliath," Cathy said, "and me with a bad pitching arm. I have to be honest, I was hoping you guys would come down on the side of the SecState job. It's not just Dennis, and not just that, locally, I feel like I can make the biggest difference. It's that I feel like that seat needs someone in it who will be true to the principles we fought for the whole time Dennis was in government. What we tried to do there, to clean things up, that can't be allowed to be undone. The Senate would be cool. But this is personal."

Miss Finn sucked the last of the silky syrup off her spoon. "As long as you don't think you're getting rid of me."

"Wouldn't dream of it," Cathy said. "I can't wait to unleash you on Louis Sulla's thugs. They're in for some serious re-thinking if they believe that being appointed to the job means they're going to get to keep it without a fight."

The press conference announcing Cathy's run for the SecState job wasn't well attended. Only one TV crew put in an appearance, and they didn't carry the speech live. They just cribbed bits for their later broadcast. After it was over, Cathy, Mom, and the twins sat on the lawn of the state Capitol and let the sun beam down on them. Below them, the grass sloped away to the street, and beyond that, Helena spread out to the horizon.

"That was a disappointing turnout," Emily said.

"Not terribly," Cathy said. "We don't need a lot of attention right now. What we need is to get rolling and get the right team assembled. There are a lot of moving parts to a campaign. We need the right people in those parts. And speaking of that, I need to put you two somewhere."

"I want to be campaign manager," Emily said.

"Tempting," Cathy said, with a laugh. "But no. I have someone already lined up for that. In fact, most of the staff is already hired, but there are a couple of slots where I need some additional manpower. Womanpower. Teenpower."

"Twinpower," Ethan said. "It's not a thing, but it sounds good."

"What are the jobs you're offering us?" Emily asked, brushing an ant off her leg.

"One understaffed part of the campaign is the political arm, where you'd be making policy decisions, writing papers, negotiating with local political groups for endorsements and support, that kind of thing."

"And the other one?" Ethan said.

"The other one is the fundraising arm. We can't run this thing without money."

"How about one of each?" Emily said. "I mean, with our telepathic powers, you're getting two people for the price of one in each job."

Mom lifted her head off the grass and opened her eyes, shading them with her hand. "As long as they're on the same schedule, that will be fine. I'm not driving them separately, and they don't have a car."

"Car insurance is expensive," Emily said, rubbing her thumb and pointer finger together. "We need cash."

"If you two can agree on which of you goes where, I'm fine splitting you up. Most of the work will be done in the office, but there might be some field work. I can arrange rides. I would really like to have the two of you on board," Cathy said.

Emily said, "I'm all about the politics. I love writing papers."

"I'm good with money," Ethan said. "I like everything about it."

"Settled, then. If your mom approves."

Mom said, "Mom is sleeping in the early summer sun. Please leave a message."

If you want to follow Emily to the political job, turn to page 236.

If you want to follow Ethan to the fundraising job, turn to page 24.

"There's no point in doing this questionnaire," Emily said. "You used to do these, didn't you? What do you think?"

"I think they can be valuable, in certain circumstances. But probably not in this one. It depends a bit on what we'd do with our time instead. Or what you'd do, more precisely, because I think I'm only here for this project. If it's not going to happen, I should be on down the road doing other things."

"Like?"

"Super cool stuff you wouldn't understand," he said.

"Like sleeping?"

Gio couldn't keep it going anymore and burst out laughing. "Dang. I think I'd like working with you, too."

"Well then, before you go off to your super cool stuff, what do you do for a living, other than muck around in political campaigns? Maybe we can come up with something that keeps you around. And paid. I'm assuming the paid part is a thing."

"Kind of, yes. I mean, yes, getting paid is a thing. I'm a political consultant. I eat during election years."

"Let's keep the gravy flowing. What else do you know besides unions?" Emily said, swiveling in her chair. It had good balance. With a good push, she could get around three times.

"I know music," Gio said. He said it like it didn't matter much, or wasn't important.

"Type?"

"Jazz, mostly. Or, not modern jazz, but dance band jazz. Also the usual modern stuff."

Emily tagged the ground with her foot to stop the swivel facing directly toward Gio. "I fail to see how that could be useful to the campaign."

"Sort of what I was thinking. Though there are musicians' unions, too."

Emily leaned back, her face skeptical. "There are?"

"Sure. Orchestras have them. Did they send us a questionnaire?"

"Not that I'm aware. I don't think the Montana Symphony is interested in making an endorsement. Do you have a lot of other consulting gigs at the moment?"

"I'm between contracts. It's still early. The big Senate campaigns haven't started wasting huge sums of money just yet."

"So you have time."

"I do."

"And I do what they tell me, which right now is filling out questionnaires and talking to various community groups about meeting with Cathy." She made a face.

"You don't say that as if it is the light of your life and existence."

"My brother chose to do fundraising. I thought political work, position papers, stuff like that would be more fun. I am not sure I made the right choice."

Gio tossed his pen in the air, bounced it off the ceiling, and caught it. "So I don't have work to do, and you don't have work you want to do. That would be a serious problem if we weren't brilliant people."

Emily smiled. Flattery. But it still worked. "Being brilliant, I already know what we're going to end up doing, but in an attempt to be equality-minded, I'm going to let you tell me."

"Have you ever organized anything before?" he said.

She laughed. "Quite a few things. Protest marches, food truck rallies, you name it."

"How old did you say you were?"

"Sixteen. But as Indiana Jones says, 'It ain't the years, honey, it's the mileage.' I've led a life of some variety."

"You're quoting Indiana Jones, too. Who are your parents?"

Emily flashed a bright smile. "People who made it seem more fun to do useful work than binge Netflix. Except classics, of course."

"I have an idea, then. Why don't we find a way to put my music together with your organizing skills?"

"This is a political campaign, not a jazz club," Cathy said. "I'm not sure what you're proposing."

Gio perched on the side of Cathy's desk, an infectious smile on his face. Emily had the loveseat all to herself, but she wasn't using a lot of it, sitting on the edge of one cushion and leaning over the coffee table. It did put the Skittles closer, after all.

"I think you should run a music festival. Sponsor the thing, mingle with the people, showcase it as the sort of thing you'd encourage as the Secretary of State." Gio waved his hands around, pointing to bits of his imagination as if he were seeing it all before him. "Over here, the rock and roll. Under this pavilion, bluegrass and country. By the food court, the jazz combos."

"Food court?" Cathy said. "This gets better and better." Her voice did not indicate that this was actually so.

"Yes. If you have people there, you'll have to have food. Emily tells me she's in good with a large number of food trucks."

Cathy cocked an eyebrow toward her niece. "That was a few years ago, wasn't it? You think they'll remember you?"

"I guarantee it," Emily said. The Food Truck Fiasco wasn't something people tended to forget.

Gio looked back and forth between the other two. "I'm missing something."

Cathy waved him off. "She'll tell you, I'm sure. Listen, all this sounds fascinating, but I'm not sure what it's going to accomplish."

Emily said, "Let me see if I can remember the three things we talked about. One, it's name ID. This is the sort of thing that gets a fair amount of earned media—free mentions in the paper and on radio stations."

"Always good," Cathy said, with a frown toward the bowl of candy. "Eat some of the green ones too, while you're at it."

"The green ones are gross. Two, we get to illustrate the kind of community outreach work that the SecState should be doing. A good number of community groups will come together at this thing, if we play it right."

"Again, good. Almost thou persuadest me."

"Thank you. The third thing is a little harder to quantify, but it gives you a chance to take your political positions and translate them to something in the real world. Truth is, nobody wants to hear what your position is on tax policy. But they are interested in jazz."

"As they should be," Gio said. "We wouldn't be the only ones involved in this event, of course, and it might put us into close contact with groups we wouldn't normally associate with. There will be some strange bedfellows here."

"I don't mind that," Cathy said. "How much is this going to cost? The questionnaire you've conveniently forgotten to mention was going to be free. I assume this will not be."

"Probably not," Emily said. "But I'm sure you can scare up a few more checks and raise the funds for it."

Gio cut in, "Even easier, I think. Donating to a campaign is one thing. Donating to a community music festival is something else."

"And you'll be making a public statement about working with special interest groups like unions," Emily said.

Cathy rolled her eyes. "Here it comes."

"We're not playing ball. The political process is not served when we are influenced by groups who only want to use the power of government to make sure their positions are secure. You're not going to play ball with them. It's the people who matter, and this is the people's campaign."

"You're overcooking my grits here. No, no, I understand what you're driving at," Cathy said. "I'm just thinking this is a bold strategy. Will people come out to a festival sponsored by a political campaign?"

"That's the best part," Emily said. "It's not about the campaign. It's the Dennis Forde Memorial Music Festival."

Cathy stared at her for a moment. "Dennis… He loved music."

"Right."

"He would have adored this idea. Though he would have hated to have his name on it."

"Too bad. He's not around to protest, and he needs to be remembered. It should also allow us to reach out to the African-American community and get them involved in something visible and positive. They've been on the short end of the political process for a long time. With Dennis, they got a fair shake for the first time.

This should send a message that if Cathy Harmon were sitting in his chair, you would continue his push for criminal justice reform. That you'd listen to that community, just like Dennis did."

"Risky," Cathy said. "But it has the virtue of truth. Politicians have been using the black community for a long time, making promises, reaping votes, then doing nothing meaningful while in office. I would never use Dennis's name to do that. I would, however, continue the *work* Dennis did. His policies were working in the community, for all races, for anyone who was really committed to justice and equality. I'm not just talking about being on their side. I've *been* on their side all along."

"That's exactly it," Gio said, bending down for a handful of Skittles for himself before Emily emptied the bowl. "No way can we out-Sulla Sulla. He's got a corner on the corruption market. You can't push for the status quo. You're not equipped to play that game."

Emily dug in. "The good news is that we *are* equipped to play directly to the voters. We have a track record and a mentor that meant something to the underprivileged community. We go to them, not to corporate interests—not that there's anything wrong with corporations."

"The fundraising people are going to hate this. Your brother is going to want to kill you," Cathy said.

"No, he won't. Not when he finds out Amy's Crazy Pizza will be there."

Cathy sighed. "The truth is, I was feeling like we needed something different to boost the campaign. We're doing fine, the polls look okay, but Sulla's getting all sorts of name ID for being the current SecState. I think we need to do something to shake things up. And I had no other ideas. We can be a second-rate Sulla, or a first-rate Harmon."

"Being a Harmon is always better," Emily said. She winked at Gio. "I hope you like jazz."

At first, and for a couple of weeks, the idea lacked thrust to get off the ground. Most of the people Gio and Emily contacted were unable to wrap their heads around the idea of a music festival sponsored by a political campaign. So they went directly to community organizers. The local Commitment to Justice chapter almost hung up on Emily when she called the first time, but when she and Gio went to their office and sat in the lobby for half an hour, they finally got the message that this was serious.

Commitment to Justice was an organization dedicated to making sure everyone accused of a crime was able to be defended competently in court and that everyone received a fair trial based on the evidence. Emily was horror-struck that an organization committed to justice was controversial, but she understood from lots of late-night conversations with her parents why such a commitment was needed.

"Frankly, we were sure that all the progress that had been made with Dennis Forde was going to go away," Patrisse Hearns said. She sat behind a small desk that would have looked right at home in Aunt Cathy's ramshackle office. "We didn't know Cathy Harmon very well. She was more behind the scenes. But that office went from being lockstep behind the street-to-prison conveyor belt to being somewhat more fair while Dennis was there. Let's just say we don't view Louis Sulla as being cut from the same cloth."

Gio explained that the festival wasn't looking for money from CTJ. All they wanted was for them to put the word through the organization and to point them to groups that could be invited to perform.

"You should know," Emily said, "We're going to invite the police to participate as well. Everyone is going to be invited. But there will be special booth placement there for you to tell people about your organization."

"Yeah, in the back," Hearns said, as if she expected it.

"Right at the entrance," Gio said. "If you help us put this together, you'll get pride of place."

"Forgive us if we don't believe you," Hearns said. "There is a long, long history of blacks being told one thing, then getting something much worse when the rubber meets the road. Our community needs to see that it's valued. That means more than just nice words in negotiation. We knew Dennis Forde, and he was a man of ideals. We didn't agree with everything he did, but we knew he was listening to us. We knew he understood what it was like never to feel safe, never to be quite sure if the people who were supposed to protect us were on our side."

"You have my word," Emily said.

Hearns smiled tightly. "You're sixteen."

Emily's phone buzzed. "I apologize," she said. "It's Ms. Harmon." She put the phone to her ear. "Yes, boss," she said. "You were right. I think you can just come in. The receptionist can show you where we are." Emily hung up.

"That was the candidate?" Hearns said.

"She's outside. She wanted to meet you."

Aunt Cathy came through the door less than a minute later, hand extended, and apologized for being late. "I wanted to be here sooner, but campaigning intruded. I'm a fan of your organization. I hope we can be of help to you."

Hearns appraised her with caution. "Your two associates here have done a good job, but I'm skeptical that they can deliver on what they promise."

"If they promised you that you'll be treated like the guests of honor, that your desires for place and for prominence will be treated with deference, and that whatever we say we will do you can bank on, then I back those promises myself, and I'll do it in writing if you like."

Hearns said nothing, but the look on her face was priceless.

"I'm not a person of color," Cathy said, pulling a chair close enough to look Hearns directly in the eyes, "so I do not and never will understand all that you're going through, all that your community has gone through for centuries. But I can promise this: Dennis Forde taught me a lot about how to listen, how to wait for understanding, and how to see and respond to injustice. I'm committed to justice. I believe in eliminating prejudice, reducing obstacles to black advancement, and being ruthless toward those who would impose prejudice in the law. This," she said, sweeping her hand toward Gio and Emily, "is a community event. You are a part of the community, and you should be featured as such. Call it a small evidence that what I tell you is true."

Hearns said, "They told me we could exclude any organization we didn't want to deal with."

Without missing a beat, Cathy said, "No, ma'am, they didn't. We don't work that way. Justice for *all* is what we believe in."

Hearns paused for a moment, then laughed out loud. "Well, I don't know if y'all rehearsed this before you came in, but I will say you could hardly have made a better pitch. As for me and this house, we'd like to see what you can come up with."

That more or less sealed the deal.

And once they were on board, it wasn't hard to get other organizations to participate as well. The huge relief organization, Jackie's Pantry, agreed to put the word out. The Rotary Club district provided volunteers. The food trucks did remember Emily Tuttle—quite well, as it turned out—and promised to assemble in force.

They scheduled the event for the week before the primary election. "Probably pretty late," Gio said. "A lot of people will have voted by mail before then."

"Then we register people to vote. I have some experience with that, too. Ethan and I did it as part of a campaign to save my grandmother's house."

Gio shook his head. "This kind of thing shouldn't keep surprising me, but it does."

Gio's favorite singer, Kassidy Evans, agreed to headline with her jazz combo. Emily managed to schedule the twins' favorite local rock band, Wonderbad. Everyone got something.

The event was a nightmare to organize, though, and it taxed their handful of volunteers to the limit. Getting all the permits, the tents, the sound equipment, and port-a-potties. Scheduling dozens of performers. Juggling hundreds of other things together to make the event successful. It all took a lot more time and

energy than filling out the questionnaire would have. Sometimes Emily remembered that and wondered if she'd made the right choice.

But the day of the event made it all worth it. At first, few people trickled in, and the early bands played to mostly empty spaces. As the day wore on, people began to come in larger and larger waves. Lunchtime saw another huge influx as people came for what turned out to be the largest gathering of food trucks in the state.

And then the bands whipped the people up, and the party got started for real.

Hundreds of people danced and sang and ate churros. They wandered by the Commitment to Justice booth and had a chance to see that these were just people looking for a chance to tell their story—not people to be feared. The CTJ booth proudly displayed a simple but large banner: "We Deserve a Chance!" When Emily saw a pair of off-duty cops laughing and joking with a pair of black teenagers, she thought that, right there, the whole event was worth it. Politicians might keep people distracted by stoking their fears of each other, but once people begin to talk with one another, they realize they aren't enemies after all.

Also quite popular was the voter registration booth, prominently placed in the park. A steady line of people queued up there all through the day to register to vote. Gio kept the campaign people away from there, but the burgundy t-shirts of the Harmon campaign were hot items nonetheless. By the end of the night, when

Kassidy's combo kicked off, the crowd was a sea of wine-red shirts.

Gio stood at the back of the crowd and couldn't wipe the smile off his face.

Emily got a moment to come stand with him. "Everything you imagined?" she said.

"Everything and more," he said. "Kassidy Evans and I are having dinner afterward."

"No!" Emily said, mouth agape. "How did you pull that off?"

"Well, I'll be honest. It was my plan from the beginning. All this other stuff was just gravy."

Emily punched his arm hard enough to hurt and went off to make sure the pavilions were being carefully dismantled.

The combo finished by calling Aunt Cathy to the stage for a thunderous ovation. The organizers and community groups had each gotten their turn to take a bow, and Kassidy wouldn't let Cathy leave the stage without making a short speech.

"This wouldn't have been possible without a huge number of volunteers of all stripes, but the real thanks has to go to Dennis Forde." Cheers drowned her out for a moment as the thousands voiced their approval. She waited for them to subside. "He was the first black man to sit in the SecState chair. What he did there, rooting out corruption, reaching out to all members of our community," she paused to reach out to Patrisse Hearns, standing just to the side, and take her hand, "changed our state for the better. That change should be permanent. It should be followed up on. Dennis would have done it, but he's gone. It falls to us. Will you carry on his work?"

Roars shook the ground. It took almost five minutes for the band to get the crowd quiet enough to play their concluding songs.

The campaign staff got together the following Monday for the post-mortem.

"In the end, it was a lot better than I thought it would be." Cathy sat behind her desk, checking through some last-minute details. "You both did brilliant work."

"Thank you," Emily said. "It certainly was the weirdest campaign event I've ever been to. We registered almost two thousand voters, and that's not nothing. They won't all vote for us, of course."

"The polls don't look good," Miss Finn said. "I'm not going to lie. But I don't think they'd look better if we played the game the usual way, kissing up to every major corporation, union, and special-interest group on earth."

"We only kissed up to some of them," Gio said. "Which is much better. We got a huge amount of late coverage in the press, and Twitter blew its top over this thing. We had several people streaming over the web during the event. If the election were national, we'd kill Sulla."

Cathy checked one more box. "It's not, sadly. But I'm not disappointed. We started something. Maybe it won't result in my election this time, but there will be other chances."

"Can we talk for a second about the election night party?" Gio said. "I had an idea for the entertainment. I think the Kassidy Evans combo would come play for us, if we asked."

Cathy looked at Gio over the top of her clipboard. Everyone else's eyes were on him as well. His cheeks colored.

"Would she indeed?" Cathy asked.

"Uh, I think so. I'd have to check," Gio said.

"Do that."

Cathy looked tired. There were bags under her eyes, and she looked like she'd aged ten years in the previous weeks. "We've done all we can. If we haven't done it the way others would have, we've done it the best we knew how. Get out of here and vote."

Kassidy Evans did come and play for the party. Gio looked like a man who'd won the lottery.

Emily, Ethan, and the whole Tuttle clan arrived in time for the dancing and food. Cathy glad-handed the crowd as it filed in, including a lot of people Emily recognized from the music festival.

Just as the polls closed, Cathy announced to the crowd that her friend Hank had donated enough to ensure that the Dennis Forde Music Festival would be an annual event and provide a place for the community to gather and get to know one another from then on. The packed crowd cheered this news as enthusiastically as if it meant that Cathy Harmon was going to win the election.

She didn't.

It was close. For a long stretch of the night, it appeared that she might be able to pull off the upset, but by midnight enough of the vote was in to know for sure that it wasn't going to happen. Not this time.

Cathy and Mom hugged each other for a long time, until they were interrupted by two African-American women asking for a moment of Cathy's time. It was Anniele Forde and Patrisse Hearns. Their hugs weren't any smaller or less lengthy.

"This isn't over," Anniele kept saying. "We're only getting started."

And Emily realized that was true. They'd already won something important, and they'd keep coming until they won it all.

THE END

"I don't think I'd like talking people into voting for anyone," Emily said. "Whatever the other thing is, it has to be better than that."

"You're sure?" Kohn said. "You'll miss being right next to the room full of snacks."

"Snacks shmacks," Ethan said, "I'm all in on whatever the secret thing is."

Kohn smiled. Emily wasn't entirely sure she liked the look of it. But she was sure she liked the next part.

"This other job is something a little different. In order for the campaign to work, we need to know everything we can find out about our opponents."

The twins exchanged a glance.

"Everything we can find out. You mean like research?" Ethan said.

"Hmm. Yes. Definitely there will be research. That's not really what I was talking about though."

"What other kinds of… Oh," Emily said.

Kohn nodded, seeing she had the idea.

"You're talking about spying," Emily said. "You want us to be spies."

Kohn waved a finger. "Not spies exactly. We prefer the term 'opposition researchers.'"

"And what do opposition researchers do?" Ethan said. "Interview staffers from the other campaign?

Pretend to be interested in the candidates so they can get secrets from the competition?"

"Yes, basically," Kohn said.

"That's spying," Emily said.

"Fine, if you insist. But oppo research has a long and distinguished tradition in this country, dating back to Jefferson and Adams."

Ethan had a quick flashback to their lesson on the presidential election of 1800, where one side paid a newspaper to print lies about the other one, and both sides' supporters violently clashed in the streets, after which the two candidates—who had been best friends for years—didn't speak another word to each other for a decade and a half.

"That was a nasty campaign," Emily said. "But we're only sixteen. Nobody's going to tell us anything."

"On the contrary," Kohn said, standing up and moving to a file cabinet against the back wall. "It's because you're sixteen the other campaigns will tell you anything you want to know."

"Isn't it unethical?" Ethan said. "I'm not sure I like the idea. Can't you just put your ideas up against the other guys' and see which the voters like better?"

Kohn stared at him, fingers deep in a file. "What sort of game do you think this is?" he said. "That hasn't really been tried since Lincoln and Douglas."

"And it didn't work then, either," Emily said. "Remember, Douglas won."

"That is precisely the point," Kohn said. "An extended series of researched debates, hours long, would be deeply educational for me and my opponent, but I fear modern attention spans would hardly stand it. Thus we will need to try something different." He drew out a manila folder, shut the drawer, and came back to the table. He put the folder in front of Emily. "Take a look," he said.

She opened it and inside was a sheet of paper, just one. It had a list of dates and places on it, and a name at the top: Bauer. Emily looked up, not understanding.

"That is a list of the places our main opponent Donald Bauer will be over the next week. These are all public appearances, which will give you a good sense for who he is, who his people are, and what sort of operation he has going on. All that is valuable. But there are more things to learn, and I hope you'll be willing to learn them and share them with me and my staff."

Emily tapped the sheet of paper, thinking furiously. Was this ethical? Could she really do this? What would happen if she were caught? And also…

"How many of the people on this campaign are actually working for Bauer?" she said.

Kohn's jaw dropped. "I don't… Well, none of them. They really couldn't be. We check everyone pretty thoroughly."

Emily smiled. "Then I think we can do this. If you can't find any of his people, then he probably won't be able to find any of yours. I assume we're not the only ones you're having do this kind of work?"

"You assume correctly, and you have a suspicious mind, did you know that?"

"*I* knew," Ethan said. "We shared a bedroom the first ten years of our lives. You can't even imagine what that was like."

"I grew up with four of us sharing a room," Kohn said. "My sisters were similarly nosy."

Ethan nodded, a shared point having been established.

"What is it you really want us to get?" Emily said. "I assume you can get the text of his speeches from the newspaper or VidNow, just like everyone else."

Kohn twirled a pen and looked down at the table for a second. "What I really want, if you can get it, is evidence that the other side is cheating. I want to know if they're buying votes or organizing in an unethical way, stuff like that."

"Do you think they are?"

"I don't. Not really. Oh, they could be, of course. It's certainly possible—"

"Just like it's possible this campaign is doing that."

"—But it's very unlikely," he said sternly, with a dark look. "Even on the other side, I don't think people intentionally try to break the rules in that way. They'll cheat, of course, in minor ways. They'll steal yard signs. They'll misquote us. They'll work hard to register people they know are going to vote for them and not do it for people who aren't. Stuff like that. But I don't think they're going to break the law. Obviously, if they do and they show it to you, I'd expect you to report it."

"So *realistically* what do you want?" Ethan said.

"The best I could reasonably hope for is inside information—what they're planning to do, what their strategies are, what their key talking points will be—so that we can prepare counters for them."

"Corporate spying then," Emily said. Her face was unreadable. "Espionage."

"More or less, yes."

"Dirt?" Ethan said. "What if we find that the candidate's car is rowed by child slaves?"

Kohn stared at him. "There are so many things wrong with that question, I don't even know where to start."

"You know what I mean, though."

He sighed. "Okay, yes, I know what you mean. If they're not paying their people, or they're violating labor law, or the campaign manager is secretly a hit man for the Mafia, then yes, I believe that information would aid the voters in making an informed choice come November."

Ethan smiled. "Fair enough. I don't have a problem with that. I won't promise that I can come up with anything useful, but there's no harm in hanging around and seeing what's what."

"Money though," Emily said. "That might be an issue. Not just pay, but like, an expense account. Suppose we have to take someone out to lunch or something."

"I'll make some *limited* funds available to you, along with a debit card for things like gas and other incidentals. Do you have a car you can use, or should I supply one of those as well?"

"Since I joined this campaign primarily to afford a car, I think you'll have to see if there's a spare vehicle in the fleet. Sorry."

He made a note on a card and tucked it into his pocket. "That's fine. I'll have it here tomorrow, and you'll start."

The twins contemplated one another in contentment. "Great," Emily said. "It should be fun to get paid for this sort of thing for a change. We've always had to do our political party crashing for free."

It wasn't until the third campaign appearance, a rally at a bowling alley in Port Hope, that the twins got the attention of someone who mattered in the campaign.

They were lined up for the free Skittles when the lady behind them in line said, "So, you two don't go to school much, do you?"

The twins turned around to find a short, smiling woman with brown hair shot through with streaks of gold standing behind them. She had a "Bauer" shirt on that had seen some washing.

"We don't go to school at all," Ethan said. "Homeschool is awesome."

"It really helps us get into the political process," Emily said.

"Plus, we like bowling," Ethan said, moving forward a place in line. "And Skittles."

"And apparently, Donald Bauer." The woman kept the smile fixed in place, but Emily had a feeling it wasn't entirely genuine.

"Why do you say that?" Ethan said, voice all innocence.

Emily elbowed him in the ribs. "Because we've been to his last three campaign appearances," she said. "And really, with the nonsensical stump speech he makes about jobs and unions and common-sense trade reform, it's obvious we aren't following him around hoping to learn anything about economics."

The woman looked from one twin to the next and back again, not quite sure what to make of the act she was seeing. They moved up one more spot. Almost to the table.

"It's true," Ethan said. "We can't vote, but Bauer does the best events, and he's growing on me."

"That's nice to hear," the woman said. "I'm Evelyn Craddock. I'm the deputy campaign manager for southern Montana. I'm pleased you like our campaign so far."

"But why do we keep coming out?" Emily said. "You might as well just ask us. It's obvious you want to know."

"Okay. Why do you keep coming out?"

"Two reasons," Ethan said, stepping to the table and picking up a pen to write on the clipboard so he could claim his bag of Skittles. "One, as homeschoolers we have to do projects for school. We chose to do one on the campaign." He stopped talking because writing his email address made it hard for him to speak coherently. And because he was shocked at how easily he was able to lie. Could a life in politics change you that fast? Was it really important enough to win that sacrificing your character was worth it?

"The other reason," Emily said, writing her name and address with no trouble at all, "is that we know a lot of people don't like Bauer in this area, and we thought we'd investigate why."

"And?" Craddock said.

"And we decided we couldn't understand it." Emily laid her pen down, got her bag of candy from the bowl, and ripped off the top. "He's not a smooth talker, but he doesn't say dumb things. He seems to have a plan for what he wants to do, and three terms as mayor of Grover's Corners is a decent way to start in politics." She did *not* say "maybe they don't like him because his economic policies are as illiterate as a wading pool full of polliwogs", but she was thinking it. She'd already mentioned it, and if the campaign people didn't already know about the job-killing effects of their "progressive" ideas, she didn't see how her explaining it to them was going to fix things.

"It beats his opponent, who hasn't got any experience at all," Ethan said through his own mouthful of candy.

"You'll excuse my curiosity," Craddock said, stepping out of line to the joy of the kids behind her. "It's not a usual thing, getting groupies. Do you plan to keep coming to events?"

Ethan smiled. "I do. The next one is at the Manticores game. Free hot dogs."

Craddock rubbed her chin. Behind her, someone shouted for a strike as pins clattered. "Would you be interested in a little closer look at things? Might help with the project."

"Closer look?" Emily said. "You mean, would we volunteer?"

"Campaigns can use all the help they can get."

Ethan popped a handful of fruity candies in his mouth and tried to say something. It didn't work. He choked and bent over trying to clear his burning throat. Emily pounded on his back.

"What my brother is trying to say is we won't do it unless we get t-shirts."

They got the shirts. And the responsibility of cooking hot dogs outside the Manticores baseball stadium. Apparently, free food was the way to go if you wanted a crowd. Since they were on the main drag into the stadium, a lot of people coming to the game stopped to pick up a hot dog, and Emily and Ethan were stuck at the grill for hours, it seemed like. Ethan had had visions of getting to see the game, but that never happened. By the time they'd shut down their operation, it was already the sixth inning, the Manticores were being slaughtered by the Angsty Pythons 14-2, and all the twins could think about was getting home to a hot shower and a cold drink.

"You did good," Craddock said, as she clicked the ratchet to lower the tent that had provided shade during the operation.

There had been six or eight people there to help most of the day, handing out literature and taking names and emails, but now that the work was down to disassembly of the cooking apparatus, they'd found other things to do. Craddock though, she was there from the beginning all the way through to past the end.

Her brown hair was matted with sweat, and her shirt had mustard, ketchup, and grease all down the front of it.

"Thanks," Ethan said, wiping grease off the grill. "Please tell me we don't have any more of these coming up."

"Nothing quite like this," she said. "Besides, we only make the newbies do the hard stuff. You two proved yourself today. That is, if you're coming back at all. Did we scare you off?"

You would have if we were really volunteers, Ethan thought, but he didn't say so.

"Not a chance," Emily said. "We're excited to do more."

Craddock pondered them a second. "Okay. That's good enough for me. Next week we're doing a picnic for likely voters at Meridian Park. You know where that is?"

"We can find it," Ethan said, holding up his phone. "We'll re-task a satellite to help us."

Craddock laughed. "Fine. Be there about eleven to help set up. You'll be manning the booth where we take delegate pledges. You showed what you could do today and that you're more than thrill-seekers. If you work like this, you'll do really well in the campaign."

But what kind of campaign was this? Free food? Face painting? What did any of that have to do with trade with China or education policy? Was this just a form of vote-buying, packaged in hot dogs and relish instead of direct payments?

But he didn't say that. "Happy to be of service," Ethan said, carrying a cooler toward the parking lot. "You want this in the back of your pickup?"

"No, better put that in the cab," she said. She turned and pointed her key fob in the general direction of the parking lot. A faint chirp sounded from out there in the forest of cars. "It's unlocked. The white one with the… Well, you'll know it when you see it."

He did. It stood out a mile. The white crew-cab truck sat in one of the nearest parking spaces, like a number of other vehicles, but this one was festooned with red-and-white Bauer signs in vinyl, like a wrap. Truly, you couldn't miss it.

Ethan opened the driver's door. The rear door opened backward, like wings, but it made a wide space for him to get the oversized cooler into. He had plenty of room; you could have used that cab as a hotel suite. It fit onto the floor behind the driver's seat. He slammed the back door and went to close up the front when he saw a manila folder on the passenger seat. It was unmarked. Might be anything.

Might be something.

He stood up on the running board of the truck and looked over the roof toward the remains of the cookout; Craddock was pulling down a canopy and had three sides to go. Her back was to him, and she was fifty yards away or more.

He ducked back inside, reached across the seat, and flicked open the cover of the file.

Inside was a printout of a spreadsheet, with large payments down one side and a cryptic notation down the other. Not dates, but something else, maybe sources. Maybe banks. No way for him to tell.

The file wasn't thick, but there were fifteen, twenty pages of stuff there. Again, might be nothing. Campaigns took in a lot of money. But just to be sure, he pulled out his phone and started taking pictures.

Kohn met with them himself.

"How's it going?" he said, jovially but with a hint of something else in his voice, curiosity maybe.

He should be curious, Ethan thought.

Ethan's eyes went to the woman seated at his left. They were in the boardroom again, this time with shades drawn so no one could see into the room. Emily nervously drummed her fingers on the polished table. Little smudges appeared before her.

Kohn saw the look and said, "This is Maria Norton, my accountant." She was a small woman with dark hair and skin. Her eyes were quick and her face full of intelligence. She sat calmly, hands folded in her lap, leaning back just a bit in her black vinyl chair.

Ethan slid a sheet of paper across the table.

"What am I looking at?" Norton said.

"I was hoping you could tell me."

Kohn leaned over to see it better, but it was Norton's eyes that Ethan watched. She was like a cat, knowing a mouse was out there, in the dark, and if she were patient and quick she could strike. She didn't touch the paper but carefully went line by line down the page. When she was finished, she looked over at him. "Where did you get this?" she said.

"From the Deputy Campaign Manager."

"She gave you this?" Kohn said, eyebrows shooting up.

Ethan squirmed. "Not exactly. It was more like just lying around."

Norton's eyes flicked over to Kohn and back to Ethan. "You don't leave something like this lying around."

"You don't?"

"I assume you don't actually know what this is."

He shook his head. "I mean, it's obviously numbers. Money. But I don't know what any of it means."

She sighed, reached out, and plucked the sheet off the table with a well-manicured nail. "It is money, yes. But I have a feeling it's a specific kind of money."

"Donations?" Emily said, leaning forward to put her elbows on the table.

Norton's mouth set in a hard line. "Yes. Probably. It's hard to know without the rest of the ledger."

Ethan put several more pages on the table and slid them across.

Norton cocked an eyebrow. "My. Full of surprises, aren't we?"

"I told you," Kohn said.

She took a minute or two to leaf through them and paused at the back page. "Ah," she said. "This will help."

"What's that?" Ethan said.

"These are bank routing numbers, nine-digit strings. It will tell us which banks the money is going into."

A long column of numbers marched down the page.

"That's a lot of banks," Emily said. "Does a campaign need to have accounts in so many places?"

"Not usually, no. This is… rare. And odd. And coupled with two or three other things on these pages, it paints a very interesting picture." She stacked the pages in front of her and laid them back on the table. She swiveled in her chair to look directly at Kohn. "How much are we telling these two?"

Kohn pursed his lips. "Maybe not everything. But something, yes. I think they've earned that much."

"It's your funeral," she said, frowning. But she looked levelly across the table and said, "Campaigns get donations from many different sources. You know that much, I believe. Most people think you fund a campaign from donations from hundreds and thousands of mothers and fathers and small businesses, people like that. And it's true that a good amount of money does come into a campaign in that way. But it's not enough. You can't make a Senate campaign out of fives and twenties. You have to have sums a good deal larger than that."

Someone walked by outside, talking on their cell phone. Norton waited a moment, then went on. "It's incredibly expensive to run a campaign for the US Senate. It takes millions to do it right. There are only so many ways you can get those millions. If you have them in the bank," she said, her hand waving in Kohn's direction, "then you can just give them to yourself. Nobody's passed a law that says you can't waste all your money chasing a Senate seat. But if you don't have them," here she tapped the pages in front of her, "you have to get them from someone who does. But there are laws governing how you get that money."

"Restrictions," Kohn said.

"Limits," Norton said, "especially in federal races like this one. No individual donor can give more than a certain amount per cycle, That's a fancy way of saying that if I love a candidate I can give her some money for the primary and some more money for the general election, but I can't just fork over millions. I'm tightly constrained."

"What about building an organization and running money through them?" Emily said.

"Good question. You can do that. Lots of people do. But those donations are also restricted. Some people get around them by donating to the candidate's *political action committee*—a PAC—rather than to the candidate directly. But there are rules for that too. People have to know about those donations. Not only do the amounts have to be disclosed, but the names of the donors have to be disclosed as well."

"Not written in code on a spreadsheet?" Ethan said.

Norton almost smiled. "No. That's not disclosure. Besides, the amounts on this sheet are far, far too large for any individual to legally give them to a campaign. If this is what I think it is, you've uncovered a massive violation of campaign finance law."

No wonder the campaign had been able to spend so much on free food and t-shirts.

"What happens to the people responsible?"

Kohn and Norton looked at one another. "It's not that simple," Norton said. "These amounts have to be disclosed, and if they're not, it isn't the police that someone has to worry about—"

"It's the publicity," Ethan finished. "I see where you're going."

Kohn smiled. "Essentially, this is the kind of story that finishes campaigns. We still need to do the forensic work here and decipher the sheets, but potentially this could destroy my opponent before he even collects a vote."

The twins sat around their kitchen table with Alannah, picking at a giant dish of caramel, strawberry, and raspberry ice cream, topped with chocolate syrup. It was a mound the size of Mount Rushmore. And nobody thought it was too much. Sometimes all that you can do is eat ice cream.

"We've been helping out the other campaign for weeks now, and we only got that one thing that Kohn was so excited about, and since then, bupkus," Ethan said, stabbing his spoon into the mass.

"Well, not necessarily bupkus," Emily said, pulling out a spoonful of her own. "We've certainly served hot dogs and collected signatures and driven in yard signs until we can hardly see straight. I'm not sure that counts as great contributions to the election though."

"And it's weird," Ethan said. "Everyone was so excited when I came back with that finance stuff, and then nothing at all happened with it. No announcements, no arrests, nothing. It's like it never happened at all."

Alannah speared a strawberry and popped it in her mouth. "What exactly did you guys find?" she said around it.

"A ledger. Campaign donations. A bunch of stuff that's probably illegal and certainly shady," Ethan said. "When we told them about it they said it was the kind of thing that could bring down a campaign."

Alannah's eyes got wide.

"What?" Emily said, pausing mid-spoonful. "You look like you've seen a ghost."

"Not *seen*," Alannah said. "Heard."

The twins put their spoons down.

"I was in the office doing some filing. They have me going everywhere and doing everything, a little bit of everything, and I was in there when some of the finance guys, the fundraisers, were having a meeting. I think they forgot about me because they didn't bother to keep their voices down at all. They talked mostly about nothing, or stuff I didn't care about, but then one of them mentioned the report Ethan found." Her eyes went wide. She put a hand to her mouth. "Holy Guac… I just realized this is what they were talking about."

"What else?"

"They were laughing about it, and one of them said, 'We'd better make sure we're not leaving any of our ledgers around. It could make that stuff look like a lemonade stand.' And another guy said, 'None of it's on paper; we're not that stupid.' They laughed and the first guy said, 'We made sure it would be pretty hard to trace, but what are we going to do? We know they're doing it. Everyone's doing it. If we don't have that money, we don't have a prayer.' The second guy says, 'With Randy's dough, we always have a prayer. But he's already poured in enough that things could get dicey if we don't come up with votes.' Then they moved off to talking about other things."

The ice cream suddenly didn't look all that interesting anymore. The three of them stared at each other over the melting mass, and Emily finally said to Ethan, "You still have the photos?"

"Of course I do."

To Alannah she said, "I wonder if Aunt Cathy is available for a discussion. I think we need advice from a pro."

Aunt Cathy came in and hugged Mom, admired the new couch in the front room, then sat on it like it was in a furniture showroom and she didn't want to get it dirty. The twins and Alannah sat on the loveseat across from her, all together, as if they were banding together for support. Nobody said anything for a long moment. Ethan traced a pattern in the nap of the sofa.

"So," Aunt Cathy said, "I take it this isn't a social invitation. I heard you wasted a lot of ice cream the other day."

"We didn't waste it. Dad ate it," Ethan said. "He kept talking about how it was going to make him sick, but he didn't slow down much."

Aunt Cathy gave a tight smile but kept her eyes on the kids.

Alannah sighed. "We all agreed it would be better to tell you this all at once, so you could help us figure out what to do."

Aunt Cathy nodded and waited for the kids to go on.

Emily led off. "It started when we took the job at the Kohn campaign. We thought it would be a lot more fun to be spies than telemarketers." She told how they got in with the Bauer campaign and how they earned the trust of the staff, and then she looked at Ethan.

"I wasn't snooping. Not really. It was just there, and I found it, and yeah, we were supposed to be looking for stuff anyway, so…" He stopped and glanced over at Mom, who was cutting something out of construction paper. Her eyes encouraged him to go on. Ethan pulled out his phone and tapped a couple of times. He handed the phone to Aunt Cathy.

She scrolled through the photos one at a time, her face getting more and more serious. Finally she looked up and said, "You know what this is?"

"We do now," Emily said. "We had a meeting with Kohn and his accountant. They explained about campaign finance limits and suchlike."

"And?"

"And we turned the stuff over to them and never heard another word."

"How long ago?" Aunt Cathy's attention was riveted to the phone.

"Two, three weeks?" Emily said.

Aunt Cathy made a face. "Too long," she said, mostly to herself.

"But there's more," Alannah said. "I overheard the Kohn people talking about doing the same thing."

Aunt Cathy sighed. "I'm not terribly surprised. I mean," she said, looking up, "that they're doing it. I *am* a little surprised that they'd talk about it when you were around."

"I think they forgot I was there. I'm... invisible, a lot of the time."

Something passed between Alannah and Aunt Cathy then, something the twins couldn't catch.

"So why tell me?" Aunt Cathy said. She looked over at Mom. "You know about this?"

Mom shook her head. "They wanted to tell you."

"You know things, Aunt Cathy. You know how politics works, and how it's *supposed* to work, and all that. You know what we should do, who we should tell," Emily said. It all came out in a rush.

Aunt Cathy was silent for a long moment and then said, "No, I don't. Not really. I didn't do much with campaign finance, that sort of thing. But what you've uncovered is serious. There are rules about this stuff for a reason. Our electoral process is one of the best things about this country, and subverting it—no matter the justification—is a serious thing that needs to be exposed."

She made sure the twins were paying attention, and then she went on. "People think the worst thing that can happen in an election is that their candidate loses. But they're wrong. The *worst* thing that can happen is that the whole electoral process is destroyed. No matter how bad we think the other side is, there's always a worse thing, and that would be to lose the chance to vote at all. Remember, we think voting is normal, but it isn't. Until very recently, almost no one in the world ever got to vote on anything. I would put my life on the line to preserve that, even if my candidates never won another election.

"I mean, imagine if people came to believe that their vote was a meaningless gesture and that the results were already decided by a few men in a smoke-filled room, or by rigged voting machines," she continued. "If people are going to be empowered to have a say in the process, then it's critical we make sure that process is protected."

"Some people already think there's no point to voting, that the whole system is rigged," Emily said.

Cathy nodded. "I know that. And it is true that there is a huge amount of pressure to regulate voting procedures and verifications in ways that benefit one party or another—or at least the people engaged in such things believe they do. One of the most important jobs of the Secretary of State is to maintain the fairness of the voting process. We worked very, very hard to eliminate voter fraud and to ensure elections are conducted fairly. We were very proud of the work we did, along with tens of thousands of volunteers across the state. No matter how badly we want our candidate to win, no victory—*v* victory—is worth corrupting the process over.

"That's exactly why what you've discovered is so important. Transparency, even-handedness, compliance with regulations, all of these things are part of ensuring we do not become one of those countries where voting truly doesn't matter, where the people have completely lost any influence over their government. Then we are lost indeed."

She handed the phone back to Ethan.

"But it's not my story," she said. "If you want to tell it, I can find the people who will be interested to hear. You have to make that call, though. I'm not going to decide for you." She shifted in her seat, back a little, settling in. Mom kept up her scissor-work and said nothing.

"You should understand, though I see you likely already do, that this is going to be a big deal. Probably, because you're all minors, your names can be kept out of it. But maybe not. Regardless, a lot of people are going to lose their jobs, and it will affect the campaigns quite a bit. It's an unpredictable element. Randall could lose, and right now, he's winning. That might even be enough to tip the balance of power in the US Senate. It could have long-term repercussions. You might be influencing the course of history. Are you sure you want to do that?"

"Isn't that a bit dramatic?" Ethan said.

Aunt Cathy shook her head. "I don't think so. It's hard to know how the Senate races will go, of course, but this is a key race. If the Republicans win this one they could hold on to the Senate, and it will be much easier for the president to get legislation passed, not to mention Supreme Court justices approved. If the Democrats take over the Senate, they'll be able to influence policy their way and keep federal appointees from taking office if they feel they're unqualified. It's more than just one race. It's potentially the fate of the nation one way or the other."

Emily looked down the couch at her brother and her friend. "It's up to us, then."

"It always was," Ethan said.

"I know what I think we should do," Alannah said. "I know what my father would do. But we all have to decide together."

If you think they should tell the whole story of both campaigns, turn to page 44.

If you think they should bury it, turn to page 76.

Aunt Cathy looked tired. Ethan hugged her a little longer than the minimum. She smelled of strawberries, but she was trembling like someone who had run a long race. He stepped back.

"Are you coming to our house for dinner?" he said. "Sunday. We always have too much. You should come, since you're in town."

She looked over at her sister.

"I should have invited you, but you know you have to come to dinner when you're in town," Mom said, looking at Ethan. "Dad would insist on it. Please come."

"Mom will make something extra good if she knows you're coming," Ethan said. Mom's mouth dropped open, but Aunt Cathy did just what Ethan thought she would do. She laughed out loud.

"I see how it is," she said to Ethan. "This is about getting a better meal, isn't it? Well, I'll play along. Count on me for dinner. Not this week, but maybe next. I'll be in town a while. Six o'clock?"

"Perfect," Mom said, and reached out to squeeze her hand. When she let go of Aunt Cathy, her hand came to rest on Ethan's shoulder. There was a pressure there, and Ethan wasn't entirely sure what it meant.

They said the right kinds of words to the widow, Mrs. Forde, whose face was a perfect mask of calm and serenity, which Ethan didn't buy for a second. She was a very good actress, though. He had to give her that. They shook hands politely and then came the kids. Most people just nodded at them as they passed by, though there was an occasional hug from someone they knew personally.

Their mother might have been holding it together, but the kids looked straight-up miserable. The first was a boy, definitely a couple years younger than the twins; then a girl who was probably their same age; and another boy who was a little bit older. Seeing them up close, Ethan could read a world of pain on their faces.

Emily stopped to shake their hands, and she said a couple of low words to the girl. Ethan couldn't make them out.

When it was his turn, he stuck out his hand for the younger kid to shake. He did, automatically, because that's what you do when someone sticks his hand out to you. His eyes came up to Ethan's, a little bloodshot, two pools of sadness tinged with the agony of having to stand there for hours as people came by to tell you how sorry they were that your dad was dead.

"This must well and truly suck," Ethan said. "I'm really sorry any of this happened. I'm Ethan Tuttle. My Aunt Cathy worked for your dad. She loved him. That makes you family. I hope… Well, I hope you know all these people loved him, too. Your family is practically the whole state."

The kid's eyes widened, and he forgot to shake Ethan's hand, just left it there a second while he tried to figure out what to do.

Ethan filled the silence. "I don't know what any of this is like, but I wish I could take your place for an hour."

"It's not so bad," the kid said, his voice small in the cavern of the Capitol. And he was totally lying.

"Yes, it is," Ethan said. He was holding up the line, and Mom gave a tug on his jacket. Ethan pumped the kid's hand. "It's the worst thing ever. And you're the bravest kid on earth for standing here like this. Your dad is proud of you. I'm sure of it."

That was when Ethan saw the tear start to form at the edge of the kid's eyes, and his sister's arm went around his shoulders and pulled him a little closer. Ethan couldn't let go of his hand anymore because the kid's grip was like a vise, pulling him in for a hug.

It was fierce, and hard, and the kid said in Ethan's ear, "It sucks worse than anything."

In the other ear, the sister said, "Thank you for understanding my brother."

Then Ethan was crying, too, and all three of the Forde children wrapped themselves around him. And then the whole world was crying, and no one cared that the line wasn't moving anymore.

The Tuttles were silent all the way to the car. Ethan shut his door and clicked the buckle on his seatbelt, and Emily hit him in the shoulder.

"What was all that?" she said. "What happened to you in there? You didn't even want to come, and all of a sudden you're a grief counselor."

"Emily!" Dad said.

"No, Dad, she's totally right," Ethan said, rubbing his shoulder. "I didn't want to come. I thought it was a waste of time."

That stopped conversation for a moment, until Mom asked, "What changed?"

Ethan set his forehead against the glass of the window. It was cool and made a cold patch against his skin. "I thought about Dad."

Nobody said anything for a while. Emily was looking at her lap, but her phone was nowhere to be seen.

"And it just seemed like if… Dad was… if Dad was gone," Ethan said, swallowing a lot, "everybody would leave me alone because they wouldn't know what to say to me, and the one thing I couldn't stand is being alone, you know? I would probably growl at everyone and say that I didn't want any people around, but I really would. So when I saw Aunt Cathy looking so sad, I thought she might want to come over. And then the boy—"

"Martin," Dad said. "His name's Martin."

"Martin, then. I thought he's got to be the saddest guy in the world, and I just wanted him to know I knew it. That was all."

"Well, you did a good thing there," Mom said. "Thanks for remembering to invite Cathy to dinner, too."

"Was that okay?"

"It was more than okay," Mom said, turning around in the passenger seat and patting Ethan's knee. "I just figured she'd know she was invited, but of course she has a million things to do. I didn't think she'd actually have time to come. That was a stroke of genius to make her think it was because you'd get a better dinner." Mom chuckled.

"Uh, Mom," Emily said. "I don't think he was kidding about that."

"Nope," Ethan said. "Your food's great, Mom, but you do try a little harder when there's company."

Mom looked at Dad. "If you say anything, dear, so help me, we're all going to have hot dogs on Sunday."

Dad kept his eyes on the road. But his laugh boomed through the whole car.

Ethan was trying to figure out a particularly tricky line of code when Mom knocked and walked into his room without waiting for a reply.

"Geez, Mom," Ethan said. "I could have been in my underwear."

"Then that would be a lesson to you that you should put pants on unless you're asleep or showering."

"That would have been so embarrassing!"

"Not for me," Mom said. "You don't have any body parts I haven't wiped with baby-soft towelettes. Anyway, I need to update you on the Sunday dinner you spontaneously organized."

Ethan tore his eyes from the computer screen and dumped his headphones in his lap. "I didn't. All I did was ask—"

Mom rolled her eyes. "Yes, fine, that you lit the fuse on, and that I am now organizing. I just thought that you'd like to know that Aunt Cathy is bringing a couple of people with her."

Ethan thought fast. Why would Mom want him to know this? What difference would it make to Ethan? Unless he was supposed to cook the beans or something. No, that wouldn't be it. It had to be something more than that.

Whomever Aunt Cathy was bringing, they were more than just friends from work. Something was up, and that something had to do with him. What had he and Mom been talking about recently, that she would go out of her way to mention to someone else?

He wanted a job. He had to get one, or he was never going to drive, and he'd always be that weird kid that stayed home and coded instead of getting a life. There was a chance that these people had a job for him. That would explain the pointed reference.

A kid can't get a reputation for being preternaturally brilliant without taking some chances. Plus, he owed Mom for the "baby-soft towelette" comment.

"Tell them I'll take the job," he said.

Mom was good. She was very good. She'd had many years experience at hiding her thoughts—always making the kids work things out on their own—doubled by the fact that she was the mother of twins. But sometimes he was really good at making intuitive leaps, and she couldn't keep her face totally blank. Ethan saw the flicker of surprise on her face before she arranged it as if she had been sure he'd come to that conclusion from the barest of hints. "I'll be sure to tell them that," she said.

"Seriously, Mom. Who are these people?"

"Seriously, I'm not sure. Cathy didn't tell me everything. She only said she'd like to bring along a couple of people and she needed to talk to us. All of us."

Ethan rubbed his chin. "All of us. Huh."

"That's exactly what I thought."

Ethan knew that he wasn't brilliant. He knew he wasn't even the smartest person in the room. So he said, "What do you think this is about?"

And Mom said, "I think Cathy is going to run for Dennis Forde's job."

Ah. "And she needs staff."

"I'm told it's a requirement for a successful campaign."

"Where better to get it than your dear beloved relatives?"

Mom turned back to the doorway. "Where indeed?"

Cathy was even better at controlling information than Mom. Maybe it came from working with all those politicians. She swept in like a force of nature and deflected all questions of a personal nature, at least those that related to the future, right through dinner prep and all the way through putting the mounds of food on the table. She had brought two friends: an older gentleman who introduced himself as Gordon Soffits and a young woman of about twenty-five named Sherise Finn.

Mom had tried to draw out what Mr. Soffits was doing there, but he simply deferred to Aunt Cathy, who told everyone he was a colleague she'd wanted to introduce to her family. He was a curious character in a sweater and a button-down shirt that hadn't seen an iron in recent history. He seemed, at moments, not to be entirely focusing on the conversation, as if what was going on in his head was more interesting than anything happening at the house. But he fielded questions without apparent difficulty, so maybe he was just the sort who didn't really need to be paying attention in order to keep track of everything. His hair was almost entirely gray, with an occasional strand of dark showing through. During the run-up to dinner, he spent long moments poring over the bookshelves, smiling every now and then as if encountering an old friend.

Miss Finn said she was from upstate New York, near the Canadian border. She was thin like a blade, with hair so short it stood out from her head on one side, and pale skin that didn't show signs of ever having been exposed to the sun. Her face wore a perpetual half-smile, as if she found everyone and everything around her faintly amusing. She was also a whiz with a kitchen knife, as they found out when Mom asked Ethan to chop vegetables for the salad and she volunteered to help. The little black-handled paring knife never did so much work in such a short time. Her hands were a blur. Ethan found himself doing more watching than chopping.

"Aren't you going to do anything?" Emily said.

"Do what? Miss Finn is so fast I can't even follow what she's doing," Ethan said. "Where on earth did you learn to do that?"

"My father owned a restaurant. He put my brothers and me to work before we could make a complete sentence. I used to carry knives in my belt, just in case I needed to chop something. I have my own set. Maybe I'll show you sometime. They're worth more than my car."

The salad had never been made so fast.

After Dad said grace, his curiosity about the mysterious guests finally got the best of him.. "Okay, Cathy, you've held back long enough. Unless the three of you are forming a commune, and you just didn't want to break it to us before we were trapped by this excellent pork roast and potatoes, you should probably tell us the big news."

Cathy and her posse took up a whole side of the table. She looked vaguely embarrassed. Mr. Soffits, though, plowed through his pork and potatoes and gravy as if he had been invited to dinner simply to make sure there weren't any leftovers. Miss Finn laid her utensils crossways on her plate and folded her hands, watching Aunt Cathy.

"It's not a secret. I don't know why I didn't want to talk about it earlier, but I guess I felt like until I told you, it wasn't real, and I could still back out if I wanted to." She took a swallow of water. "I'll just come out with it. I'm going to run for office."

Mom winked at Ethan.

Cathy saw it. "What?" she said. "Don't tell me you guessed that."

"Not for sure, no," Mom said. "But remember, we've been sisters for a long time. It's really hard for you to keep secrets from me. Possible, perhaps, but not easy. And truth be told, I was hoping you'd do it."

"You were?" Cathy seemed incredulous. "You *want* me to do this?"

"Sure. Why not?"

"Because it's expensive and I'm going to lose."

Mom laughed. "Depends on what seat you run for. Regardless, there's no doubt you'll lose your shirt. Winning any serious race takes huge money. But if you feel like you should, then go for it."

Cathy was dumbstruck. Miss Finn found this as amusing as anything so far. And Mr. Soffits, under his breath, was chuckling like a running brook, his shoulders shaking.

Cathy elbowed him.

"What?" he said. "Family is weird. You never can tell what they're going to do. Don't expect me to be able to tell you."

"Okay, well... I'm... so much for my big announcement."

"Don't take it hard," Mom said, passing the rolls. "Eat up. It always takes the edge off the shock. And when you come up for air, you can tell us what motivated this and what office you're going to run for, and then you can tell us what you want from us because clearly that's part of the dinner arrangements."

Over the next half hour, Aunt Cathy talked about the day she got the idea. "It was actually your fault, Ethan," she said. "Why did you ask me to dinner, anyway?"

Ethan shrugged and tried to swallow a huge chunk of meat. The gravy was perfect, salty and filled with flavor, and he was taking his time. "It just... I don't know. Seemed like the right thing to do at the time."

"You didn't think you should check with your Mom first?"

"No. Not that it's not ultimately her call. But I knew if it was the right thing to do, she'd back me up."

Cathy stabbed the air between them with her fork. "That's what I thought. In fact, when you did it, I said to myself, 'See, that's how it's done. If it's the right thing to do, just do it. Don't think about it. Just go.' And then I watched how you were with the Forde family, and how sad they were. The next couple of days I had to go around to all the staff at SecState—that's what we call the Secretary of State's office—and tell them they were probably not going to have jobs much longer."

"What's the deal with that?" Emily said. "You guys were doing a great job."

"According to some, maybe," Cathy said. "But it's a political job, and the vacancy is filled by appointment of the governor. Everyone knows that Governor Macrinus and Dennis didn't see eye to eye on things. Dennis kept his eye on the finances of the state, and I think the governor would just as soon he didn't. Anyway, it all didn't matter because Friday we got the word that Macrinus is going to appoint a successor to Dennis on Monday."

"Who?" Mom said. Her voice was cold. Suspicious.

"Louis Sulla."

Dad dropped his knife. "*Sulla*? And so soon? I thought he had to wait a month or so."

"The state constitution says nothing about any time period. The tradition is that you wait at least a couple of weeks. But Macrinus is in a hurry. It's an election year. The longer he waits, the less time Sulla has in the job to get comfortable and let people get used to his being there. The longer he's there, the more likely he'll be to get elected in November. So he's going to make the announcement on Monday, and Sulla will move right in, I expect."

"You're out of a job," Mom said.

"Both of us are," she said, pointing to Miss Finn. "Sherise is one of our crack auditors. She knows more of the shady secrets of government than the people who are involved in them."

"What about Gordon, here?" Dad said. "He doesn't strike me as the government type."

"I'll let Gordon tell you himself."

Mr. Soffits put his knife and fork down and wiped his mouth with a napkin. "I'm afraid there's nothing much to tell," he began. "Dennis Forde and I were friends. I don't know that I ever had a better one. My kids got used to him calling and asking for me—this was long before he became Secretary of State—so they recognized his voice. Our monthly lunches were some of my favorite times. When he ran for SecState I tried to stop him. But when he wouldn't be dissuaded, I went to work for him. I have certain skills in that line. I've been in politics in one form or another for fifty years or more."

"Gordon is being modest; he's one of the best political strategists I've ever seen, and Dennis almost thought of Gordon as his conscience. He used to say to me, as he was slipping out to a lunch with Gordon, that he knew he could never get too far off track as long as Gordon was around to call him on his bad decisions."

"He didn't make many," Mr. Soffits said, with a catch in his voice. "I never knew a better man. He wanted to do the right thing every time, all the time. No one could have worked harder to make this government a good one, and the idea that his successor is one of the most corrupt, self-serving politicians I've ever known is nothing less than sacrilege. But it might have happened anyway because Dennis was thinking of running for the US Senate."

This caused much surprise on the Tuttle family side of the table, but it was clear Cathy knew this.

Dad said, "He was, huh? Not a bad move for him. He wasn't going to get to the governor's mansion, that was for sure, but he had good name identification—most people knew who he was—and even though he and the governor didn't see eye to eye on things, it might have been that Macrinus would have helped him. You know, by way of getting rid of him."

"The Senate is a funny way of getting rid of someone," Emily said. "Wouldn't that be more power?"

"In a way," Cathy said. "But Macrinus doesn't care about the federal government. He just wants to make sure his power base is secure here in Montana. If Dennis were back in Washington, D.C., he couldn't be keeping an eye on things here."

"But which of the two are you going to run for?" Mom said. She got up without waiting for an answer and said, "I have to check the peach crisp. I'll be right back. You can have a minute to think about that answer."

"I don't know," Cathy said. "But nothing should get in the way of making a perfect peach crisp."

Mom exited, and Cathy fixed Emily and Ethan with a pointed stare. "You two are also part of this. You know I've been following your adventures for years now, all the political exploits you've been getting into. I know you as two of the most intelligent, hard-working kids ever, and I need people like that on my campaign."

"Summer job," Emily said, rubbing her hands together.

"We're expensive," Ethan said.

"But we might be able to come to an arrangement," Emily said. "Given certain considerations."

Miss Finn burst out laughing. "Holy moly... You warned me, Cath, but this is really something."

Mom returned. "What did I miss?"

"We were getting ready to extort raises from Aunt Cathy," Emily said.

"Extortion?" Cathy said.

"Or blackmail," Ethan said. "We know things. We're not fussy about vocabulary. We just need money for a car."

"Mercenaries are so straightforward," Mr. Soffits said. "It's refreshing, in a way."

"Shush, you two," Mom said to the twins. "Cathy was going to tell us which seat she wants to run for."

"These two represent each side of the coin," Cathy said. "Gordon here is one of Dennis's oldest friends. He thinks I should run for Dennis's seat. Miss Finn was part of Dennis's brain trust at SecState and the most insistent voice that he should push for a federal job."

"And you came here together. That's impressive restraint," Mom said.

"They've both made their pitches to me. I can see both sides. What I wanted was for them to tell you what they told me, and then you could share what you think I should do."

"Kind of like a debate," Ethan said. "With us as the judges."

"Exactly."

Mom said, "We have six minutes left on the crisp. So you each get three. Who goes first?"

Mr. Soffits said, "My mother would have my head if I went ahead of a lady."

Miss Finn laughed. "Ah, chivalry."

Mr. Soffits shrugged. "Rock, paper, scissors, then."

He threw paper. She threw scissors. "Your choice," Cathy said.

"I'll go last. That's the best position, I think," Miss Finn said.

Mom said, "Okay, Gordon, you tell us why you want to support my sister as Dennis Forde's successor."

"Simple. Because Dennis wanted it."

"You know this?"

"With certainty."

At the end of the table, Cathy's mouth dropped open. "You didn't tell me this."

"You didn't ask," Mr. Soffits said, getting another slice of pork roast. Apparently the pressure of the debate wasn't of much concern to him. Or else the roast was just that good. "But yes, Dennis and I discussed his successor from the very first minute he thought of moving to the Senate, and again when he knew he was sick. One thing he made me promise to do was to support Cathy if she decided to go for the position. But I couldn't tell her that he wanted her to do it because the desire had to come from inside her, not from Dennis, or she'd never have the guts to see it through."

"Dennis said that?" Cathy said in wonder.

"Essentially verbatim." He chewed another mouthful of roast. "Mrs. Tuttle, you can make a pork roast, I'll say that. This is excellent."

"Nice flattery at the end there too," Emily said. "This guy's a real pro." She had known him less than an hour, but she loved the way he thought. He didn't have to spell it out for you. He sort of wandered along and made you want to come with him. He let you decide for yourself. Emily found herself hoping his side would win.

"Not so fast," Miss Finn said, rising to her feet. "Now it's my turn."

"I can tell this is going to be good," Emily said. The timer went off in the kitchen.

"Is that a penalty?" Miss Finn said. "Now I have to wait until we've had dessert because no way am I getting in the way of a peach crisp."

"With ice cream," Dad said. "I'll get the crisp out, but it's going to need to cool for a bit. Long enough for you to make a good speech, I think." He got up and went into the kitchen. There was a banging, and something beeped, and he returned, tossing an oven mitt into the center of the table.

"And, go," he said.

"What's the issue you care most about?" Miss Finn said to him.

Dad looked at Mom. "Civil liberties? War?"

"Rising taxes, maybe. The economy? That's pretty important." Mom pursed her lips, the way she always did when she was thinking hard.

"Healthcare," Emily said.

"Immigration."

"Foreign relations, treaties, trade policy."

Miss Finn smiled. "You got all the big ones. That's what everyone is worried about. Who declares war?

Congress. And who helps oversee all the government agencies doing surveillance and impacting our civil liberties? The Senate. What about taxes? The economy? Everything is connected, globally. Those treaties, foreign policy. All that is decided by the Senate. They have to ratify any treaty that gets signed."

"Not that they get any chance, these days—everything is signed by the president as if he were king," Mr. Soffits muttered under his breath.

Emily and Ethan exchanged a glance. They knew all about this from talking with their parents. The President used executive orders instead of letting Congress draft laws. Even though the orders apply only to the executive branch, these days the executive branch had its fingers in everything. The president had tremendous power—and he used it, no matter which party he was part of.

"Shush," Miss Finn said, but obviously with affection. "Immigration is a federal issue. So is healthcare. So pretty much everything you named is controlled by the federal government. That's where the action is. I want Cathy Harmon to be there to do something about it."

Dad whistled. Mom applauded. It was an impressive performance. Even Mr. Soffits rose from his chair and executed a little bow in Miss Finn's direction.

"Kids, go get the crisp and bring it out here," Mom said. "And don't forget the ice cream. Then we'll have a judges' meeting."

The twins went with no argument because it smelled divine, and their bellies, so full from the excellent dinner already, had mysteriously acquired new room for additional food.

Emily picked up the crisp, making sure to keep the hot pads centered because the glass pan was still very hot.

Ethan stopped her and leaned in close to keep his voice from carrying. "So, what do you think?"

"Close," Emily said. "Miss Finn made a great case."

"But what Gordon said mattered. Dennis knew Cathy and what she can do. Maybe she'd be better here in Montana."

"You know where Mom and Dad are going to come down on this," Emily said. "It's up to us to be sensible."

"Good," Ethan said. "That's settled. We vote together."

"Absolutely."

If you think the twins should vote for the Secretary of State job, turn to page 118.

If you think the twins should vote for the Senate seat, turn to page 334.

"Isn't this what we wanted?" Ethan said. "We're moving up the ladder. More responsibility, more interesting work to do. Probably more money, too, if we ask for it."

Emily swiveled in her chair, as if the energy inside her wouldn't allow her to sit still. "It's *a* thing we wanted, but it's not *the* thing. I'm doing this because I want to buy a car, not because I want to end up like Ed. And..."

"And what?"

"I like what I do. It's not a big thing, but working with Alannah is a blast. She's great, and we're good friends. You know how hard it is to make a real friend."

Ethan did know, and he was thinking of Dara. She was tough. She'd do fine without him. And maybe he was imagining the lift he thought he saw in her step when she came in for her shift and he was there, but he certainly wasn't imagining the flip in his own gut when she smiled at him, coming through the door.

"This isn't a career," Emily said. "It's a great summer job."

"And fall job too."

"Even better, so we don't have to go get a shift at Chicken-on-a-Stick and deep fry everything we eat."

Ethan scratched a spot on his arm. His mouth twisted this way and that. "So... We tell them thanks, but we'd like to stay in the place we are?"

"If you're okay with that. I mean, you could take the step up, and I'll keep plugging away in the sign-and-t-shirt-and-phone mines. I'm sure we could talk Kohn into that, if you really wanted."

Ethan shook his head. "That would put us on different work schedules. You think Mom and Dad would be excited to drive us down here separately when we're already hearing their sighs of resignation about doing it twice a day?"

Emily's smile was rueful. "No, I guess not. Sorry to be the anchor that drags our ship back, little brother."

"*Big* brother. That's okay," Ethan said, trying to hit just the right note of martyrdom. He waved his hand as if fanning her away. "My job is cool. I'm good with it. Really. And... This is going to sound really odd, but I have this weird feeling like we're supposed to stay where we are."

"Really?" Emily said. Her eyes shone. She put her hands flat on the table and leaned toward Ethan. "Because I do, too. I was afraid to say something. Thought you'd call me crazy."

A moment later Kohn re-entered, sliding his phone into his jacket pocket. "You two ready to start?" he said.

The twins' eyes met for a second.

"Uh," Emily said.

"Ready to continue, actually," Ethan said. "We're going to say no to your very interesting and generous offer and keep doing what we have been doing, if it's all the same to you."

Kohn stood for a moment like a mannequin, as if he'd lost motive power. "Well. Okay. If that's what you want," he finally said.

"I think it is," Emily said. "There are lots of reasons—"

"Which I don't want to hear, really," Kohn said. "No offense. You're not idiots, so I'm sure there's math here I'm not able to do. If I didn't trust you, I'd have just ordered you to do it instead of giving you a choice. So, yes. It's okay, and you can go back to doing what you were doing because you're good at it, and I know you'll keep putting your formidable selves into the work with a will."

He really was very good at this, Emily thought. He clearly had been disappointed, but he recovered himself with speed and then made it a compliment that they'd done something he wished they hadn't. She could see how a man like that could amass a fortune—and want to spend it running for public office.

"Thank you again for the offer, sincerely," Emily said. "We're flattered you'd want us to be part of the management team."

"And one day, maybe the offer will come round again. You never know," Kohn said, and the flashing smile was back, and the radiant charm, as he shook their hands and ushered them out of the boardroom. As they walked down the hall back to the phone room, Kohn bellowed out behind them, "Ed! I'm throwing these back! They're under the size limit."

Ed met them at the door, holding it open and standing in the way, blocking it. His eyes were beady and suspicious. "Are you two, in fact, insane?" he said.

"Probably," Ethan said. "It's a hard thing to test for."

"You just failed it," Ed said. "But welcome back. I'll do my best to make you regret it."

But he really didn't. For a couple of days he was prickly but not much more than usual. Prickliness seemed to be his default setting anyhow.

Dara showed up at the usual time and sat next to Ethan in her usual chair. He looked for some sign that she was glad he'd stayed, but then he realized that she hadn't been part of the decision. She didn't know about the heroic sacrifice he'd made just to sit next to her and hear her say, "Thank you, ma'am. I'm so happy we have your support." He wanted to tell her, but it really ruined the magic of the sacrifice having to explain it to someone who didn't know.

The twins settled into a routine. They'd get to the campaign at about 1pm, just after lunch (though Ethan often grabbed a second one from the leavings in the Cool Room—the break room with its foosball and air hockey tables, plus a fridge full of soda pop). Ethan would walk the well-worn path to the phone room and take his seat, clicking up the list of numbers to call for the day.

Emily cut left at the beige metal door, heading down another short hallway to a dark brown wooden door. Through it was a large room piled high in yard signs of all sizes, from the "microsigns"—hard backed paper signs no bigger than a piece of paper for posting in small windows, in cars, and suchlike—to the huge, twenty-foot banners that could be hung over a city street. On the wall, a series of racks held lists of places signs were to be delivered. Not having a car, she wasn't able to do the deliveries, but she excelled at packaging the signs for pickup. She put bundles together, tied them up with string, and attached the relevant list of delivery destinations.

A couple of times a week, a new shipment would come in, and she'd spend most of the day taking bundles of signs from the dock to the storage room and racking them in their various categories. Inevitably, those days she'd be short of temper and covered in itchy cardboard and vinyl shavings. They got everywhere despite her best precautions: down her pants, inside her shirt, in her mouth and ears and nose. She showered hard those days.

In fact, she would have regretted her decision except that Alannah was there. Usually with people she'd just met, Emily was shy and compensated for it by being extra exuberant, which most people found annoying.

That tended to make the relationships not work well. But with Alannah it was never like that. There was no initial awkwardness, no tentative feeling-out. It was as if they'd been friends for years, right from the first minute.

Emily found her a true friend—"a kindred spirit" in the true Anne Shirley sense—despite their very different upbringings. Alannah had been born to a man with political ambitions, someone who was in the public eye a great deal as the highest-ranking African-American official wherever he went. He was used to cameras, recording equipment, reporters, anything anyone could use to capture a weak moment. Everything he said was picked apart, analyzed, criticized, looking for anything anyone could use to destroy him. In spite of this, Alannah said, he managed to live a fairly normal life with moments of truly carefree living.

But in the middle of this, Alannah was born. "I never remember a single day when I could just do whatever I wanted, without worrying about someone watching, judging, reporting. I couldn't—not anywhere—say what came to mind, without thinking first about how other people would interpret it. I haven't ever gone out for a run by myself. Not once. It even gets into the music I listen to, whether I post on Instagram about some boy, or a band, or a historical figure I admire. There was always a second when I wondered if someone was going to grab that and use it against my father."

They carried a huge box filled with plastic yard signs and stacked it in the back corner, where they could get at it later. Wiping her brow, Alannah sat for a moment on another box, her battered tennis shoes sliding back and forth along the smooth concrete floor. "It wasn't all bad. I mean, it wasn't bad at all. I live a lot better than most people."

"It doesn't sound like it to me," Emily said. "I don't know how you could stand it."

"That's because you didn't have to. If you had grown up this way, you'd handle it. You already handle things in a way I totally admire. The way you talk to Mr. Kohn or Mr. Ed like an equal... I don't even know where to start on that."

Emily didn't want to think about how she'd never given that a second thought. She just talked to them like they were people. Like she talked to everyone. It was the way her parents spoke to *her*—like an equal. She realized again how very lucky she and Ethan had been to be raised by people who trusted her and allowed her to take risks so she could grow.

But then, she could. She knew nothing seriously bad was going to happen to her. Nobody was going to come after her father to destroy his career if Emily were mouthy. She had to beg people to pay attention to her Instagram posts. What would it be like to have people looking for any way to take her nonsense and make something horrible out of it?

Was this what it was like for public figures everywhere? Was it worse because Alannah's father was a Black politician, and so few others were? Or was it just horrible no matter what?

"Thing is," Alannah said, and her voice was so quiet Emily could barely hear her over the big industrial fans, "since Dad died, I haven't exactly stopped thinking about that, but sometimes I start posting something, and I hitch, do a self-check like always, and then I remember he's not there any more, and no one is watching. No one cares now. And just for a moment, I feel a weight lift off my shoulders. It feels incredible. But then… It's so awful, because I don't want to feel good that my father is gone. It feels so wrong to be happy. Is there something wrong with me?" In the dim overhead light, her eyes were wide and white.

Emily felt the weight of it. This was her friend's darkest secret. It pressed down on her. The despair in her friend's face overwhelmed her. What could she possibly say in the face of such pain?

And then something happened in her heart, and she knew what to do.

Emily stepped toward Alannah and knelt on the floor, her hands on Alannah's knees. Emily looked up into her friend's face. "You're not a monster. You're a teenage girl living through one of the worst things that could possibly happen to her. You feel how you feel. There's nothing you can do about it. I like marshmallow peeps and One Direction. Sometimes I'm ashamed of it, but what can I do?"

Alannah laughed, just once. Her eyes never left Emily's face.

Emily said, "Do you think your father ever wished he wasn't forced to live like that?"

"I think he wished it all the time."

"But then he got up and did the thing he needed to do because that was who he was. You can feel whatever you like about anyone or anything, and it doesn't matter because I already know that you're going to *do* the right thing. You loved your father. You did. You don't have to prove that to me or to anyone. You don't need to prove it to *him*. Whatever you feel like, you never betrayed him. You never got him in trouble."

"Well, there was this one time..." Alannah said.

"Wait," Emily said. "I want to hear this story, but I'm so thirsty I could crack and blow away in a high wind. I'm going to the Cool Room for a drink, and then I'm coming back, and we have thirty more boxes for you to tell me all about your most embarrassing moment."

Emily paused at the door to the main building. "And I'll tell you mine. But you don't want to be drinking anything when I do because snorting Pepsi is really painful."

"Can you imagine what it must be like to live like that?" Emily said. They were in the car on the way home from work. Dad drove sedately, carefully, and slowly enough that they could have the whole conversation before he got them home.

"No," Ethan said. "I can't."

"In a fishbowl every second. Under a magnifying glass. Dad, promise me you'll never be anything more than a minor figure in an obscure company."

Dad glanced over. "Oh, I promise. I've achieved my level of mediocrity, and you have nothing to worry about. You'll never be pursued by rapacious paparazzi because of me."

Emily reached over and patted her father's shoulder. "We love you, Dad."

"I know it. And I love you. It's only because I love you that I didn't hit this button here and eject you from the car."

"That's the CD eject, Dad."

"So you believe. My master plan remains a secret." And he belted out an evil laugh.

When order was restored, Ethan said, "I'm really glad you and Alannah can talk about stuff like that. Do you think that was why you felt like you shouldn't take the other job?"

"Maybe. It's a sure bet she hasn't told anyone else the stuff she's telling me. And I've never told anyone the things I'm telling her. Not even you."

"You don't have to tell me," Ethan said. "I was there for all of it."

Emily arched an eyebrow.

"Okay, most of it. But seriously, I'm glad that she has you."

Emily turned back toward the front, looking out the windshield. "What about you and Dara? You're always sitting together."

"Dara, huh?" Dad said.

"No, Dad, not '*Dara, huh,*'" Ethan said. "She's on the phone bank just like I am."

Emily said, "And the two of them are top of the list, battling back and forth in completed calls, donations, signs placed. You name it, there they are."

"Right. It's just a competition. She pushes me. She's good." From outside, the smell of fresh-cut grass wafted into the car. Ethan remembered he hadn't cut their lawn yet this week and hurried to keep the subject hot so Dad wouldn't be reminded. "Anyway, I get the feeling there's something to her, you know, something more than she's almost eighteen and pretty."

"Like what?" Emily said, swiveling back.

Ethan shrugged. "I don't know. She doesn't talk much, except on the phone. I don't even know where she lives. But once in a while, I get the feeling she *wants* to say something and just doesn't know how. Or doesn't trust me. But I hope she'll share it one of these days. I have the weirdest feeling it's something important, something she doesn't normally share."

For a few minutes, nobody said anything. The hiss of the tires on the pavement, the creak of the seat as

Dad maneuvered the car, the rush of air over the chassis were the only sounds.

Dad broke the silence by saying, "Both of you are talking about sacred things. I hope you understand that."

"Sacred? As in religious?" Ethan said.

"No. Religion is a formal thing, a set of beliefs. An exercise program for coming closer to God, as it were. But God can come close to you without religion, and what you're talking about, people sharing with you their most important secrets, their true selves, that is a sacred trust. Take it seriously. There is no more important thing you could be doing."

Emily said, "I thought, you know, being in the top level of the campaign would be a lot more important since the campaign affects millions of people. This is just one or two."

"That's math," Dad said. "But this situation isn't math, it's spirituality. A small effect on millions doesn't necessarily equal a life-changing moment for two people. You may have been put where you are because only you could do what you're doing. I'm just asking you to be open to God while you do it. If He has something to say to you, listen."

"Dad," Emily said. She practically whispered. "It was like that when I was talking to Alannah today. She was so sad and in so much pain, and she looked at me like she had no hope at all. And I didn't know what to say. But then... I did. I can't explain it."

Dad smiled broadly and turned onto their home street. "I could," he said. "But that would spoil the fun. I'm proud of you, though. You've taken a step into a larger world."

Ethan, in the back seat, thought it would be a good idea to pay close attention in the next few days, just in case.

Ethan was just wrapping up a phone call when Dara came in the following Monday. She was dressed as usual: rock-band t-shirt over jeans, flip-flops, long strawberry-blonde hair pulled back in a ponytail. No makeup. Ethan didn't think she needed any. He couldn't think how she could look any better than she already did.

But there were things in her face today that spoke of trouble. First, without even waving to Ethan, she walked over to Ed's closed door and knocked. A moment passed and Ed showed his face through the open crack. Dara said something, and Ed scowled and said something back. Dara nodded, and Ed closed the door again. Ethan thought he saw her shoulders slump a little, but when she turned around, her face was set and she looked the same as always.

Now she smiled at him and came toward her seat. Ethan's stomach set up a revolt, and he felt his pulse tick up. There were several people in the office this afternoon, and a couple of them called out to her or waved as she marched by. She waved back, bantered. Same as always. Carefree, loose.

So what was that with Ed?

"Hey," she said. She settled on her swivel chair as lightly as a bird, the chair rocking gently as if pushed by a sudden breeze. Long, white fingers tapped the keyboard, waking it up. Right hand on the mouse, slim wrist flicking it this way and that, clicking, scrolling. The clear blonde hairs on her forearm caught the light and seemed to glow.

He didn't say anything to her.

"*Ethan.* Hey."

"Thank you, Mr. Gardener. It's been a pleasure talking with you," Ethan said into his microphone.

Dara laughed and reached across him to tap his screen. She smelled of spearmint. "Not Gardener. You're on Garland. At least, you would be if you were even talking, which you're not." Her shell-pink nail tapped the screen where the "connection" button was grayed out. "And anyway you shouldn't try to make a call when you're staring at me. Looking out of the corner of your eye, okay. Angling your screen so you can see me reflected in it, I can see that—it's clever, actually—but you don't connect well with people when you're distracted."

It was bad enough when she leaned over him, heat radiating from her like a gas oven, but to have her list off things he had been absolutely sure she did not know he had been doing—things he refused to admit to himself he *had* been doing—that made him want to sink through the floor. So he said, "Whatever. Flatter yourself if you like, but I'm going to put your donation record to shame with the numbers I'm going to hit."

"In your dreams. Which I probably am, come to think of it."

"You wish. I like brunettes."

"Who says that's not my natural color?" Her screen came alive and showed her the next ten names in the dialing queue.

"Nobody, but that wouldn't matter, would it? I don't like the *species* brunette; I like the *look* of brunettes." And that was true. Except now it didn't seem to matter, but he wasn't going to admit that, not for any money.

"Fine. Have it your way," she said. She scooted her chair a couple of inches closer to his, to where their armrests were nearly touching. Her arm lay there, long and cool and slender, and Ethan had to tear his eyes off it. He could just put his arm there, next to hers, no biggie. On his own armrest, of course. It *was* his armrest. Wasn't he entitled to it? He was sure if he did it, their arms would be so close he could feel the fine hairs on her arm. And his hand would be right there, if she wanted to hold it…

Dude. *No. Not what you're here for.*

Besides, he needed that arm to click on his mouse and dial the next number. Which he did. He swiveled his own chair a bit anti-clockwise, putting her on his back quarter, and dialed.

Just before the call connected, he heard her low chuckle, deep in her throat, like a tremor in the earth.

But distracted or not, he absolutely crushed the next hour. The scoreboard—updated electronically via the team's reporting software—was directly in front of him on the 72" flat-screen pegged to the wall next to the door leading to the Cool Room. It rotated through the categories—signs placed, endorsements, donations. The resolution was dialed up so far and the magnification so high Ethan was sure it could be read from space.

He wasn't in first in any category at the moment. But Rhonda, who led in signs placed, was a morning caller, so she was already in the clubhouse, so to speak. She wouldn't be posting anything more today. Endorsements was not Ethan's specialty, but he managed to hang in the top 5, and he was only thirty sign-placements or so from the top. That was a couple days' work at his normal pace.

The biggie, though, was donations, and everyone knew it. With donations, everything else became possible. And here, he and Dara were locked in mortal combat. No one else was close, although a big donation or two might get Corwyn into the mix. Dara led, but it was close. A thousand dollar donation would get him even with her.

But she was calling too, furiously, as if a yawning pit would open and swallow her if she didn't get through her list. Out of the corner of his ear, he could hear her voice rising and falling, cajoling, persuading.

Ethan had a different style entirely. He didn't really want to persuade people. He was all about the vision of the campaign. The script kept him relatively on target with the first part of the call—the whole call sometimes. But there often came a moment when he could sense that there was an opening, where the person on the other end showed something, just a flash of the person they really were. Those were the opportunities he was waiting for.

"Are those children I hear in the background?" Ethan said. They definitely were, or she was under attack by pixies.

Mrs. Twitchell laughed. "Yes. They're such a handful. All I really want is for them to sit for a minute and do their schoolwork."

"Do you homeschool, by any chance?" Ethan said.

A pause. "Why, yes I do. How did you know?"

"I'm homeschooled myself. You sound just like my mother."

Mrs. Twitchell gave a little exclamation of surprise. "I thought you were much older, Ethan. You sound so mature on the phone."

"I'll tell my mother that. She'll be thrilled," he said. "But what I especially wanted to mention was Randall Kohn's position on education. Most people think there isn't anything to talk about on the federal level, but there is. The Department of Education has a huge influence on education curriculum and disburses billions in funding every year. Mr. Kohn would love to see the federal government take a much smaller role in education policy and leave it to the states to decide how that should be handled. He would also propose legislation making it legal in all fifty states to homeschool without interference from state governments."

"Really? I wasn't aware of that." More shrieking. "Sorry! It's crazy here."

"No problem. One of the reasons I'm calling is that we're trying to raise money to run a series of ads dealing with education policy. We think it's important to get our policy out there, regardless of whether it helps Kohn get elected or not." He remembered something his parents had taught him about education funding, and thought it might tip the scales with this woman.

"We believe," Ethan said, "that education funding dollars should follow the child. Wherever that child goes to school—even if it's at home—those dollars should belong to the child to spend on their education. This is happening on the state level, but there is work to be done at the national level as well, especially with special-needs kids. Their education is funded significantly by the Department of Education. Flexibility in where those dollars could be spent would be a big boost for those kids."

The woman's voice changed, warmed. "I would *love* to see something like that. You probably know we're under a lot of fire as homeschoolers."

"I know it very well. I hear it from my friends all the time." Time to make the pitch. "Look, you're busy, and I don't want to take up any more of your time. But I'd love to get your support on this campaign. Are you where you can pull up our website?"

She was, and he took a second to walk her through it. "Right there, top left, you select the drop-down, and that lets you put your funds directly toward this project."

A deeper voice in the background. There was some kind of back-and-forth. Ethan waited.

She came back on the line. "My husband says he's very impressed with Kohn's positions on trade and taxes—my husband does shipping overseas—and if his education policy is what you say it is, we have $2000 to donate right now."

Ethan swallowed. "That's great, Mrs. Twitchell. We're so close to being able to launch the ad. Will you make that donation while we're on the phone together?"

Moment of truth. He wouldn't talk until she did. Three seconds. Four. Five. Getting into the uncomfortable range. Then, faintly, he heard the click of a mouse.

"Done," she said. "And please send us a yard sign and put our names on your endorsement list. Carol and Vern Twitchell."

Ethan tapped keys and checked boxes. "And that's done, too. Thank you, Mrs. Twitchell. And good luck with those homeschoolers. Homeschool kids are a rambunctious lot."

She was laughing as she hung up.

The board flashed, and there he was, Ethan Tuttle, on top of the donation list.

"Bang!" he said, standing up and punching the air. A smattering of applause sounded behind him.

But next to him, Dara said, "Wonderful, sir. Let me send you the link to the donation page. And I'll see if I can arrange to transfer you to the candidate. One moment."

She clicked her screen, and Ed came bolting out of his office as if he'd been sitting there waiting for the signal. Dara waved, and Ed came at a sprint. "Potential PAC donor," she said. "He might be willing to give to the National Committee, and they could send it to our candidate committee. Low five figures."

Ed turned the screen so he could see the name. "Huh. Never heard of him. You think he's on the level?"

"I do. A little nutty. He's a gun guy."

"Guns do not make one nuts," Ed said. "But yeah, Randall's on phone duty for the next, uh, thirty-eight minutes." He squinted at the big, red, digital clock at the front of the room. "Send the call."

"Got it," she said, and clicked her headset back to live. "Sir? I'm transferring you to the candidate now. Please hold on for a second—all this technology! If you get cut off, I'm going to call you right back, okay sir? Hold on."

She clicked the buttons. The lights blinked, connected, and the call was gone. Ed migrated through the floor like a homing pigeon that had forgotten how to home.

Dara swiveled in her chair, slowly, achingly, revealing her face and its Cheshire-Cat smile.

"Not in the books until the check clears," Ethan said.

"Which is lucky for you. Because when this goes through, you'll never catch me. You'll be looking at my shapely behind for the next nine weeks, trying vainly to catch up."

The color drained from Ethan's face. That was some image she conjured up.

She realized what she'd said, and all the color from Ethan's face ended up in hers. Her skin turned the same color as her hair. She turned back to her screen.

But their calls were off-cycle. The screen said, "Break. 20 minutes."

Ethan recovered first. "I can beat you in air hockey too."

"But not pool," she said.

"Want to put something on that?" he said. "I think there's just one bag of Skittles left in the box."

"You're on."

A couple of their co-workers sat in the far corner of the wood-paneled Cool Room chatting about baseball. Otherwise, they had the room to themselves.

Ethan lost at everything.

When the fifteenth goal ended any chance he had at a comeback, Dara said, "You lost on purpose."

"Never," he said, but it wasn't quite true. He hadn't actually set out to lose, but one long strand of hair had come loose and hung next to her face, shadowing it, and he wasn't always looking at the tabletop anymore.

Dara danced over to the bar and held up the prize bag of Skittles. "Not sharing," she said.

"You won. No reason to share."

She tore the bag open, selected a single Skittle—red, naturally—and tossed it into her mouth triumphantly. Ethan watched the whole thing, a slightly stupid look on his face.

She sighed. "Look, Ethan," she began.

"You don't have to say anything," he said quickly, abruptly, before she went any farther.

"Yeah, I do. But not here. Come with me." She took his hand—*took his hand*—and led him out of the Cool Room, across the phone floor, and out the rear doors into the blast furnace of the west-facing wall of the office.

"This way," she said, and led him around to the north-facing side, where the brick and concrete hadn't been absorbing the sun's rays for the last ten hours.

It would have been dramatically cooler there, except for one thing—Dara hadn't let go of his hand. Sweat prickled the back of his neck, and it didn't have much to do with the temperature.

"Since you watch basically everything I do, I'm sure you saw me have a chat with Ed when I came in." She put him with his back to the wall, and she stood a heartbeat away from him, facing him, his hand still loosely in hers.

"I, um, without admitting to the rest of what you said, I did see that, yes."

"You want to know what it was about?"

"Of course I do."

She turned her head, and he could see that she was embarrassed, hurt even, but also that this was something she needed to say.

"I have to quit the campaign."

"What? No. You can't do that. You're one of the best we have." Ethan squeezed her hand, maybe a bit harder than he should have.

She pulled her hand away. "I have to. It's not… I don't want to. But I need to take care of some things at home, and being here isn't going to work out anymore." She wouldn't look at him.

"What things? I mean, I know it's none of my business—really I do—"

"That's right. It's none of your business." Now she could look, her eyes flashing.

But now he was angry. "But you felt like you had to bring me out here and tell me. Yet it's none of my business."

She opened her mouth, and shut it. But she didn't look away. She opened it again. "I wanted to tell you."

"That you were leaving?" he said, voice hot and bitter. He almost said *Good. Now you've told me. Goodbye.* But there was a weight on his heart that wouldn't let him. So he just reached out and took her hand again. She wrapped her fingers around his and held on like she was drowning.

"No, not that. I mean, yes, that. But also… I've been ripping on you about how you're crushing on me."

"I noticed."

"Yeah, but… Oh, man, boys are so dense." She shook her head, bouncing her ponytail from one shoulder to the other. "Did it ever occur to you to wonder how I know you're watching me all the time?"

"Well… Uh, yes. Absolutely. Occurred to me right away."

"Liar. Stick to the truth. You're better at it." She smiled right into his eyes, and the weight on his heart made it difficult to breathe. "You're not the only one with a crush."

"That's… That's great," Ethan said in wonder.

"Yeah," she laughed short, filled with rue. "Great. It wasn't going to work anyway. I'm too old for you. And I'm leaving, so that's that. I just thought you should know."

The abyss opened beneath Ethan's feet, and his stomach dropped. A moment ago, he thought he'd have floated over it, but the wings were gone.

"Really. Dara. Tell me. What's the thing with home? You can tell me. You know I care."

She shook her head. Her eyes shone, and she wiped at them with her free hand. "No, I can't. You couldn't do anything anyway." She pulled her hand away and shuffled back. "So now you know. Our break's over. We need to get back." She walked to the corner of the building. Ethan wanted to follow her, but his feet were stuck in the pavement. He didn't know if they'd ever come loose.

"It's been fun, Ethan," she said, pausing with the sun on her face. "Maybe some other time it could have gone on being fun. But—" she seemed on the verge of telling him what she'd so far backed away from twice. "No," she said. "It's just not going to work out." And she was gone.

When he got back inside, Ed had the phone team up at the front of the room. "We're going to have a minute here with the campaign technical director. He wants to know what we think of some ideas they're playing with as far as policy. You guys are talking to hundreds of people every day. So it would be useful to know if there are things people keep bringing up."

"Who's the technical director?" one of the callers said.

"Tank Abrams," Ed said. "He's good people."

"I thought you were the director," another voice said.

"Naw, not me. I'm Co-Campaign Director, with a fella name of Pascoe. He does the political, fundraising, tech, and communications—each one of those has a director—and I do field work and data crunching. Every campaign has to organize itself more or less like that to keep its head above water. The political director is the one that develops the principles the campaign wants to get across to the people, and the tech director is the one that figures out how to know what principles to recommend we work on."

The door opened, and a small man, no bigger than Ethan himself, came in. "This is Tank," Ed said.

"Howdy, folks," he said, in a thin, reedy voice that carried like the squeak of an oboe to every corner of the room. "Sorry to take you away from the most important part of the campaign, but we have to use the people we have, and you're it. The campaign has been working out some new talking points. If we decide to use these, you'll be re-doing your scripts, so here's your chance to tell us what you think."

He drew up his tablet, tapped it a couple of times, and the big board changed to show his screen instead. "Here are the big five: military, trade, legal equality, health care, and education. Thoughts?"

Dara, who had positioned herself on the far side of the group, said, "I think legal equality belongs at number one. Almost everybody I've talked to has brought that up."

Ed looked over the group. "Anyone else?"

Lots of head nods. "Comes up all the time," someone said, and everyone else seemed to agree.

"It's a big topic. Give me specifics. What are people looking for?"

Ethan's hand went up. "The law is already pretty clear—there's to be no discrimination against people because of their color or race or religion, etc. The problem people have is how that law is *applied*. In many places there's a culture of 'us against them,' police against parts of the community, government against small business, picking sides, winners and losers. Poor people get public defenders who are overworked or incompetent; rich people get the best legal talent there is."

"Sentences for blacks are longer for the same crimes. I hear that a lot," Aziz said.

"Outrageous use of force for non-violent crime." That was Dara.

"Criminalization of things that aren't hurting anyone."

"Excessive jail time."

"Overregulation."

"Whoa," Ed said, tapping away as fast as he could. "Gimme a sec."

It went on for another twenty minutes or so, swapping in new ideas for bad ones and refining the message. Ethan didn't hear a lot of it because he was concentrating on Dara. Not that he hadn't been before, but this was different.

What could take her out of this job, one she was obviously so good at? He brought up and discarded a dozen possibilities and finally concluded that he couldn't possibly guess. But that only made him more determined to find out.

Sure enough, Dara didn't show for work the next day. Or the next. Ethan poked his head into Ed's office and said, "Hey, where's Dara? I'm getting tired of winning everything all the time."

"Gone," Ed said, without looking up. "She's left the campaign."

"Left it? Why?"

Ed glanced at Ethan over the rim of his glasses. "Because she didn't want to keep working here, I suppose. I wasn't curious."

"Well, I am."

"Get used to disappointment," Ed said. "Close the door on your way out."

Ethan stood for a moment outside the office and thought. He needed information. If he were going to find out what was going on with Dara, he was probably going to need help. There was a way he could think of to get it. It was risky, though. A little risky. He knew he was meddling in things that could get him in trouble.

If Dara really wanted him to know what the story was, she could have told him. She *would* have told him. Therefore she didn't want him to know. Therefore he should be satisfied and move on.

But he couldn't. He liked her. He thought—his gut did a little dance just thinking about this—that she liked him too, a little. She had almost come right out and said so. Regardless, this wasn't really about that. When she left, she hadn't seemed relieved, or enthusiastic. She'd seemed sad. More than sad. Trapped. Embarrassed, even. It looked like she was in trouble.

And if she were in trouble, and he was her friend, didn't he have a responsibility to try to help her?

Sure he did.

Even if Ed didn't want him to. Even if it exposed him to a certain level of risk. Even if it got him a reputation for being nosy. This was a thing he couldn't explain, but he knew was right. He was supposed to do this.

So he went through the door into the main office and went looking for Tank.

He found him eventually, tucked back in a corner of a smallish room made even smaller by a warren of cubicles made of fabric walls. Six, seven data collection geeks crammed into an office half the size of the Cool Room. Three of the desks appeared occupied based on computer keyboard clacking coming from over their walls. At one of them, farthest from the door, was Tank.

Ethan stood in the opening of the cubicle and waited for Tank to say something. He didn't. And then he didn't some more. Ethan cleared his throat. That did not appear to change the situation at all. Tank had to know he was here. Why didn't he say something?

With a heavy clack, Tank put the period to something and clicked his mouse. He swiveled in his chair and said, "I'm not sure who you are, but you clearly haven't been briefed on protocol here, so I'll tell you, and in the future we can avoid these pointless little dances around etiquette. I work in this space. If you want something, don't stand there and hope for an invitation. Come to the door of the cubicle and state your purpose clearly and as briefly as possible. If I care, I'll acknowledge it. If I don't, I won't, and you can go away. Clear?"

"Clear." Better than clear, actually. Ethan thought he might like this guy a lot. "I want to find someone and I want you to help me."

"Interesting. Possibly worth considering. Except I'm working for the campaign and have duties."

"It's a campaign matter."

"Is it? Then why is it being brought to me by a junior staffer from the phone floor?"

Ethan looked surprised. Tank waved that away. "I said I wasn't sure who you were, not that I didn't know things about you. Whom do you wish to find?"

"Dara Zundel."

"Name unfamiliar. Who is she?"

"Junior staffer from the phone floor. Was. She left this week. Quit."

"Tragic. Not my problem. Not your problem. Ed should be the one to bring me this, if it matters, and it probably doesn't."

"Ed doesn't care, but I do."

"Ed is wise, and you are probably sixteen. I don't see the relevance to the campaign. Goodbye." Tank swiveled his chair back toward his glowing screen and another world where Ethan knew he'd never find him again.

"Losing her is costing the campaign a lot of money," he said. He tried to keep his voice reasonable, but he knew he sounded shrill and desperate.

But it worked. Tank stopped, his hands poised over his keyboard, and said, "How?"

"You have the statistics from the phone floor on that machine, I bet. Look them up. Look at how much money Dara has raised just in the last couple of weeks."

Tank cocked his head sideways, like a bird listening for predators, but then he typed away on his keyboard, fingers flashing so fast Ethan couldn't follow them at all.

A screen lit. Ethan couldn't see it from his vantage point, but he watched Tank's eyes move sideways, then down, then sideways some more.

"You're Ethan Tuttle," Tank said.

"I… Yeah. That's right."

"I know why you're really here, Ethan Tuttle, but you're fortunate because I do not care that you're in love with this woman as long as you're right about her leaving costing the campaign money."

"And?"

"And you're right about her leaving costing the campaign money. It's not a huge amount in the grand scheme of things, but it's enough to be worth a couple of phone calls. Which I take it Ed has not made?"

"I, uh, actually don't know if he has. He just told me to get used to disappointment."

Tank grunted. "Ed is wise. Come with me."

Ethan stood aside for Tank to go past him, then followed him down the cubicle hall, through a door, and into another hall. Like rats in a lab, they slowly made their way back to the light—the main office, where, to Ethan's surprise, Tank turned *right*, not left; heading toward the phone floor, not toward Kohn's office.

"Where are we going?" Ethan said, as they approached the door that led to his own workspace.

"Unnecessary question since we'll be there in seconds."

Ethan thought it would have been a lot simpler just to answer rather than make a sarcastic comment, but he knew better than to say *that* to a fellow he was asking for help.

As it was, he could have simply thought, 'what is the worst place he could be taking me?' and gone with that answer because ten steps later Tank was knocking on Ed's door. Ethan tried to ignore the quizzical looks from the few phone workers scattered about the floor. Their eyes burned on his back as he waited for the door to open.

But even when it did, it took a moment for Ed to register that Tank was there, and then that Ethan was behind him. "Glory. What's this? No, no, don't tell me. Come in."

They did, and he closed the door behind them.

Tank said, without preamble, "Ethan didn't ask me to come here with him. He's probably not too happy that we're here, actually. But you need to know what we're doing, and besides, you can give me info that will save me time."

Ed said, "Dara Zundel."

"That's right. Her leaving is costing us money. This boy wants to know why she's gone. Now I do too."

"I asked her. She refused to tell me."

Ethan said, "So did I. Same result."

Tank squinted. "So she wouldn't tell her boss, which makes a little sense, or her boyfriend, which makes no sense at all. Therefore I am curious because it's unlikely to be something simple."

"You actually care what it is?" Ed said.

"No. I care that it's costing us money. And I suppose I care because there's a chance another human being is in serious trouble."

"You suppose," Ed said in a voice so dry it sucked moisture from the air.

"I *am* human. No matter what you think."

Though the train of conversation seemed to have left the station, Ethan felt compelled to say, "I'm not her boyfriend."

"Pointless quibble over semantics," Tank said. "I need the girl's file."

Ed said he'd email it. Tank said he'd do a little digging, see what came up. Both of them wanted Ethan to go back to work and stay there until further notice.

"But... I'll get notice, right?" he said.

Tank looked at him like he was insane. "I'm not a field agent. I don't go places. Ed's too busy. If there's something we can do, you'll be the one doing it."

There was. It took only a pair of days to find.

Monday afternoon, while Ethan was busy reinstalling himself at the top of the sign-placement list, the door opened and Tank came in. His eyes locked onto Ethan's, and he pointed to Ed's office, marched across the floor and vanished inside.

Ethan wrapped up the call—he did not place the sign, as it turned out, having been thrown totally off his game—and went over to Ed's office. He knocked. The door opened, and he slithered inside.

Tank said, in his usual manner, "She's at home, taking care of her three little brothers and one sister."

Ethan gaped like a fish. "Why? What..."

"Father lost his job. Had to get two to replace it, so he's day laboring and driving Uber at night. The family can't afford child care. Dara is it."

"How did you—"

"I don't answer questions of that nature," Tank said.

"So that's that," Ed said. "Explanation provided. Mystery solved. Back to work."

By this point, Ethan had recovered. "No, that's not *that*," he said. "Dara was good for us. She made money. She pushed me to make money too. I'm sure you've seen my numbers fall off since she left."

Ed made the kind of face that said he had and hadn't wanted to say anything.

"She's good for all of us. And this job was good for her. We need to do something to help her get it back."

Ed scowled. "Not our business. This is a personal matter."

"Of course it's personal. Everything's personal. What is it you tell us to do when we call, keep it as robotic as possible?"

Ed admitted that was not what he advised, no.

"So let's help her."

"I offered to have her work from home, and she said no."

"Of course she did. How old are these siblings?"

Tank said, "Twelve, eight, four, and two."

"Impossible to call people on any kind of schedule with that many kids of that age," Ethan said. "We need to help her."

"How? You have a handy free babysitter?" Ed said.

"No. But I have an idea." He looked at Tank. "What did her father do? I mean before, when he had a good job."

"Machinist," Tank said.

Ethan smiled. "I happen to know someone who owns a machine shop. I wonder if he needs an experienced machinist there." And he turned, went out the door, and headed for the office.

Because he did it so quickly, it took a moment for the other two to figure what he was doing. Once they did, they were mobile enough, but Ethan was bold, determined, and fast. He was already walking past Karen at the receptionist's desk before they caught up with him.

"You can't go where I think you're going," Ed said.

"Sure I can. It's right here. There's a hallway. With nice carpet. Leads right to the door."

"Which you can't go in."

"It's okay," Ethan said, with a bright smile. "He's on phone time and his light is green."

He opened the door and there was Randall Kohn, sitting in his chair behind his dark cherrywood desk, reading something off his laptop. He looked up. Then he looked harder as three people crowded into the room.

"Excuse me, Mr. Kohn," Ethan said. "I need to talk with you for a moment."

"He really doesn't," Ed said.

Kohn looked at Tank, who said, "I'm an appendage, sir. I may have no function here at all."

Kohn said, "I cannot wait to find out what this is all about."

Ethan's mouth was dry and his hands were wet, but he was here now and he might as well get it over with. "Once upon a time you asked me to come work on your personal staff."

"I recall that. I also recall you told me no."

"This office invasion has to do with the reason why."

Ethan began relating the entire story, being on the floor, making phone calls, and the relationship that began with Dara—plus Emily's relationship with

Alannah—leading them both to conclude that as cool as the offer was, the place they really belonged was in the place they already were. And then Dara left, not because she wasn't good, or because she didn't want to be there, but because the family circumstances demanded it.

"So she did the noble thing, but it's hurting her. And the campaign," Ethan finished.

"And you, clearly," Kohn said. "But let that go for now. Why is this something I need to get involved in?"

"Because you have the power to fix it."

"I do?"

"Her father is a machinist. You own a machine shop. There's potentially a match there," Ethan said. "I know it sounds like I'm committing you to something, but really I'm not. I'm really just trying to find something that works."

Kohn let him finish then fixed him with a stare for a long, and increasingly uncomfortable, moment. "You realize," Kohn said, "that there are people who would resent your meddling in their lives."

"I, uh, I've been told that, sir."

"You realize that you're asking for something you have no business asking."

Ethan took a deep breath. "With all due respect, sir, I don't think that's true."

"Explain," Kohn said, and Ethan heard Ed exhale explosively behind him.

"You talk about running for Senate being a chance to use your power to help people. Well, here's a person.

Right here on your staff. She's in a tight spot, and she needs help that you can provide. Power over millions of people and billions of dollars is one thing, but power comes down to one person doing something for another person. I'm not… I don't know how to say this next part."

"Let me try," Ed said, very quietly. "Randall, you're a good man in a bad game. If you weren't running for Senate and this were one of your businesses, if something like this happened, what would you do?"

"I'd look into it," Kohn said. He ran a hand through his hair and all of a sudden looked very tired. "At least I like to think that I would. Once, I definitely would have."

"Then do it now," Ethan said. "Stop running for Senate and for ten minutes run for 'best dude in the world.' No one will know. Well, no one but me and these guys here. And we all already think you're a great guy, but I think it wouldn't kill you to prove it. That's… That's all I came to say."

And for a good minute—which Ethan discovered was a really long time when nobody was talking—the only sound in the office was the ticking of the grandfather clock behind Kohn's chair and the beep of the phone system outside at the receptionist's desk.

"I can do that," Kohn said. "And what's more, I think it would be a good idea for me to at least take a look—no promises—to see if there's some way to help this family get right again."

Everyone started breathing again. "Thank you, sir," Ethan said.

"Don't thank me, son. I should be thanking you. A long time ago you wouldn't have had to come here and remind me what power is good for or why I wanted it in the first place. I guess I got distracted," Kohn said. He looked at Ed. "Thank you for not stopping him."

"Have you tried stopping this kid? From doing anything?" Ed said.

Kohn looked at Tank. " Unless you are a very different person than the guy I thought I hired, I believe you have a file for me."

"Of course I do. In three minutes it will be in your inbox. Can I go now?"

"Not quite. What's the situation?"

"Father's working two jobs, making half what he used to."

"Where did he learn to be a machinist?"

"Army."

"Active duty?"

"Two tours. Iraq."

Kohn nodded. "All three of you, get out of my office and go back to doing the work I'm paying you for. Tank, two minutes, I want that file."

And then nothing happened. At all. Ethan went back to his phones. He dialed like a madman because every hour or so Ed would come out, walk the floor, stop in front of Ethan's computer, and listen to what he was saying as if he were trying to catch the smallest possible error. Tank did not send Ethan a message. Kohn did not send Ethan a message. No one, in fact, talked to him at all.

"That's because you're an idiot," Emily said, as they drove home a week later. Ethan slumped in the back seat, watching the world go by the window. Even the smell of Chick-fil-A wafting through the car couldn't revive him.

Emily reached back and gave Ethan's knee a squeeze. "But you're a noble idiot. Like Don Quixote."

"He died broken after giving up on his dream because he was convinced it was a delusion."

She patted his knee and turned back toward the front. "I know."

The next day, Ethan was halfway through a call when the office door opened and Dara came through it, eyes narrow and possibly red-rimmed. She didn't look right or left, just marched across the floor to Ed's office, knocked once, and went through the door.

Ethan had lost the thread of the phone call.

The man in his ear said, "I don't know why I should vote for Kohn. I don't really like rich candidates."

"I understand that," Ethan said, trying to recover his balance. "But I think you'll find that this rich candidate hasn't forgotten us little guys. He's willing to do some very kind things. I've seen it."

"Huh," the man said. "What else can you tell me about him?"

Ed's door opened.

"Can I send you a link to some information?" Ethan said. "I believe I have your email address." He confirmed it, and hung up the phone just as Dara came through. Backward.

Ed said something to her, and she said something back. Ed nodded and shut his door.

Dara pivoted on her heel, fixed her eyes on Ethan, and stalked across the floor like a heat-seeking missile. Seeking Ethan's face, which had flushed so red he was sure it could have been used as a barbecue.

She stopped next to his chair, reached down, grabbed his collar, and hauled him out of his seat.

"Hey, Dara—" Ethan tried to say, but Dara wasn't having any. She frogmarched him through the telephone bank and out the back door.

Where it was raining. Not hard, but the kind of summer shower that could wet a guy through in less than a minute. The door banged shut and Ethan heard it latch.

Dara grabbed him by the shoulders and pinned him to the wall, her arms straight as pokers. Water speckled her face and matted her hair. Ethan felt the raindrops steaming off his flaming face.

"What did you do?" she said. "You tell me right now. What did you do?"

Ethan's gut was a yawning pit. He had thought not seeing her day after day was the worst thing that could happen to him. Now he was seeing her like this, furious and close to tears, and he realized not seeing her at all was far better.

What did she want him to say? How could he have thought his meddling in her life was a good idea? What had happened?

"I..." he started. He stopped. He had been embarrassed, and now he was ashamed. He had hurt her when he would rather have died than cause her pain.

"Let me make this easy on you," she said. Her voice cut through the rain like a whip. "Did you follow me? Did you come to my house and spy on me?"

Ethan winced. "No, I would never do that."

"Did you hack into my computer system? Bug my phone?"

"What? No! I don't even know how to do that."

"Did you bribe someone to give my father a job so that I would come back to work here?"

That was a tougher question, but still, he shook his head. "No. I didn't do that."

"So what *did* you do?"

"I... went to Tank and asked him to check how much money we were losing by not having you here. Then I went to Ed and told him what Tank found out. We were losing a lot."

"And Ed took it to Kohn." Her voice had lost some of its menace, but her arm hadn't lost any of its considerable force.

"Uh, no." Ethan swallowed and tried to blow some of the rain off his face. Rivulets flowed off the front of his hair and made it hard to see. "No, that was me. I went to Kohn."

"And what did you tell him? Don't you dare lie to me." She seemed oblivious to the rain running down her face. That was rain, wasn't it?

She needn't have added the warning about lying. He could never have lied to her, especially when she was like this.

"I just told him I didn't see the point of having power if you couldn't make someone's life better when they needed your help. If he wanted to sit in the Senate and help millions, what difference would that make if he didn't help the people closest to him?"

She searched his face. "And that's all. That's all you said."

"I swear it. And I haven't heard anything since and it's killing me. But if I hurt you in any way, I'll walk out of here right now and never see you again."

Her eyes peeled the skin from him. She leaned in, closer, closer, her eyes narrow and her face wet, until they were nose to nose. "Don't you dare," she said. Then with no warning at all she tilted her face sideways half an inch and kissed him on the mouth.

She had been gone for five minutes before Ethan unstuck himself from the wall and wandered, as if in a thick fog, around the side of the building to where there was an open door and he could get out of the rain. Everyone he walked past gave him a long, worried look

as he dripped on the floor, oblivious, his face frozen in a disbelieving grin. He didn't see any of it.

For two months, Dara and Ethan tore up the manual for how to work a phone bank. At one point, Ed had to shut their phone lines down and kick them out for half an hour. No other caller, volunteer or professional, could come anywhere near them in results. And if, while walking by, you might have thought Ethan's right hand and Dara's left hand were suspiciously tucked out of sight, what of that?

Dara reported that the machinist's job her father had taken paid somewhat better than his old one, was closer to their house, and allowed them to hire back their old caregiver at a bit of a raise. He was still surprised at how the company found him. "He says they emailed him and asked for a resume. It was only there for about an hour before they called him back, and they hardly interviewed him. He says they already seemed to know all about him."

Ethan had by this point learned that saying nothing at all in these situations was a solid choice.

Kohn won the primary in a landslide. The polls were looking good for the general election. Emily reported that Kohn himself had come to the sign storage room and moved signs around for an hour, talking with the two girls and asking them questions. The next week, Alannah's brother Martin was hired, along with four new staffers in varying levels of responsibility. All of them were from underprivileged parts of the city, and most of them were African-American or Latino.

Alannah was shocked, yet so hopeful. "I wondered if there would be anyone to replace my father one day. This is the kind of opportunity underrepresented and underprivileged people need," she said. "I know a bunch of these people from school and such. They're good workers—the best of the kids. Kohn knows talent, that's for sure."

"Well, he hired us. So obviously."

Alannah laughed. Emily saw that Alannah had become much more cheerful and fun since the hirings. "It's all well and good to talk about being color-blind," Emily said. "But it's a lot less pressure when there are more faces around that look like yours."

Of course, it was too good to last.

In late August, Dara came through the door again, and went to Ed's again, and came over to sit heavily in her chair again.

"We've done this before," Ethan said. "You're leaving?"

She just nodded. "I got in. I didn't think I possibly could, but I got in."

"Got in?"

"To college. Pepperdine. I'm going to be a lawyer." She said it in wonder, the way someone would if they'd been chosen to be on the cover of *Time* magazine.

"That's... great," Ethan said. "I'm very happy for you." He did a good job of keeping the breaking of his heart out of his voice, and he was quite proud of himself for that.

She smiled at him, and this time there was no snark in it, no teasing. "I don't leave for two weeks. Let's not waste it."

They didn't, although it was true that their numbers were not quite as good as they had been. Ed grumbled, and Ed growled, and Ed gave them the evil eye, but in the end he didn't actually do anything until the day Dara's chair was empty once more.

Ethan had done nothing whatever that day, made no money and placed no signs and barely made any calls at all, when Ed came out of his office and pointed at him.

"You," he said. He crooked his finger, summoning Ethan to the dungeon.

When the door was shut and Ethan was sitting like a skittish mouse on the very edge of the chair, Ed gazed at him sourly and said, "Oh, come off it. I won't eat you. Relax."

Ethan tried, but his insides were in too much of a mess.

Ed reached into his desk, pulled out a box of Oreo DoubleStuf and slapped it onto the desk between them. "If you want to keep working here, you will match me cookie for cookie while we eat this entire tray."

Ethan couldn't make himself smile, but he did sit forward a bit and sigh.

"I get it, kid," Ed said. "Carbs. Makes the whole world better. Even binds up a broken heart."

Ethan managed a weak grin. "Thanks, Ed. But I don't think I can eat these."

"Why not?"

"I only eat Oreos if I can dunk them in milk." He shrugged. "Sorry."

Ed bent down, pulled up a jug of milk and two glasses and thunked them on the desk next to the Oreos. "Who do you think you're talking to, kid?"

It took almost an hour. But darned if Ethan didn't feel a whole lot better when they were done.

THE END

Emily swiveled in her chair, staring at the industrial ceiling tile above her. She tapped her lips with a pencil, thinking of the right words to write. The office wasn't terribly quiet for thinking. Every few minutes, a light rail train came by, shaking the floor and rattling the blinds.

"It's not how fancy the office is," Cathy had said. "It's about the quality of the people working in it. We don't have to impress anyone. Everyone interested in this race knows who I am already."

That had proved true so far. Once she'd announced that she was running, there had been a steady stream of local officials traipsing through her office, sounding her out, quizzing her on her policy stances on everything from the proposed ballpark in Malantown to the recently passed bond for highway maintenance and construction.

Emily's keen eye had discerned that most people had left her office unhappy. They'd discovered for themselves that Aunt Cathy wasn't your typical politician. Hence the pressure on her to put this memo together.

Cathy herself hadn't given Emily a lot of direction. "I need both sides. Research. Get me opinions from all over the political spectrum. You'll have to dig, because—you might not be aware of this—the internet isn't overly excited about the minutiae of governmental interactions."

That had been an understatement. Numerous searches had turned up nothing at all. But she had been persistent, and gradually she'd found what she'd been looking for. It wasn't a simple Republican/Democrat divide—it was kind of like different branches of physics. On one level, gravity was a thing, but on the quantum level, it wasn't. Parties mattered a lot on the national level, and a good deal on the state level. But the smaller one got in terms of political units, the less important party affiliation seemed to be. There wasn't a lot of difference between a Democrat and a Republican on the city council, for instance. It seemed that when local issues were on the table, the principles the parties talked about on the national news went out the window. Republicans voted for more taxes. Democrats proposed regulations making it harder for poor people to start their own businesses. Both sides seemed very happy to spend as much money as they could get their hands on. It made no sense to Emily at all.

She leaned forward and typed the last few sentences of her report. She sent Cathy the document and sat back in her chair again. A train came by and rattled the window. She wanted to open it—there was lavender just outside, growing through the cracks in the ancient asphalt—but the noise of the trains was too much. So she settled for imagining she could smell the flowers while keeping her teeth in her head.

Her laptop pinged. It was an incoming message from Cathy. "Come see me."

Nothing easier. Emily got up, opened her flimsy wooden door, turned left, and went down the dim hallway with its broken fluorescent baffle shining flickering light onto twenty-year-old industrial carpeting. At the door at the end, she knocked.

"Come in," Cathy said.

Emily pushed the door open and stepped into the only decent room in the building. The carpet was probably only about ten years old, an attractive light blue and cream, and the office was spacious, with windows on two sides that let in plenty of light. Unfortunately the view out the windows was of a parking lot, but what could you do? At least there was a Russian Olive tree growing where it shouldn't, right on the corner. It lent shade and greenery to the scene.

Cathy was on her couch, against the left-hand window, her shoes off and her feet propped up on the coffee table. Her skirt was immaculate, as if it had just been pressed, and Cathy looked fresh and energized, even though it was nearly four in the afternoon and she'd been working all day. Emily was sure she herself looked like a rat with mange; she couldn't understand how Cathy pulled it off.

"Sit," Cathy said, waving a pen at the loveseat to Emily's left.

"You can't have read my paper already," Emily said, obeying the instructions.

"Of course not," Cathy said. "Though I'm sure it's terrific. I have something else I want you to do for me."

There was a knock at the door, and it burst open before Cathy could say anything. A man stood there, a fellow in his late thirties or early forties, the same age as Aunt Cathy, in dress pants and a white shirt open at the collar. His face was friendly, if a little flushed, as if he'd been running, and dark matted curls decked his head.

"I'm late," he said.

"You are, but not very," Cathy said. "Sit there next to my niece Emily."

Emily scooted to the far end of the loveseat, closest to Aunt Cathy. The man perched on the other end, like he wasn't sure he wanted to commit to the cushions.

"Emily, this is Gio Cardona. He's a specialist in unions. Gio, Emily, one of the whip-crack smartest kids you'll come across in your life."

He held out a hand. "Charmed," he said. "I love meeting smart kids." He had a thick accent from someplace back east.

"Thanks. I like specialists."

"We're gonna do great, then."

Cathy said, "You will, and you'll have to. One of the biggest political players in Montana is the MTUT—that's the Montana Union of Teachers, Emily—and they've sent me a questionnaire they want me to fill out." She pointed to a quarter-inch-thick stack of stapled paper on the desk.

Gio reached over and picked it up. He leafed through it. "Are they serious?" he said, looking up.

"Deadly," Cathy said. "I'm not going to fill it out. I'm not telling *you* to fill it out. But I am telling you to figure out whether we should fill it out, and if so, then with what. Your job is to get the unions on my side, or at least to keep them off Sulla's. You're working together on this because Emily might be able to get information you can't, Gio. You're pretty well known to the bosses, but Emily isn't. She could be useful for research purposes. Your call. Get out of my office. I have to talk to the governor in a few minutes, and I don't want my niece to hear me swear."

She picked up her phone and began tapping.

Emily and Gio got up and went back into the hallway. "I take it we're using your office?" Gio said. "Seeing as I don't have one?"

"I don't really have an office, but there's a space nobody else wants because it's right next to the train tracks. We can use that, I guess. Or we could sit in the lobby here and shout back and forth at one another."

"I usually need to know someone for at least twenty minutes before they start shouting at me," Gio said. "Let's try the office."

Gio had to drag in one of the battered metal-and-plastic chairs from the lobby or sit on the floor. As it was plastic carpet over bare concrete—with no pad—he went for the chair.

"Who are you?" Emily said. "I mean, I know who you are, but who are you?"

He laughed. It was rich and full, no falseness or pretense in it—the laugh of a man comfortable in his own skin. "I'm from back east originally, you might be able to tell from the accent. I moved out to Helena a few years ago to go to grad school and met Cathy. She's your aunt?" Emily nodded and he went on. "We were working on a project that required some delicate negotiations with the teachers' union. We've kind of collaborated since. I think that's why she called me. Now, who are you?"

"I'm from Spoonerville. I'm sixteen and I need money for a car, plus my Aunt Cathy doesn't take no for an answer."

"Excellent," Gio said. He waved the sheaf of papers. "This looks like a chore. But it's pretty standard. They like to really grill their candidates before they make endorsements."

Emily craned her neck to get sight of the papers. Gio saw it and simply ripped the bottom half of the stack off the staple. He held it out to her. "If we answer it, we'll have to unstaple it anyway. If we don't, then who cares what we do with it?"

She smiled and took it from him.

The first item on her sheet was, "Describe the function, duties, and responsibilities of the education liaison in your office, should you win the Secretary of State seat."

"Wow," she said, looking up.

"That bad?" Gio said. She told him what was on her paper. "Interesting. My first one was, 'Outline in detail your educational experience, both as a student and as a teacher or administrator.'"

"That one's pretty simple. Aunt Cathy went to college, got a degree in political science, then a masters degree in business. That's it. She's never been a teacher."

"Where do you go to school?" Gio said.

"Right here." Emily waved her arms around at the four walls of the office. The ground shook a bit. "Incoming," she said.

The train rumbled by.

"I see the appeal of this office," he said.

"You should open the windows for the full effect."

"Back to my question," he said. "You don't go to school?"

Emily eyed him for a moment. "Do you want the short answer, or the speech?"

"Uh," Gio said, "What the heck. You have me intrigued. Let's have the speech."

Emily put her hands in front of her, stood primly up, and made a little bow. "There are many kinds of alternative schooling—homeschool, unschool, nonschool, lifeschool, worldschool, and several others—but they all boil down to the same thing. Schooling is just one way to learn, and it's not necessarily the best way, especially when a child is young and the most important thing is to get the tools for learning and to love learning, not necessarily to memorize a textbook full of facts. I am homeschooled, but that means that everyone is my teacher and everywhere is my class."

Gio's face spoke volumes. "Wow. Shows what I know. Maybe I should have gone for the short answer."

"Here's that one: I go to school everywhere. I'm homeschooled. Most people think it means I don't ever go to class, but ask any homeschooler—it really means I'm *constantly* in class."

"I take it your personal experience with teachers' unions is pretty small, then." Gio moved his finger down the page to the next question. "What are the key attributes of a Secretary of State with regard to education policy?"

"Please tell me you don't understand that any better than I do," Emily said. "I would have no idea at all how to answer that."

Gio flipped through the rest of his pages. "A lot of more of the same here. What about you?"

"My next one is 'What should school districts address in their academic programs and policies? Specifically outline a sample curriculum.' Are they serious? Do they really think that a bunch of people in an office somewhere can decide what every kid of nine in the whole state should be learning right now? Nobody learns like that."

"My experience is they *always* think they should decide. This isn't terribly surprising. I've seen questionnaires much like this before. They take a long, long time to answer."

"For the millionth time, I'm so glad Mom and Dad decided to homeschool us."

"The good teachers manage to get the job done anyway. Didn't you ever have one?"

"Mrs. Miner. I do miss her sometimes. Even so, this is better." Emily rocked back in her chair. It groaned as if it would come apart at any moment. She ignored that and stared at the ceiling. "So do we take the time?"

"How important is it to Cathy to win the race?"

Emily sat back up. "How important are the unions to her winning?"

"Are we going to shoot questions back and forth, or is one of us going to break and give an answer?"

"Would you like to go first?"

He burst out laughing at this. "Okay, okay! I'll go. The unions can be make-or-break in a campaign like this one, which is going to turn on a small number of votes."

"It's very important that Aunt Cathy win. You might say it's personal."

"Then, Miss Emily Tuttle, we probably should answer the questions and try to get their endorsement."

Emily scanned the rest of her pages. "I don't know that we can get it. Even if we could answer all these, could we do it in the way the unions want us to without lying?"

"Lying would bother you?" Gio said, offhanded, his eyes on his page.

"It wouldn't bother *you*?"

Gio sighed. "If we're going to do this every time, our discussions are going to take forever. Yes, it would bother me, but I've done worse. There are always ways to spin things so they sound better to the people asking the questions."

What a process, Emily thought. Even good people had to all but lie in order to get votes, to get elected. Whatever happened to just being yourself and letting the voters decide? "I don't know if Aunt Cathy would go along with that."

"She'll have to, or she's going to lose this endorsement."

Emily picked up a pencil and used it to try to peg the ceiling, flipping it up end-over-end, hoping to get it point-first, like throwing a knife. She couldn't get it to stick. "'There's the rub,' I think Hamlet would say."

"Aye," Gio said. He pulled a pen from his pocket and tried the same thing. "Let me ask this: How much do you know about Sulla? Are his answers going to be any more acceptable to the Union than ours?"

"Probably," Emily said. "He's very capable of giving whatever answer is going to get him closer to being elected."

"I'm going to go out to my car and get my laptop. That one's yours?" he said, indicating the desk. Emily nodded. "Okay. Then we're going to look up everything we can find about Sulla and MTUT. It might be that he's already in their pocket. In that case, we can move on to something else."

An hour's searching turned up a couple of interesting things. One, the unions had no opposition to Sulla's campaign. Quite the contrary, they seemed likely to be in favor of it. One of the former union organizers was on Sulla's campaign staff. A minor position, but still.

But the second piece of information was even more interesting. "His wife's a teacher," Gio said, eyes glued to the screen.

"*Was* a teacher," Emily said. "She was fired. Look here." She swiveled her laptop around so he could see the article. "Just a couple of years ago."

He read down a bit. "It doesn't say what she was fired for—but it's not easy to get fired as a teacher. It might have been something serious. That's not unusual, but it's disappointing. Oooh, but it says here she filed a union grievance. There could be bad blood there. Probably is."

"You're the specialist. I don't understand unions like you do."

Gio blew out a breath. "Where to start? Well, truth is that the idea of unions—workers banding together to get better working conditions for themselves—isn't a bad one. There have been some bad people to work for in history. Some jobs are seriously dangerous, and workers have every right to organize to protect themselves." He tapped a finger on the desk, as if trying to decide what to say.

"But teachers' unions are, and almost always have been, somewhat different. The job itself isn't dangerous except in rare circumstances. The hours can be awful, of course. The pressure is high. Teachers should—and do—have the right to band together to make things better for themselves. Remember, though, that this isn't like working as a plumber or a coal miner. There is only one employer, realistically, and that's the government. Whether we should have or not, we've allowed the government to set working conditions. Most of the things a union would have been necessary for aren't really a problem for teachers.

"So instead of arguing for *teachers*, mostly what the teachers' unions do is argue for funding."

Emily cut in. "That should help teachers though, right?"

"It should," Gio said. "And sometimes it does, at least a little. But more often it goes to administration.

To staff outside the classroom. In most school districts, half or more of the payroll for the district goes into the hands of administrators—not to teachers. And that," he said, winding up, "is why they will want a man like Sulla in charge. He can funnel money to the union and the administrators while making it look like it's 'for the kids.'"

"Wow," Emily said. "How much money are we talking about?"

"Billions. With a 'b.'"

Emily whistled.

Gio gave a big nod, eyes wide. "So, on the one hand, Sulla sounds like the kind of guy that unions love. He's into big government control of schools and beefing up contracts with the unions. On the other hand, his wife is a former teacher with a checkered record and a union grievance in her recent past. That might give us an opening we could exploit."

Emily looked over the rim of her computer. "How? What does that have to do with us?"

"Suppose for a second you're the union. Some of the membership has a bad taste in their mouth over this woman. The rest are in favor of her husband being elected. What if we come in with a set of answers that are pretty good—not quite what they'd like, but better than they thought they'd be, given Cathy's reputation. They might decide to withhold endorsement. Or make an endorsement but no sizable donation. That could be big for us."

"Playing defense, in other words."

"Right. It's not just about getting good stuff for ourselves. We can also keep good stuff from going to the other guys."

Emily frowned, thinking. "But... Really... How big a deal is it? Most of the teachers are not going to vote for Aunt Cathy. They should—they'd love her as SecState—but they're not going to, no matter what the unions do. So does it matter if we don't get their endorsement? Even if it goes to someone else? How many votes is that going to move?"

Gio got up and paced a little. "Sharp thinking. Maybe we don't lose those votes, because we never had them. But there are a lot of people out there—most of the population, sad to say—who don't do their homework on the candidates. They rely on shorthand, picking up their cues from their party or from organizations that they trust. For better or worse, most of the population has a very high opinion of the teachers' unions. They think 'the union' means 'the teachers.' If they give their endorsement to someone, that carries weight. It moves people."

"Okay," Emily sighed. "We're back where we started. Or I am, anyway. It might be a good idea to fill this out, and it might not."

"What do we have to lose?"

"Time," Emily said. "This is hours of work, hours we could be spending doing other things. Time is the most important resource we have."

Gio stared at her. "You're sixteen? How did you learn that?"

Emily quoted, "'Don't act like you have ten thousand years to live; death is close to all: while you live, while you have time, be good.' Marcus Aurelius. We're lousy with stoic philosophy at Chez Tuttle."

"Explains a lot," Gio said, apparently to himself. "Okay, well, here we are. What do we go back and tell Cathy? Are we going to do it, or not?"

If you think they should do the questionnaire, turn to page 285.

If you think they shouldn't, turn to page 124.

“Troops,” Emily said, “I didn’t get into this race to be a wind-up toy for any political party. If I didn’t think I could handle the race on my own, I would never have gotten into it. So the RNC, the DNC, the Libertarians, the Greens, the Communists, and whoever else has a party these days can keep their advice to themselves if it comes with hooks and leverage. As a very famous puppet once said, ‘There are no strings on me.’”

She stopped and looked at Kohn for reaction. Apparently he was dead. He showed nothing on his face at all.

Finally he said, “Oh, you were done. I don’t think that speech sounded much like me at all.”

“I’m not sure what you want me to say,” Emily said. “So instead of guessing, I’ll just tell you what Alannah’s father would say: don’t promise what you’ll feel terrible about delivering on.”

“That sounds like one of Will Pascoe’s rules,” Kohn said.

She shrugged. “Maybe it is one. I have no idea. All I can tell you is that if it makes you feel icky, you probably shouldn’t do it.”

“That’s just it,” Kohn said, tapping that pen of his on the table like a drummer. “I think I probably shouldn’t. But I don’t know why not. They haven’t actually asked me to do anything yet, and if they did, I can’t say that it would be something I wouldn't want to do. What if they never ask me to go against my gut feeling about what's right? Am I blowing the whole reason I want to get into the Senate?"

"How can we know that?" Ethan said. "We're sixteen. We don't even have a car. You want us to forecast how your Senate term is going to go?"

"Of course not," Kohn said, getting up and pacing. "But how do you *feel* about what they said?"

"Icky," Emily said, without hesitation. "There *are* good reasons to go along with them. They have money, and money would probably be helpful. We're really expensive."

"And likely to get more so," Ethan said.

"But what happens when they *do* ask you to do something you don't want to do? What if you have to stand behind a policy you genuinely disagree with? Will it be easier to do that before you take their money, or afterward?"

Kohn made a face. "Afterward it will be impossible."

"But it isn't now. So maybe you can tell them to jump in a lake. Metaphorically speaking," Ethan said.

"I wouldn't do that," Emily said. "But I would tell them thank you, and their money would be welcome, if they're willing to spend it without imposing conditions on it."

"They'll interpret that as a declaration of war," Kohn said.

"Maybe a declaration of independence," Ethan said.

Kohn shook his head. "Don't you see, though? It amounts to the same thing. The handcuffs might be golden, but they're still binding. If I put them on, we're friends. If I don't, we're not."

"You'll make other allies," Emily said.

"Maybe," Kohn said. "You're familiar with those rules Will Pascoe keeps trotting out, so here's another one for you to think about: You can't make friends of your enemies by making enemies of your friends."

"I like that one," Ethan said. "Why didn't he quote that one at us?"

"He probably hasn't gotten around to it yet. Which number is that?" Emily said to Kohn.

"I never remember the numbers. But that's the one I think of most often. It seems applicable."

There was a silence then, inside the room. Shadows passed the blinds from passersby in the hallway, people scurrying back and forth, carrying the campaign to victory.

"The question I have is, which kind are the RNC people? Are they friends or enemies?"

Finally there was a meeting Emily and Ethan weren't invited to. Kohn, Ed, and Pascoe went into Kohn's office with the RNC people and shut the door. Emily wondered if they'd hear shouting, banging, gunshots, something... but no. The place was very quiet. With no one to give them orders, the twins were left to figure out something to do, wondering what sort of conversation was going on behind the deep oak door.

They settled for going through old campaign event social media work and trying to gauge interaction. Just as they'd come to the conclusion that people didn't care what you put in your tweets as long as you included a good photo, the door opened and the six inhabitants of the room came out. Ethan studied them for signs of violent confrontation but didn't see much to get excited about. No red faces from heated argument. Everyone looked not just calm but pleased. How could *everyone* look pleased?

They shook hands at the door, and the RNC people said they needed to get back to their hotels, but they'd be out in the evening for the campaign event before they had to fly to Denver the next morning. They went out the front door into the warm sunshine and left the top campaign brass with bemused smiles on their faces.

"Ready to go?" Ed said. "I'll get Melissa."

Kohn slapped Pascoe on the shoulder and retreated to his office, closing the door once more. A faint smell of sweat reached the twins, evidence that at least some hard work had gone on behind those drawn shades.

"What happened?" Emily said.

Pascoe looked blankly at them. "What do you mean? We had a campaign meeting and exchanged information and ideas. What do you think happened?"

"Did Kohn tell them to go jump in a lake?" Ethan said.

"What are you talking about?"

"That... We just..." Ethan pointed to the conference room in confusion. "He asked us, and we... We said..."

"You said, 'I exist but to serve you, my liege.' At least you better have. That's about all the statementing you oughta be doing around here."

"Um, yes," Emily said. "That's exactly what we said. C'mon, Ethan, let's go wait outside."

Pascoe let them go. He must have had a lot on his mind. Emily wanted to talk about it, but Ethan didn't. Neither of them, it seemed, was having any success figuring out what the scene after the meeting had meant. Maybe they had both completely misunderstood each other, because there was no way those three from the RNC had just been shooting the breeze when they said that their support depended on Kohn's being willing to play ball. And it sure sounded like Kohn had intended to tell them they could pound sand. So what could have happened to make them all be happy about things?

"In the end," Ethan said, as they stood wilting in the sunshine, "it doesn't matter what happened in there. We have a job to do, and we better do it."

They stood in the parking lot for five minutes, getting nowhere, before a woman came out with the keys to the white truck. "You two ready?" she said.

"Sure," Ethan said.

She introduced herself as Ed's daughter Melissa, and she turned out to be a fun person to spend a few hours with while setting up for the event. She worked tirelessly with them the whole day and made sure the twins got a break and some food before they went to change for the event itself.

Pascoe showed up an hour before the event officially began and said that the body wouldn't be there until about thirty minutes after the event had started. "It's good for people to see him as very busy and squeezing out time to show up. Besides, it makes the visuals good, and everyone will already be seated when he gets there, so he can go around to tables and greet people, get some photos, all that."

The twins nodded and said nothing.

"This is impossible," Pascoe said. "You two haven't stopped talking for this long since the Carter Administration."

"Which we weren't alive for," Ethan said.

"So you could hardly be talking, could you? What's up?"

"What happened in the meeting?"

"You're not still on about that, are you?" Pascoe said, pushing past them to get into the venue. "Nothing you need to worry about. Let's get to work and get this job done."

But they did worry about it. They worried all through the dinner, through taking hundreds of photos of the candidate with the Rotarians, matching those photos with the people in them and making sure they had email addresses and contact information to send the pictures to.

Pages and pages later, Pascoe was impressed. "You thought of all this?"

"Melissa helped. We did the social media stuff, but we also talked about getting to each of these people individually, because who doesn't like to have a photo of themselves with the next US Senator from the state of Montana."

"Gives us another touch. Nice. That's gonna make some donations, for sure." Pascoe checked his watch. "The body is on in fifteen minutes. Hustle him backstage, Emily."

She threaded her way through laughing tables of Rotarians to Kohn's side. He sat munching on the remnants of his dinner, listening to one of his tablemates tell a story about his humanitarian trip to Guatemala. The dinner smelled divine—grilled chicken on a bed of rice with fresh asparagus. Emily's stomach rumbled. She'd had a few fries and an overcooked burger from one of the local fast-food joints, but that had been several hours ago.

The woman at Kohn's left looked up at her and said, "You're one of the twins, aren't you?"

"Yes, ma'am," Emily said, surprised. "I'm sorry I don't know who you are." But then she remembered the seating chart from the event prep. "Wait, you must be Mrs. Kohn. I didn't recognize you." Emily didn't know whether to curtsey or bow or offer to shake hands, so she settled for a bright smile. That seemed to be the right thing to do. Mrs. Kohn smiled up at her with teeth so perfect they could have been used for a dental commercial.

She pushed back from the table and swiveled in her chair until she was mostly facing Emily. "Call me Daniela. Don't be surprised that I know who you are. Randall has been talking about the two of you for a month straight. You've made quite an impression on him."

"I'm very glad to be working for the campaign." Emily put conviction in her voice, but she wondered if it were still true.

"It's probably time for Randall to get backstage for speech prep. I'll cut the story short here and be the bad guy. Give me a second."

Daniela turned back to the table and laid a slim, tanned hand on Kohn's stark white sleeve. He leaned his head in her direction without taking his eyes from the table's storyteller, a grizzled older man about five feet tall bearing a strong resemblance to a garden gnome—whose name was apparently Dollar. Like the money. Daniela whispered in his ear.

He gave the barest nod, and a moment later, as the raconteur paused for breath, he cut smoothly into the flow and excused himself. "But Dollar, I want to hear the rest of this story. There are some things we can discuss, I think. Will you stay a moment after the festivities?"

"I have nowhere to be and all night to get there," Dollar said. "I'm happy to play squire to you, sir knight, as long as you need me."

"Great," Kohn said, obviously meaning it. "I must go make a speech now, but would you allow this lovely young lady to take my place for dessert?"

The men at the table stood up and enthusiastically welcomed Emily to the dessert course. A brown-clad waiter with a white shirt and a towel draped over his arm took away Kohn's plate and set a triple-layer chocolate cake in its place.

Emily did love a chocolate cake.

"I'd love to join you," she said, "but I don't want to get in trouble with the campaign. I have a job to do tonight, and I can't leave my team high and dry."

Kohn was already gone, heading for the curtain that led to the backstage area. Pascoe was there to greet him, so that assignment was accomplished. But Ethan and Melissa and the others were still working...

Daniela's dark eyes lingered on Emily's face. She got up. "Excuse me, gentlemen, but Emily will never be able to enjoy her dessert unless someone makes sure her duties are taken care of. If you'll give me a moment, I shall return with a get-out-of-jail-free card."

She patted Emily's arm. "Sit. The next half hour is not going to cost us the Senate. You look like you haven't eaten all day. Take a minute and enjoy these people's company. I'll be right back."

Daniela stalked off in the direction of Pascoe. Emily couldn't see Ethan anywhere. Probably somewhere uploading photos to the internet.

Dollar said, "Emily, it's so nice to have you join us for a few moments. Are you the one responsible for the photography here tonight?"

"Partly. Yes, sir."

"Sir! My lords and ladies, you look upon one who has been knighted by the queen herself!" Dollar said. "Nay, milady, I am but a humble jester, and you may call me Dollar." He leaned forward conspiratorially. "But you may hear others refer to me as Bartholomew Bloodworth. Believe not a word of it, milady."

What sort of man was this?

"She's wondering how on earth you get from Bloodworth to Dollar," the man to Dollar's left said. "I'm Bob Packer, the District Governor. I'm not colorful like Dollar here."

"I'm sure she couldn't care less about my nickname, Bob."

"Actually..." Emily said.

"It's like this," Packer said. "What's blood worth? Get it?"

Emily thought for a second. "I think it's like $130 a pint these days."

The District Governor stared at her a moment then burst out laughing. "How old *are* you, Dollar?"

Dollar seemed to be enjoying himself as much as anyone. More, even. "It's not how old I am, it's the poor quality of the serum that runs in these tired veins," he said. "But when I started donating blood, it was pretty cheap. One of the nurses thought my name was ironic and teased me about it. But I had the last laugh—-she ended up taking my name." Dollar winked at her.

Emily couldn't help smiling.

The others introduced themselves as the assistant district governor and her husband, the district governor-elect, and other people with lofty titles. Dollar alone seemed to be just, well, himself. Emily wondered what he was doing there at the head table.

Daniela returned before Emily had a chance to put a forkful of cake in her mouth. It smelled divine, like a cocoa factory milling chocolate right under her nose. "You're in the clear, Emily Tuttle. Pascoe says Rule number 25 is 'the mind can absorb no more than the seat can endure,' which probably means something deeply wise, but for the moment it means that you've done all you need to do, and you can finish your cake and listen to the speech from here."

"But—"

"And your brother will do the speech's social media outreach, in return for which he gets a triple slice. It's all arranged. You're famished. Eat."

Against such an iron lady, Emily decided she had no chance and might as well put a forkful of cake in her mouth. She did, and the one bite was worth all of the work that had gotten her there.

"Did I hear Mrs. Kohn—sorry, Daniela—say your last name was Tuttle?" Dollar said.

"Uh, yes. It is."

"Are you any relation to Susan Tuttle, by some wild happenstance?"

Emily stared. "How could you know that? She's my mother."

"Ah, that explains a great deal. I know your mother. She's one of the dearest souls in the world and a force for good everywhere she goes. Apparently her powers are concentrated in her daughter as well."

Emily's face broke into a huge smile. Dollar had that effect.

"When you're finished, you must tell me why you've decided to support Mr. Kohn," Dollar said. "Knowing that the daughter of Susan Tuttle is on staff with Randall Kohn tells me a lot about him. But don't do it now because talking politics over chocolate cake is sure to summon the trickster god Kumokums."

Daniela laughed, a beautiful sound, like the chimes of a handbell choir. "You made that up."

"Not at all, gracious one. Kumokums is the god of mischief among the Modoc Indians of California, of which I am an honorary tribal member. His arms are long and his fingers light. It would not do to tempt him."

So Emily got to eat right up to the introduction of Kohn as the main speaker of the evening and right through the speech.

Which wasn't bad. It focused on the good that one person can do by simply refusing to quit in the face of opposition. He used several examples, from Marie Curie to Jackie Robinson to Bessie Coleman, an African-American pilot of whom Emily had never heard. Based on the faces around her, Emily would have bet nobody else in the arena had either.

But all through the speech, Emily couldn't help thinking about the meeting in Kohn's office, where he was supposed to have taken the examples of these people he praised and done the same thing—stood up to people who wanted him to compromise, to be less than he was. Yes, they were powerful, and yes, they could probably shove him to the margins of things as they were—but didn't Kohn want to get into the Senate to change how those people used their power?

And if he didn't, or didn't anymore, how could Emily put her heart and soul behind him?

The speech was inspirational, and the crowd rewarded it with several long ovations. When Kohn finished, he announced a $5000 donation to the Rotary

District to fund clean water projects in Africa, and that was greeted with a standing ovation.

Emily stood. But she couldn't applaud. Before the clapping had died down, she excused herself and went to find her brother. She couldn't stand the whiff of hypocrisy under the piped-in aroma of heroism.

As she thought, he was backstage, laptop open, face illuminated by the telltale blue screen of Twitter.

"Hey," she said.

"Hey," he said. "Some speech, eh?"

"You thinking the same things about it that I am?"

"Probably. Although I'm thinking them deeper and more substantively."

"While sending out social media messages on Twitter. Highly unlikely."

"Yeah, well. My last tweet got retweeted sixty times in the first two minutes, so take that. Anyway, I think I'm done here. We've got cleanup work to do, don't we?"

She nodded. "But not that much. Most of the cleanup is supposed to be done by the venue staff, if I remember right. I'll find Melissa. We'll want all the campaign signs back, of course, and probably any loose literature. We can re-use those things.."

"I'll do the outside if you do the inside. I need some air," Ethan said, closing the laptop. He stood and uncricked his back. Then, without warning, he gave Emily a hug. "Don't sweat this. Nobody's done anything wrong."

"Has anyone done anything right though?" she said.

Emily handed over the camera to Melissa, who said she'd take care of taking exit photos.

As Emily exited the backstage area, the three RNC people, who had been hanging back on the fringes of the event, approached Kohn. They shook his hand warmly, and Eastman clapped him on the back. They waved to Pascoe and went out. Emily rubbed her face and tried to get enthusiastic about doing one more thing for the campaign.

Emily went around, table by table, and collected all the loose campaign materials, especially those that were donation envelopes. Around her, venue staff and campaign people pulled down bunting, removed glassware, and folded up tablecloths.

Except at one table. Pascoe hovered there like the ghosts of A Christmas Carol, wanting to intervene, but not having the power. Mr. and Mrs. Kohn sat, leaning forward in close attention, listening to Dollar, who was obviously relating something of great importance, punctuated with a lot of hand waving and table thumping. Emily couldn't hear what he was saying, but whatever it was, it must have been important because even Pascoe couldn't get the body and his wife to so much as stand up from the table, much less leave. He was supposed to have been gone.

But he wouldn't go.

Emily was working on her last table when Pascoe loomed up behind her and slapped his hand on a campaign brochure just as she was reaching for it.

"You're wrapped. No more cleanup," he said. "They want you at the head table."

Emily stared at him. "Me? What for?"

"You remember how you wanted to know what happened in that meeting earlier today?" His face was completely blank. Emily could read nothing in it at all. "Randall told me what you said in your little meeting beforehand. That wasn't what he said in the meeting with the RNC, and if you tell anyone, anywhere, that you heard that from me I'll fire you so fast your britches will burst into flame from friction before you can get out to the parking lot."

Emily dropped her gaze to the tablecloth. "That's what I was afraid of."

"It was sense, girl, and don't forget it. I won't stand here and tell you I liked it, but I've been in politics since before Methuselah learned to crawl, and sometimes you have to hold your nose to get the thing you came for."

"It makes sense," Emily said, thoroughly miserable. "I just can't… I don't like it. I don't see how we're going to change things if we keep backing down."

"Slowly," Pasoe said. "Ah, you can't possibly understand. I was like you once. Forever ago."

From across the floor, above the din of cleanup, a voice carried to them. "Emily!" It was Dollar's voice. He waved her over.

Emily said to Pascoe, "We made a commitment. We'll stick to it. We'll do the work, but I don't know that I can be happy about it."

Under his breath, Pascoe said "Rule number 31." He put his hands flat on the table and leaned on them, his shoulders hunched and his eyes closed.

"What's Rule 31?" She ignored Dollar's repeated call.

"Never fully trust someone until they've stayed true to a good cause even when they saw it was losing. You broke something, Emily Tuttle. I don't know what you did, but we were going one way, and now I don't know what on the green earth we're doing." He blew out a long breath. "Go. They're waiting."

Emily left her box and her sense of security and walked slowly across the polished concrete floor to the one table that still looked as if it were set for dinner. Kohn's face showed quizzical interest, but all she saw on Daniela's and Dollar's faces was warm, smiling welcome.

As she approached the table, Dollar stood and pulled out a chair, the one between himself and Kohn. It would put all four of them in a crescent moon on one side of the table, with no one sitting opposite. She wondered if that was deliberate.

Dollar sat down and said, "We were discussing a piece of advice you gave to Randall earlier today. You remember what that was?"

She certainly did. She hadn't thought of much else all day. But she felt that her usual habit of blurting things out would not be appropriate here. There was an air of solemnity at the table, as if something momentous were being hashed out. So she simply said, “I do.”

“And you expected Randall to listen to that advice?”

“I… Well, I thought he would.”

“Even though you’re sixteen and he’s a multi-millionaire running for the Senate.”

“When you say it that way, it sounds silly. But otherwise, why ask me in the first place?”

“Why indeed. You didn’t find it unusual that he would do so?” Gone was the high tone, the joking plays on words. This was someone different, and Emily could see that despite his lack of title he was someone to be reckoned with. Dollar kept his voice low, even, and calm. He wasn’t conducting an investigation. He was talking to her as a friend.

“At the time, no, but I can see that to ask me something so important probably would be.” Emily scratched at the tablecloth, uncomfortable despite the friendly tone from Dollar and the close interest from the Kohns. Across the floor from her, a custodian pushed a wheeled plastic trash can heaped with spent bunting.

“So thinking about it now, why do you think he would ask you and your brother to give your opinion?”

Emily’s mind tried to latch onto something that would explain it, but finally she turned to Kohn and said, “Why *did* you ask us? It can’t have been because you thought we’d give you experienced advice.”

Kohn laughed and laced his fingers through his wife's. "I asked you because you *weren't* experienced. I thought you'd give me advice from principle, from your gut, not from any calculation about keeping your job or getting promoted or even winning the seat. And that's what you did, didn't you?"

"I don't know much about any of those things. But I know what I think is right."

"Precisely," Dollar said. "And then something happened that upset you."

How could he know this? She looked at Kohn, whose face was calm and gave away nothing, and at Daniela, who winked. Daniela? Was this conversation her work?

"It's all right," Kohn said. "We'd like to hear about it."

"Well, it wasn't just me," Emily said. "Ethan, too. We started the day getting invited to a meeting we didn't really belong in, and then to one where we *definitely* didn't belong, and then there was another meeting we weren't invited to. That meeting should have had fireworks and arguing, but it didn't. When it broke up everyone seemed... happy. But if Mr. Kohn had told the RNC people he wasn't going to do their bidding, they should have been ticked off. They weren't, so I assumed—"

"You assumed I hadn't said that. You assumed I'd given in to their demands."

Emily nodded and didn't trust herself to speak. She dropped her gaze to the tablecloth.

"You assumed correctly," Kohn said.

Her head whipped up. He was admitting it? She was sure her face transparently showed her shock and dismay.

"Right. I told them I was prepared to do whatever it took to win the race, that the most important thing was to get into office because that's where the power is. And once you have the power, you can put things right."

Emily opened her mouth to say something, but then she couldn't. Not in front of these other two. She couldn't just quit right here.

"But then some things happened. And they, uh, changed my mind a bit." Kohn leaned back in his chair and fixed his eyes on Dollar.

"The first one was Dollar here. Bartholomew, I believe, is his given name, and thanks to the excellent prep work of my team," here he winked at Emily, "I knew a lot about him before I sat down. What I didn't know was that five minutes of conversation with him would completely change the direction I was going to take my campaign."

"What did he say?" Emily said, turning to Dollar, wanting to know what could possibly have had that big of an effect.

Kohn said, "He said he was dying."

"*What?*"

Dollar gave a modest shrug. "It has the virtue of being true, but it is very often a conversation killer.

Randall here, however, got *more* interested, not less." Dollar blew out a long breath, and Emily thought she could see how tired he was under the friendly exterior. "Emily, everyone has so much time on the earth. We don't get more. We don't know when the jug of milk hits its expiration, if you get me. And that should help us make decisions. I told Randall that I had gone to Guatemala on a clean water trip for three months, even though I knew I was dying already."

"And I asked him what would make him do that. Why wasn't he ticking things off his bucket list and sipping cold drinks on the beach and visiting family," Kohn said.

That sounded reasonable. Emily wondered what she would be doing if she knew she only had a short time to live. Guatemala didn't sound like it would be anywhere near the top of the list.

"So, why wasn't he? I mean," Emily said to Dollar, "Why didn't you?"

"Because I was sure I was doing the right thing. And if you're doing the right thing, don't *stop* just because of a little thing like cancer. But if you're *not* doing the right thing, you better make a change as soon as possible because tonight might be the only night."

Daniela said, "This is what you said to my husband earlier today, Emily. The right thing doesn't become the wrong thing just because you're out of time. And the wrong thing doesn't become the right thing because you're going to try to do better later. What if there *is no later?*"

"Right," Kohn said. "What if I lie and cheat and steal my way to the Senate—meaning to do good when I get there—and find that I die of a stroke before I can do any of those good things? Then what? I never did the good stuff. All I did was lie. While Dollar was telling me his story, all I could think was that this night might be the last one. I was not going to waste it doing something I didn't believe in."

"You weren't watching me during the speech," Daniela said, "but if you had been, I doubt you'd have missed the surprise on my face. I knew what speech Randall had prepared, and what he gave wasn't it."

"But I was watching *you*," Dollar said to Emily. "And you couldn't wait to get out of here. I thought you might throw up right on the table. You thought you were listening to a classic hypocrite."

Emily failed to suppress a small smile. "I did feel pretty sick about it."

Kohn said, "I couldn't help remembering all these people I'd read about all my life and their unwillingness to quit just because it was hard. I realized that this was my moment, and I'd already been told what to do earlier in the day. I should have listened."

"I wasn't that wise," Emily said. "I just told you not to do what made you feel icky."

"That's pretty wise," Dollar said. "A lot of people would benefit from that kind of advice."

"You're probably sick of the rules Will keeps trotting out, but when I quoted one at you this morning, I quoted the wrong one. I said, 'You can't make friends of your enemies by making enemies of your friends.' But I should have quoted you a different one instead: 'Better a snake in the grass than a viper in the bosom.' Then when you came to the table with your face pale and looking like you had the flu, I knew you were going to be loyal to me no matter what. You were going to work hard even if you thought I was wrong because you made a commitment. And I knew I couldn't ask you to do that."

"I might have quit," Emily said. "I was trying to figure out how to do that."

"Don't you dare," Daniela said.

"What if I made it so you didn't have to?" Kohn said. "What if I told the RNC and everyone else that I'm going to be my own man, and they can make a contribution if they like, but I will promise nothing but to do the right thing as I see it?"

Emily's smile grew until it overcame her whole face. "I think… That sounds pretty good to me."

Dollar gave Emily's hand a quick squeeze. "I knew you were going to be something special when you told me who your mother was. She's one of those people who's made my life worth living in the first place."

"This is real? No fooling?" Emily said.

Kohn held his arm to the square. "Scout's honor."

"And he really was a good scout," Daniela said.

Dollar staggered to his feet. "I think we probably should let these good people finish their job so they can go home. Emily, would you be so good as to walk me to the car?"

As he held the door open for her, Emily asked him, "Aren't you afraid of dying?"

"No, Miss. As Marcus Aurelius said, there's no country, even beyond the grave, where there are no gods. And besides, my Antonia is waiting for me."

"Her name was *Antonia* and she was giving *you* grief about your name?"

Dollar laughed and adopted Dr. Frankenstein's assistant Igor's famous pose and voice. He had the frame for it, that was for sure. "Yeeeeesssss," he said, "but remember, Master, that I look like theeeeeesssss!"

So it was that the very best photo anyone took all night long showed a balding man walking a bit bent over, with his hands out like the claws of Quasimodo, and a sixteen-year-old girl beside him, with her head back and her mouth open in wild laughter, free and as happy as a person can be.

The twins didn't quit. Kohn had a few frank conversations with the RNC both in person and on the phone, and in the end the party made a small contribution to the race, ran a couple of ads, but by and large stayed out of it.

One day backstage, Emily asked Kohn why he didn't take their money. He looked at her, and over her shoulder her brother, for a long minute. But all he said was, "I figured I already had the best advisers money could buy right in my office."

As the campaign heated up, the press repeatedly asked Kohn if he was going to endorse the president for re-election since they were from the same party. Kohn was ready for that. "The president and I don't yet have anything to say to one another. I doubt he needs my help, and I'm confident I can do without his. The time will come when we can sit down and talk to one another in a spirit of goodwill, and that will be an interesting day. Until that day, I'd rather focus on the race ahead and doing good for the people of Montana."

Kohn earned a nickname that day. The press took to calling him "Maverick." And Kohn did nothing to discourage it. He even had a jacket made up with "Maverick" in script over his heart.

Not endorsing the president did hurt. The president was very popular in the state—with the half that was likely to vote for Kohn, anyway—and those people didn't like that he wouldn't come out in support of the party's leader. Kohn's lead shrank.

The Bauer campaign, by contrast, rode a wave of support that carried him to first in the polls by the middle of October. Both locally and nationally, the news was full of the Senate race and the cautionary tale of "Maverick" Kohn and how bucking the party was a sure way to get beat in November.

But inside the campaign, there were no regrets. None that got expressed, anyway. The twins practically did not sleep the last few weeks, going from event to event with hardly a pause. More than once, they came back to campaign HQ early in the morning to find Pascoe slumped back in his chair, snoring. He hadn't even gone home.

Still, even with all their hard work, Kohn's poll numbers continued to fade. For many people, it was too difficult a task to split the man from the party and to consider him on his own merits. The writing was on the wall.

"Polls lie," Pascoe said, one very late night as they sat around the table eating Oreos after an event. It was too late to call anyone, the place was empty, and Mom wasn't here to pick up the twins yet. For a moment, there wasn't any work they could think of to do. Ethan checked social media every couple of minutes, just in case, but people were arguing over the ethics of rhino-killing, and for once no one was talking about #maverickrand.

Emily itched all over. When was the last time she'd had twenty minutes for a proper shower? "What do you mean, 'polls lie'? People lie to pollsters? Pollsters lie? Media lies about polls?"

"All of those are true," Pascoe said. He scratched at his scalp. Maybe he was itchy, too. "In different ways.

People do lie to pollsters. They tell whoppers. Nobody wants to be the fella who won't vote for a woman, or suchlike, so they lie about their vote. Media, as y'all know, lie about anything that brings ad bucks in the door. Bigger the lie, the more eyeballs. Fun game, media. Prob'ly why I love it."

"I thought you loved it because you are seriously ill in the head," Ethan said. Nothing out there on the campaign. He exchanged his phone for a cookie.

"That too. But the coolest tall tales are the ones pollsters tell. Nah, they don't fudge the numbers—that's too easy to check—but do they make their calls on Friday night? That underrepresents people who go out partying. Sunday? Undercounts religious people. During the big game? Sports people don't answer the phone then. So you get a 'sample' of the population, but it's colored in the way you want, blue or red. Not completely. Jus' a little. Enough. Then you sell that to the media and presto, your fella's ahead."

"But don't people see that and stop listening to your results?" Emily said. Lights swung into the parking lot. Had to be Mom.

Pascoe laughed until he choked on cookie crumbs. Emily figured that meant no. "Lemme ask you a question," Pascoe said when he could speak again. "For all the Oreos left on the table, can you name one polling company not reporting our campaign?"

"Um, ABC News?" Emily said.

"Reporters are calling folk asking for their votes? No. They contract it out." He scooped up the Oreos. "Sorry, kid. But nobody remembers when a pollster is wrong—or if they do, everyone else is wrong, too, and it's forgotten. Meanwhile, you get what you really want, which is push for your fella. Momentum. Good old mo.' Like gold in your pocket."

"Or gold in Bauer's pocket, more like," Ethan said sourly, gathering his things.

Pascoe waved a coal-black cookie. "No. You watch. Polls lie. I know this state. We're doing better than it looks."

The twins paused at the doorway, looking back at the rumpled, unshaven, bleary-eyed man who had become their companion—their friend—over the past months. Drawing to a close, now. Emily had a lump in her throat. He might talk big, but she saw fresh lines of worry carved in his sharply-pointed chin.

"Will it be good enough, do you think?" she said.

Pascoe glanced up at her, just for a moment, then popped the last cookie in his mouth.

He never did answer the question.

Election night had been planned as a big party in the largest downtown hotel, but a week before, the campaign canceled it and decided to hold the party in the HQ instead.

"There's plenty of room," Ed said glumly, "and we could use it to keep our costs down at this point."

The night before the election, Kohn made a surprise appearance to the working staff in the big phone room, where a few dozen dogged volunteers kept the lines humming, looking for more votes. "I won't make this long," he said, standing at the front of the room by the white board in his "Maverick" flight jacket. "But you need to know why we're here and why I wouldn't change a thing we've done."

Ed, without being called, moved to stand next to the candidate, his presence offering support just by being there. Kohn smiled tightly at him and turned back to the volunteers.

"At the beginning of the campaign, we had a chance to throw ourselves on the mercy of the party, take their money, and agree to carry water for them, whatever they asked. I almost did it. Maybe if I had, we'd be looking at an easy win instead of rolling the dice and needing to hit sevens tomorrow."

He swept his gaze around the room at his people. All his staff, everyone who was there, kept eyes on him. There was no sound other than the whirring of disk drives. Emily, Ethan, Melissa, Pascoe, Ed, everyone. Exhausted, but proud to be with this man.

"But I didn't. I realized that I had to do what I thought was right, and there was no reason to sit in a Senate seat if I weren't going to do that." He looked briefly at Emily, who nodded. "So we may lose, and we may win. But I would rather have you all with me, no matter what. I'd rather lose as my own man than win and belong to someone else."

He paused, and swallowed hard. For a long moment, he couldn't speak. Then he finally said, "Thank you. You're the best people a man could ask for. If we come up short, it won't be because of you."

"Or because of *you*," Melissa said from near the back. "It's been an honor and a privilege."

The room exploded into applause and cheers. They went on and on. Ethan thought his hands would blister from clapping, but he didn't want to stop.

Emily wasn't clapping, but she had a really good reason. Her hands were busy with something else.

"Good morning, Montana," the woman said, her face carefully made up, and the coffee table in front of her artfully arranged. The camera's red light was steady,

and the producer behind it made a circling motion with his hand. "This morning we have something unusual for you. It's election season, and we've all been treated to an endless barrage of polished statements, both positive and negative. A record amount of money has been spent on campaign ads in this election, and both candidates have spent endless time presenting a crafted message to the public.

"That's why this morning's video is, well, it's refreshing. At least to me, it is. You may be aware that the polls have Democrat Donald Bauer narrowly in front of millionaire Randall Kohn, the maverick Republican. And maybe, like me, you were wondering what it would be like in the last few hours of a campaign that looks like it's going down to defeat. After all the money and the work and the late nights, what is Randall Kohn saying to his campaign people? Well, we have a chance to see because late last night, a video was leaked from the campaign—a young lady recorded the actual speech. Take a look."

The producer said into his headset, "Roll film."

"I won't make this long," said Randall Kohn, in a grainy, wobbly, poorly-lit cell phone recording.

The polls closed at 8. By 9 it was clear that it would be close. By 10 the polls had been torn up and tossed away because it was clear that something different had happened in the voting booths than what the pollsters had anticipated.

At 11, the major cities reported, and the gap between the two candidates shrank to less than a thousand votes. But Kohn still had the lead.

And it wasn't much after midnight when that same TV anchor, the one who had opened the day with the candid video, said with a brittle and very tired smile, "We're ready to call the election for US Senate in Montana. In a race much tighter than expected, the lead of Republican maverick Randall Kohn has been shrinking all night, but it now appears that it will hold up. In the biggest upset of the evening, the maverick is going to Washington—"

Probably she had more to say. Her mouth was still moving on the screen. But nobody at headquarters could hear anything over the hysterical cheering.

THE END

They knocked on Cathy's door. There was silence for a moment, and then a quickly muttered "Come in."

Cathy was still sitting on the couch, the phone to her ear. She waved them in and pointed at the loveseat. "Hank," she said, "I'm putting you on speaker. I want you to hear something."

Emily and Gio sat down, and Cathy put the phone on the coffee table. She picked up a piece of loose legal paper and tore it in half. "You hear that, Hank? That was your check for $5000. I just tore it in half. You ought to be ashamed of yourself."

"But Cathy!" the voice came from the speaker, "You can't... That was..."

"It was insulting, is what it was. You and I have been friends for thirty years. I've done business with you and put more business your way than you could earn in a year, haven't I? And I ask you for a contribution and you send me $5000? What kind of friend is that?"

A moment of silence. Then, "You're right, Cathy. You're right. That was pretty low. I'm making out a $10,000 check right now. I'll put it in the mail tonight."

"No, you won't, Hank. You'll get that nephew of yours, what's his name... Davis, and tell him to get in his car and bring it to me."

"Davis is out running an errand," Hank said.

"Find another nephew, Hank. I want that check over here in an hour. So long, and tell Gina I said she needs to invite me over for pie one of these days." Cathy picked up the phone, hit the red button, and tossed it on the couch next to her.

"That wasn't a check," Emily said.

"No, but it sounded like one over the phone, I bet. What did you decide?"

"Wait. Did he really send you $5000?" Emily's eyes nearly bugged out of her head.

"Sure."

"And you didn't tear the check up."

"Tear up $5000? Are you nuts? I'm only going to tear it up when Davis arrives with a better one. Why are we still talking about this? What did you decide?"

"We're going to fill out the questionnaire," Gio said, seeing that Emily was temporarily too stunned by her aunt to function.

Emily made a mental note not to get on Aunt Cathy's bad side. If this was how she treated her oldest and dearest friends, what would she be like if someone crossed her?

Cathy nodded slowly. "You think that's wise."

"We do."

"All right then." She sighed. "I'm not going to write those answers, so that's something you're going to do, and then I'll read it and edit it and we'll see. The deadline is Friday. That gives you two days. Whatever you're going to do, do it."

Thursday afternoon, Emily thought she was going to jump in front of one of those trains. She lay flat on the rock-hard floor, the scent of plastic carpet in her nose, and tried to come up with a convincing answer to the question on the paper before her.

"If I have to invent an answer to 'Describe the tradeoffs between improving quality of education and raising tax revenue,' I think I might go mad," she said.

"You want to work on 'Detail the ideal program for special education in a school district, complete with budget requests and staffing' instead?" Gio was also on the floor, sitting in the far corner, his laptop glowing gently next to him.

"No, thanks. I just wish we didn't have to write any of this. I wish I knew it was going to make a difference."

"I've been thinking about that," Gio said. "It's possible we could get a little more information before we have to spend the next twelve hours writing some drivel about how we are committed to the individual student's specialized learning style."

"Why *is* it that we want children to grow up ignorant, anyway?" Emily said.

Gio put his head in his hands. "If I had a dollar for every time someone asked me that..."

"How do you answer it?" Emily said. "It seems like that's how we do political discussion in this country: if you think drug possession shouldn't be a criminal offense, you must be in favor of handing out drugs to kids in the school cafeteria."

"Or if you think we shouldn't be bombing Syria, you hate the military."

"Or if you think farm subsidies are bad, you want people to starve."

"Sheesh. Yes." Gio thought for a second. He fanned himself with his sheaf of papers, though it wasn't particularly hot. "I guess I'd say that there really isn't any way to answer it. Sometimes I'd say something like 'Children are terrible. Educating them only makes them terrible and *smart*. But I found that sarcasm wasn't effective with people like that. They didn't really get it. They thought I was serious."

"Strawman, I think they call that," Emily said. "I had a summer where I studied logical fallacies for days. I had to stop when I interrupted my father six times over dinner, calling out things like 'irrelevant thesis,' 'whole to part,' and 'ad hominem circumstantial.'"

"Irrelevant thesis is when I say, 'That's just your opinion' after you demolish my argument. Whole to part is where I like hamburgers and ice cream and you ask me why I don't want a burger sundae. But that last one, I don't know what that is."

"Ad hominem circumstantial? You wouldn't understand. You're in politics."

"Hey! *You're* in politics."

Emily's eyes twinkled.

Gio raised an eyebrow. "Wait. You implied I was stupid because I hang around with people who are, let's face it, sometimes kind of stupid. Which is dumb. If I hung around with Latinos, would that make me Latino? That's exactly what you were talking about."

"Bingo. Which proves to me that you are *not* stupid, except that you responded with a *tu quoque* fallacy—answering my accusation with a counter-accusation, rather than addressing my point."

Gio laughed. "See? Terrible and smart. I was right after all."

"You were saying something about having an idea before I distracted you."

Gio got up off the floor and held his hand out to Emily. "Yeah. Get up. We're going for a drive."

"Can we grab my brother? He'll want to come along. He's just down the hall."

"More the merrier, actually. I'll be out in the parking lot. But bring your paperwork."

Twenty minutes later, they pulled up in front of a small rambler with a house-length front porch and daisies lining the walk to the stoop. On the porch sat a rocking chair, and in the rocking chair was a man of about seventy, cleaning some sort of disassembled gadget. Delicate chains, gears, parts of some kind of works were scattered all over the blue-painted boards of the porch. Next to him on a low table, a jar of something noxious held small metal gizmos, having a soak.

The man didn't even look up when they stopped.

Gio got out and went around to the walk. "Permission to come aboard?" he said.

"Granted. Wish you'd been here twenty minutes ago. Had a bolt stuck that was the devil to get loose."

"Sorry."

"You bring your friends?"

"They're afraid of you."

Emily and Ethan opened their doors, and Emily's hit Gio in the rear. "Gio told us to stay in the car until he could be sure you weren't dangerous. Said it was a day-to-day thing."

The man grunted. "At least he got that right. Come on up. If you move even one part, I have a lever here that will dump you into my spacious dungeons."

The twins settled on the steps of the porch. Gio tiptoed his way through the minefield to a creaky metal chair with a thick, worn pad and sat down gingerly. The chair groaned but did not appear in imminent danger of collapse.

Gio stretched out a sheaf of papers to the old man.

His deep gray eyes flicked over to it, back to the car part in his hand, and then in a classic double-take, back to the sheaf. He rumbled, "You did not bring me a candidate questionnaire."

"I did. I thought you could help us with filling it out."

His laugh boomed off the front of the porch and echoed down the street like a great surfing wave. "Never. You know I won't do that anymore."

"But we're suffering through it, and you could make our lives so much easier."

"We?"

Emily raised her hand. "I'm a partner in crime."

"What's criminal is those questionnaires. It ought to be a violation of the law to have a child work on those."

"Ordinarily I'm not a fan of 'there oughtta be a law,' but in the case of this questionnaire, I might be willing to make an exception," Emily said.

"C'mon, Douglas. For me. For old time's sake," Gio said.

Ethan mouthed to Emily, "Douglas?" with a question in his eyes.

Apparently those eyes missed little. "Yes, young man, Douglas Cartwright is my name, and once upon a time I used to write these things for the teachers' unions. Apparently your friend Gio thought it would be a shortcut to bring one here."

"If you used to write them, you know what they want to hear," Emily said. "Gio's right. You could save us a ton of time."

Cartwright finished brushing the grime off the part in his gnarled hand and dropped it into the jar with a plunk. "Now listen to me, you two." He paused for a moment and looked over at Gio. "Before I wax eloquent, who are these people?" He waved a hand at the others.

"Emily Tuttle. Ethan Tuttle. They work at the Harmon campaign where I am consulting."

"Consulting? Since when?"

Gio checked his watch. "Since about Wednesday."

"Oh, you silly little man." Cartwright looked back at the Tuttles. "Listen to me. Let's replay what you just said and think about it a minute. You asked me to help you fill out the questionnaire because I know the right answers. But think for a second about the purpose of the questionnaire. What would that be?"

Emily didn't have to think very hard. "It's so the teachers unions can know the positions of the candidates before they choose whom to endorse."

"Wrong," Cartwright said. "Or, exactly right, if you have a camera in your face and someone's taking notes. But it's not why the questionnaires go out. The union already knows very well which candidate it's going to endorse."

"The answers don't matter?" Emily said. "Then why are we answering at all?"

"The *answers* don't matter—not a lot, anyway—but *answering* does. It's power for the union, getting candidates to dance. It establishes the appropriate relationship. They want to make sure you know who's boss. That's the first thing. The second thing is that the answers *do* matter, a little. If you take the time to do a thorough job, they can tell the union a lot about the candidate's thinking, how sophisticated the candidate is, what kind of staff they're putting on this kind of job."

"It's intelligence work," Emily said, getting it.

"Kind of, yes. And it is true that in certain circumstances, the answers are illuminating in other ways. They can tell the union whether this is someone who can be influenced. The sophistication of their answers can indicate whether the candidate can be moved at all."

Emily rubbed her chin. Gio seemed to have gone to sleep in his chair. Emily found a handy dandelion, plucked the head, and tossed it at him. It hit him square in the nose. He spluttered, batting at it.

"What the—" he said.

"You brought me here for a civics lesson, and you're falling asleep in the middle of it?" Emily said.

"I've heard it before," Gio said. "It goes on for a while."

She waved her part of the sheaf at Cartwright. "So filling this out is showing something to the unions, but what is on the page is only a small part of what we're showing them."

"Bingo."

Ethan spoke up. "I thought the union was supposed to look out for the interests of the teachers. How can they do that if they've already pre-made-up their minds about whom to support?"

"They can't. But assisting teachers is not really their primary function." He spread his hands over the scattered parts on the porch. "Do you know what this is?"

Ethan looked over the parts. Gears, springs, shafts. But what was that under his chair?

"It's a clock," he said. "I can see the face there underneath you."

"Good eye," Cartwright said. "It's a clock. In fact, it's a grandfather clock. A big one. Old. Broken. Or it was before I started working on it. What does a grandfather clock do?"

"Tells time."

"So does that thing on your wrist. And those phones in your pocket. Much cheaper. Smaller. Lighter. Quieter. So why have a grandfather clock when you can wear a watch?"

Ethan shrugged. Emily said, "It's... impressive? Looks nice when you come into the room?"

"Right," Cartwright said. "But it doesn't tell time any better than any other clock. Worse, in fact, because it has a million things here that can go wrong. So why do we have them?"

"I have no idea."

"How long have we had watches?" Cartwright says. "Did they come before or after grandfather clocks?"

"Well, judging by the 'grandfather' part, I'm guessing it's older than the watch."

"Much older. When grandfather clocks came around, we didn't have any other clocks at all, except the gigantic ones like Big Ben. So putting a grandfather clock in your house was a pretty big deal. If you wanted to know what time it was without going to the town square, that's what you had to do.

"Now, a long time back, many workers wanted unions to help keep from being taken advantage of—the 'safety in numbers' idea. It was very difficult for workers to get a different education and switch careers. But just like times have changed and we have watches to replace clocks, there are many other ways for workers to exercise their power today. People change careers all the time. Education is everywhere. But the union is still there, still in the room, taking up space, and bonging big and loud whenever it has a mind to. Sometimes people hang on to the past, I guess."

Emily thought of other things that did that—child labor laws that made it almost impossible for a teen to get a good job, expensive licensing for things like hair extensions that hurt people trying to do entrepreneurial work, and mandatory seat time in school, regardless of what a student already knew.

"And it does tell time," Gio said. "If it works. But it's eating up a huge amount of space compared to a watch. It takes forever to wind it, dust it, repair it. It eats up resources. Once there was a purpose to that. Now? Not so much. It's much more a statement than it is an effective way of telling time."

"And that's why it doesn't really matter if the unions already decided. It's not really in the business of protecting teachers from exploitation now. It's about creating power for the unions and the education establishment. You don't need a questionnaire for that—it's very obvious which of the candidates is going to help you do that."

"So we shouldn't fill it out," Emily said. "We should refuse to play that game."

"But we're already playing it," Gio said, "whether we fill the forms out or not. The question is *how* we play it, and that's why we're here."

"You didn't want Mr. Cartwright to fill out the forms, did you?" Ethan said.

"Clever boy."

"So, Mr. Cartwright," Emily said, a playful smile on her lips. "If we're not trying to get the unions to love us, because they're not going to, what *could* we do with this questionnaire?"

"Ah," Cartwright said. "*Now* we have a good question."

They worked on the questionnaire with Cartwright the rest of the day while Ethan scrubbed ancient grandfather clock parts. They were even there when Cartwright began to put the clock back together, which Ethan thought was the most interesting thing that had happened in a while. Unfortunately, he didn't get to finish it. "It's a two-day job. Sorry," Cartwright said.

Emily, seeing the disappointment on her brother's face, suddenly felt quite sure that she must have left some of her part of the questionnaire back at the office. "Could we come back tomorrow and finish up?"

"Gio, these kids are quick. I'm surprised you can keep up," Cartwright said. Emily began to doubt that he had a dungeon at all.

The three campaign staffers returned in the morning and got the clock fully reassembled and placed in its perfect spot in the middle of the western wall of Cartwright's living room. They wound it with long chains inside the walnut box, and it began tick-tocking right away.

Cartwright clapped Ethan on the shoulder. "Nice work. You have good hands."

The questionnaire finished, Emily and Gio went to the office to type it all up. It took the rest of the day, but they finally had it in a form they could send to Cathy for review.

Emily took care to jog down the hall and say, "We sent it to you, but you don't really have to read it because it's not going to matter very much."

"It's not?" Cathy said, as if that were the most surprising thing she'd ever heard.

Emily suspected sarcasm. "No. But we think that your excellent ideas about alternative education and homeschooling will make them want to reach out to you and explain how schools are going to improve their results so that those alternatives are unnecessary."

Cathy smiled, slowly and with obvious satisfaction. "That's very good to hear. I'm looking forward to reading my excellent ideas for myself."

A month before the election, the Montana Union of Teachers announced that for the first time in their history, they would not be endorsing any candidate in the Secretary of State race. The union urged its members to carefully read the material written in the questionnaire, and decide for themselves.

Louis Sulla had already printed material that claimed his endorsement of the MTUT—a massive mailing that cost him a great deal, and then required two weeks of explaining away. Cathy Harmon was quoted as saying, "The state is best served by robust discussion at the highest level when the subject is something as critical as education. Everyone knows that Governor Macrinus is a friend of the unions. I'm fully behind the students. I look forward to working together to create a plan that makes our entire education system stronger for everyone."

In November, she got her wish.

THE END

Ethan stuck out his hand. Aunt Cathy's eyes were bloodshot, and there were new wrinkles at the corners of her mouth. Of course, Ethan hadn't seen her for a while, except a moment here and there at reunions. She was always too busy to come to family gatherings except when everyone got together.

"You've grown up a lot," Aunt Cathy said.

Ethan smiled a little. "I'm really sorry about your boss."

"More than my boss," Cathy said. "My friend and one of the best men I've ever known. Let me introduce you to Anniele Forde, his wife."

Ethan and Ms. Forde shook hands as well. Her grip was very firm, and she looked him in the eye. "Cathy has told me a lot about the famous Tuttle twins."

"I'm sorry for your loss," Ethan said, because that's what you were supposed to say. Wasn't it?

"Thank you," she said. "These are my children—Martin, Alannah, and Carter." Smallest to biggest. Ethan went down the line, a single pump for each hand. The kids looked tired and very sad. Probably bored as well. This had to be torture for them. But what was there to say? Sorry you lost your dad? Sorry you have to stand here for hours while people remind you your father is dead? What kind of comment was that?

Mom stood at the end of the line, watching him. He turned to her and said in her ear, "Should we invite Aunt Cathy to dinner on Sunday?"

Mom pursed her lips. She looked surprised that he would ask. "Why not? I think it's a good idea."

Ethan nodded and tried to cut back in line, but he had to wait for an elderly couple who were clearly friends of hers. They murmured their condolences, and Ethan waited until they were finished. Aunt Cathy caught his eye and tilted her head, wondering what he wanted.

"I asked Mom if it was okay to invite you to dinner on Sunday," Ethan said.

Her smile, if anything, got a little sadder. She appeared to consider for a moment. Another man stepped in front of her and drew her in for a quick embrace. They exchanged sorrowful condolences, as she must have done now a thousand times. The line inched forward, and he saw her look out and take in how long it was.

"I, uh, I'd like that. It's going to be really hard to get away. Tell your mom I'll text her."

Ethan nodded, feeling like there was something else he should say, but nothing came to mind, and he turned back to his family. They made their way through the clots of people back out into the sunshine.

"She looks really sad," Emily said, threading her arm through Dad's.

"I'm sure she is," Dad said. "They've worked together for a while now. I'm not sure I ever saw her happier than she has been the last three years."

Mom put her arm around Ethan's shoulder. "I don't think I have either."

"She said she'd text you," Ethan said. "Maybe she'll come over."

"She always says that. But she's very busy, and it's kind of a long way to come just for dinner."

Emily snugged up a little closer. "What happens if you get sick, Dad?"

He shrugged and didn't look at Mom. "Nothing much. I don't come home from work one day, is all."

Mom grunted at that, as if she didn't think it was very funny.

"We've made some arrangements," he said, "and you guys would be okay for college and stuff—or whatever route you decide to take."

"That's not what we're talking about, Dad, and you know it," Ethan said. "We don't just want you around so we can go to school."

"Especially not that," Emily said.

Dad ran a hand through his hair. Ethan saw it was thinning a little on top. He ignored that. Dad was immortal. He was going to live forever.

Dad reached the car and unlocked the doors. He slid into the driver's seat and adjusted everything for his frame. Then he sighed and sat there a moment without turning the car on. The car was very quiet. "I know… I know what you mean. The answer is, you do what everyone does when someone they love dies. You breathe in and out. You get up and do the things that have to be done that day. Look at those wonderful people in there. What were they doing? I'm certain they are so sad they can hardly bear it, but they have jobs to do, and they do them. That's what you would do." He turned so he could see both of the twins at the same time. "It *is* what you would do, isn't it?"

This was not a question. Mom laid a hand on Dad's shoulder, backing him up.

"Yes, Dad," Ethan said. Emily nodded.

"But," Emily said, "Dad. *Don't*."

"All right. You keep your part of the bargain, and I'll keep my part. No dying."

Mom blew out a huge breath. "If this trip doesn't require a massive vat of ice cream, I don't know what would."

Dad pulled out his phone to ask it for directions, but before he uttered a syllable, Mom plucked it from his fingers. "Way ahead of you. Up here at the light, turn right."

Aunt Cathy, true to Mom's intuition, did not come to dinner on Sunday, not that one, or the next, or the next.

"She's busy, but we're having guests anyway. I think you'll be surprised when they get here," Mom said.

"Who's coming?" Emily said.

Mom cocked her head and looked at her. "I would have sworn we had 'surprise' as a vocabulary word a couple of years ago. Do we need a refresher?"

Emily laughed, and didn't ask any further, but she still wondered. Eventually, someone did come, and it was as big a surprise as Mom had promised.

The doorbell rang, and because she was closest, it was her job to go answer it. It was Sunday afternoon, with everyone just back from church. Mom was in the kitchen, strapping on her special leather apron and wielding knives.

Emily opened the door and there were four people she didn't know.

Wait. She *did* know them, didn't she? They were somehow familiar.

"Is your mom here? Or your dad?" the mother part of the group said. Three children stood behind her in a group that told Emily they were only there to please their mother.

Emily realized she'd been staring at them for an awkward moment and hadn't answered her question. "Oh. Yes. She's here. Come in."

They filed into the front hall and stood there waiting, a mom, one daughter, two sons. Ah. Dennis Forde's family, of course.

Mom was already on her way to the door, using her I-know-we-have-company pace, and her face lit into a bright smile. "Anniele! You came!"

"Well, you invited us." Her smile wasn't quite as bright.

"You must have hundreds of invitations," Mom said, pulling Anniele in for a brief hug. She stepped back and regarded the children. "Let me see if I remember. You're Martin, right? After Dr. King?"

The shortest one—not that he was short, he was about even with Emily—nodded and tried on a smile.

"And you're obviously Alannah, and that makes you Carter," she said to the other two.

"Yes, ma'am," they said in chorus.

"Fine. Now I know you were dragged here against your will, but we're having pork chops and mashed potatoes and this green bean casserole I discovered the other day at a restaurant. Plus... Oh. I should ask. Dessert? What's your pleasure?"

"Anything will be fine," Anniele said.

"Not today!" Mom said, leading off toward the kitchen. "Come along. Don't stand in the doorway. If you're here, you're family, and that means I'm putting you to work." She bustled them into the kitchen and stood them around the bar in the middle of the floor, facing arrayed troops of unpeeled, unwashed potatoes. She handed each of the three children a peeler and pointed them at the big composting box on the floor.

"Peel five each," she said. "But before that—favorite dessert?"

They looked at her as if she'd spoken French. "Favorite dessert. You have one, I presume."

"I have one," Alannah said, "but you don't have it here."

"Try me."

"Baked Alaska," she said.

Mom held her glance for a long moment, then burst out laughing. "Okay. We don't have that. But that's not your favorite dessert, anyway. You're just having me on."

Alannah's smile got a little deeper and a little more real. "Okay. That's true. Really, I'm a fan of tres leches, but I don't suppose you have that, either."

"There you would be right, but we'll fix that in half an hour," Mom said, turning to a cupboard and opening it, revealing serried ranks of canned goods. She selected two cans of sweetened condensed milk and set them on the counter. Over her shoulder, she said, "Carter? Your turn."

"I like tres leches too, but I'm more of an ice cream guy."

"Chocolate, vanilla, strawberry?" Mom said. She handed Anniele a wooden spoon and pointed at a pan in which some dark liquid was bubbling. "Stir, please," she said.

"Chocolate," Carter said.

"Two vats outside in the freezer," Mom said. "Now, Martin. You look like you need dessert in the worst way. What's your pleasure?"

He jabbed at his potato, barely doing any damage to the skin. "I'll have some of each of theirs," he finally said.

"I bet you will. But there's something you want more."

Emily couldn't figure out why Mom was pushing this. Also, did she really have all this dessert stuff lying around in case someone wanted some?

Martin looked at the potato, and kept looking at it.

Emily went over and stood by him, picking up a stray peeling and dropping it in the box. She grabbed a potato. "She won't let this go, you know," Emily said. "You don't know her. She's relentless."

"Well, we used to have this pancake when I was little. It's real thin, and it cooks in like two seconds, then you roll it up with jam and stuff inside."

"Blintzes," Anniele said.

"Crepes," said Emily.

"Norwegian pancakes," Ethan yelled from the other room.

"I didn't think you remembered that," Anniele said. "It's been a long time."

"I made them with Dad all the time when we did our mornings together," Martin said. The tone in his voice was so sad Emily thought her heart would break.

Mom stepped right in before any of that could get too serious. "Fortunately," she said, "I not only have the ingredients, *and* the world's finest recipe, I also have a crepe maker." From deep in the recesses of the cupboard below the towel rack, she drew out a device about the size of a ping-pong paddle, only bulging outward as if it were pregnant. A cord trailed behind it. Emily's hands were full, so she called out,

"Ethan! Front and center!"

"Aw, Mom!" Ethan said.

"I wonder if your phone would survive an encounter with my blender," she said. Two seconds later, Ethan was standing at attention before her, his phone lodged securely in his back pocket. She gave him the crepe-maker. "You know what to do with this, I believe."

"Yes, ma'am, I do," he said, and latched on to Martin. "Hand Emily your peeler. We have more important things to attend to."

It didn't take very long before the Fordes were old friends. In fifteen minutes the five kids were chattering away as if they'd been pals all their lives. In time, they sat to dinner and plowed through what looked like three separate hogs, plus half the state's potato crop, with thick, rich gravy drizzled over it. Conversation, ribbing, even arguing, but all of it was as friendly as could be. The Fordes fit right in as if the two families had been cut to size.

With perhaps one exception—Carter didn't quite mesh. He was older, and that was surely part of it. Off to college, he said, a rising freshman at George Washington University. He wanted to study—

"Political science," Ethan supplied.

Carter shook his head. "Not really, no. I think architecture. I'm not much for politics."

Ethan didn't say anything, but his eyes shifted from Carter to Anniele Forde and back.

"Yeah, I know," Carter said. "With Dad and all, everyone figures I'll be in the same game." He shrugged. "I dunno. It's not really for me. I know it's important and all, but I'm not interested, or not as interested as I am in other things."

Dad pushed his plate away, stomach bulging. "There's nothing wrong with that," he said. "I'm not in politics."

"Yeah, but Dad," Emily said. "Politics is the work of every man, isn't it?"

"'What better subject of study can there be than government?'" Mom said. "George Washington."

"George is a good man," Dad said, "and you'll never hear me say differently. But I'll see your quote from the first president and raise you one from the second. John Adams said, 'I must study politics and war, that my sons may have liberty to study mathematics and philosophy. My sons ought to study mathematics and philosophy, geography, natural history, naval architecture, navigation, commerce and agriculture, in order to give their children a right to study painting, poetry, music, architecture, statuary, tapestry, and porcelain.' I think Dennis would be proud to think that he'd done his bit, and proud that his son wanted to study architecture."

Alannah folded her arms, "I don't think the work is done. Far from it. There are a couple of big races right here in this state, in fact, and I want to get involved in them."

"One of them, anyway," Carter said.

"Which one?" Emily said. She glanced over at Ethan. "We've done some stuff. We're helpful."

"What my sister means is that we could use jobs. I can't get a car until I can pay for the insurance, and since I am a boy—"

"And therefore mortally certain to wreck whatever vehicle you get behind—" Mom said.

Ethan ahemed at her and kept going, "—and insurance companies hate boys, I have to make some serious scratch, or I'm walking everywhere until I'm thirty."

"Thirty-five," Mom said.

Ethan closed his eyes but didn't let go of the point. "So if you've got an in with a campaign somewhere, do they have more than one job, and if they do, how do we prove we should be the ones to get it?"

Alannah glanced at Martin, almost as if she were asking permission to go on. He gave the minutest shrug, and she took that for an okay. "The Senate race."

"The US Senate? As in, there are a hundred of them and this is one percent of it?" Ethan said.

"Right. The incumbent is retiring, and the seat is open. We know the guy who's going to run for it from the Republican Party. He's looking for staff."

Dad cut in. "It can sometimes be hard to be a person of principle working for a political party."

Mom nodded. "The parties have... their own rules. They do have tremendous power, but sometimes maintaining that power can cause them to make compromises and do things that aren't in the best interests of the nation."

"He's a good man," Alannah said. "Dad thought so."

"I'm sure he is," Dad said. "The question is can he stay that way. But go on—it's not like there are a lot of viable options for major public office outside the two major parties—at least at the moment."

Ethan just had a practical question. "Is he paying?"

Alannah smiled. "He is. Not much, of course. We're not exactly top-level operatives."

"Still. Beats the StuffMart."

"Which is hiring, I saw," Dad said.

"And which was robbed last week for the fourth time this year," Mom said. She smiled sweetly at Dad, who broke out laughing.

"Okay, perhaps that's not the best idea," Dad said. "But national politics? Wow. That's... different."

Emily's heart beat a little faster. A Senate race! They'd worked on the small stuff: referenda, the odd city council race, ordinance-level politics. But this was the big time! The one who won that race would be in Washington, speaking on TV all the time, making a real difference—and they would know him! They would make a difference, wouldn't they? Emily had to admit she couldn't really name anything her current Senator had done, or any legislation he'd passed. Maybe she just needed to study more. Surely a US Senator would be involved in lots of important decisions that would affect millions of lives. He would have to. Wouldn't he?

She could see the idea appealed to Ethan every bit as much. He leaned forward, risking his sweatshirt dredging a passage through his potatoes, and said, "How do we get in on some of this?"

"Wait," Emily said, something just occurring to her. "I just remembered. Your dad was a Democrat."

Now Alannah looked over at her mom. Anniele lopped an edge off the last chop, popped it in her mouth, and chewed. She gazed levelly back at her daughter as if to say, "You started this; you get to keep going as far as it takes you."

Mom got up from the table, taking her plate and Dad's. "Cake's done. Time to make some leche."

Alannah plowed ahead with whatever she'd been going to say. "He was, yeah. And the Democrats have some great ideas, especially on the state level. But nationally..." She stopped for a second.

Martin took up the thread. "There are things in both parties we don't agree with. But it's not just that because there are things we agree with, too. The problem comes not just with what the parties claim to believe but how they actually govern when they're in power. Neither party seems to be great at delivering on their promises, so it comes down to the people, not the party. We think this guy would be a better senator than the one the Democrats are going to run."

"Who's our guy?" Ethan said, apparently choosing sides without difficulty.

"Randall Kohn," Martin said. He pronounced it "cone."

Dad squinted. "I know this name."

"You should," Anniele said, deciding it was time to get involved anyway. "He owns a third of the property in the state."

"Kohn... grocery?" Emily said.

Anniele nodded. "And Kohn motors. And—"

"Hannah Kohn Theater, in Helena!" Ethan said. "We've been there to see *Dear Evan Hansen*."

"Hannah Kohn was Randall's mother," Anniele said. "I knew her. One of the best, most genteel ladies I ever met. When her sons became millionaires, she always seemed astonished she had money to spend."

"But she did," Ethan said. "Randall must be loaded."

Dad put his head in his hands. "Right to the heart of things, aren't you, Ethan?"

"Well, it's got to be a major qualification for senator. Those campaigns aren't cheap. Great staffers like us cost a bundle."

Dessert landed on the table in waves like a surfing beach, so for a long time there wasn't much chance to discuss things.

As the evening wound down, Emily found herself helping Alannah find her jacket and took the opportunity to say, "Look, my brother's kind of excitable, but we really would be interested in anything. He's right; we need jobs. And working a senate campaign sounds so exciting."

Alannah said, "I can ask. We're supposed to start working there 10 hours a week sometime before the end of March. There's a lot to do before the election. It seems far, but it's really not. In some ways, Randall says, we're already behind."

Emily pulled her cell phone from her pants pocket. "What's your digits?"

Alannah found her phone in the pocket of her coat and read her phone number off while she unlocked her phone. "You on Instagram?" she said.

Emily pursed her lips. "I don't like to be on it much—what a time suck!—but of course I have an account. How could I know what was going on with my friends otherwise?"

"It's going to be a big part of the campaign," Alannah said. "Social media is where the battles are these days."

"Doing it as work is different. I wouldn't mind it so much, then."

There was a lot more hugging and laughing and chatter, exchanging numbers and promises, before the Fordes got through the door and went down the walk to their car. The twins waved from the front window until they were out of sight.

Alannah texted the very next day. "Talked to Randall."

Emily almost dropped her phone. "And?"

No answer for ten minutes, which Emily thought was essentially the end of the world. "He says he knows you."

"What!?" Emily yelled. It was loud enough that there came a pounding of feet down the hallway and her door burst open.

"What what?" Ethan said. "Is there a spider on your book?"

"No! It's Alannah! She just texted me. She says Randall Kohn *knows me*."

Ethan scowled. "That seems, uh, kinda unlikely."

"She said it," Emily said, holding up her phone, screen toward her brother. "Right there."

Ethan read it. "English is funny, you know. That 'you' could be singular or plural. It's too bad she didn't say 'he saith he knoweth thee,' which would clear up the ambiguity."

Emily ignored him and tapped the screen furiously.

"What are you saying?" Ethan said.

"I'm asking her how that's possible."

"Sounds like the right question. But I have a bunch more when you're done."

"Text her yourself."

"I can't. She wouldn't give up her number."

"Ha."

"You're a girl. I'm not. I think there was some kind of privacy involved."

Emily's phone dinged.

Ethan bit his tongue.

"She says, 'Remember the food trucks?'"

"What kind of question is that," Ethan said. "Of course we remember."

"I am now telling her that."

Ethan grabbed the phone from her and pressed the call button.

"HEY!" Emily said, snatching it back. "What are you doing?"

"Using the phone the way God and Alexander Graham Bell intended."

A tinny "hello" erupted from the little speaker on the phone's face. Emily put it to her ear. "That was my very aggressive brother," she said. "He doesn't understand how these things work."

Alannah said, "I get that, sister. But put us on speaker. This has to do with him, too."

Emily tapped the button.

"Hey, Ethan," Alannah said.

"Hey, Alannah. That was fast work," Ethan said.

"He called this afternoon after school, and I told him I had these friends. He asked about you, and I told him what I knew, and he started laughing. 'Wait... the Tuttle twins?' he said. 'Ethan and Emily?' and I said, 'Yeah, that's them; how did you know?' and he didn't stop laughing for like half an hour."

Ethan looked at Emily. She was thinking the same thing he was—was this a good thing or a bad thing? Did they really want their prospective employer laughing about who they were?

"You guys are probably wondering how he knows you," Alannah said.

"And whether that's a good thing," Ethan said.

"Apparently you all did a food truck thing a while back? Some regulations or something?"

The twins exchanged a glance. "We did, yeah," Emily said.

"He was one of the people who helped write those regulations."

Emily closed her eyes. "Great. Well, it's Burger Barn for me, then."

"Apparently he's not a guy who holds grudges. He wants to talk to you."

"With or without the police?" Ethan said, slumping against the wall.

"Come on, guys. He's not mad. He thought it was funny. You impressed him. He even changed his mind because of what you did."

"Well, we can't get in any deeper, I suppose," Emily said. "When does he want to talk?"

The office was definitely one of the nicer ones the twins had seen. All the chairs were clad in leather, with knobby tacks holding them together, the kind you see in fancy banks. The carpet was so deep and soft you couldn't hear people walking over it. And the table in the conference room was polished like a mirror. Ethan caught himself checking his hair. Emily sat down in one of the plush chairs and almost disappeared.

Alannah laughed at their expressions. "It's not all like this, believe me. But this front area he keeps pretty nice. There are a lot of important people coming to see him."

The heavy oak door swished open, and a man came in. He wore a dark charcoal suit, a white shirt, and a red tie with a glittering tie tack. His glossy dark hair was parted on the side. Just a touch of gray showed at the temples. His smile was powerful enough to use as a searchlight, and he turned the full wattage of it on the twins right away.

"Emily! Ethan!" he said, coming forward with his hand outstretched. "I'm so glad you accepted my invitation to come in. I've been looking forward to meeting you."

Ethan dumbly took his hand and shook it. Emily followed suit. It was like she couldn't speak.

"Please, sit. This isn't an inquisition. Alannah, will you have Hank get us something to drink?" To the twins, he said, "Are you guys soda drinkers, juice, water?"

That unlocked them. "Just water for me," Ethan said.

"Sprite?" Emily said, hopefully.

Randall Kohn nodded at Alannah, who went out.

"Now, before we go any farther, did you or did you not have something to do with the International Baseball Association deciding whether or not to come to Malantown?"

Ethan rigidly refused to look at his sister.

"We, uh, we might have had something to do with that," he said.

"Not very much," Emily said. She examined the table rather than looking at Kohn.

"We probably would have minded our own business if Emily hadn't been such a great hitter."

He raised an eyebrow. "You'll have to tell me about that someday. Anyhow, in preparation for our meeting today, I did a little digging. I think Alannah must have told you about the food truck fiasco, which was the first time I had come up against the kind of work you two can do. But then I got curious and made a few calls. You two have been very busy for kids who are only just able to drive."

Ethan scowled. "As if."

"Driving? Oh—expensive, I bet," Kohn said. "You're sixteen, aren't you?"

"Yes," Emily said.

"The most expensive age to try to drive. Hence the looking for jobs. There aren't a lot of those around for people your age, which is something I'm working on as a senator. Hopeful senator."

"Working on… as in what? You're actually going to try to make it possible for teens to get jobs? I thought you were a regulations guy. No offense. Because of the food truck thing."

He actually looked a little guilty. "Can I confess to you that being beaten makes a man reconsider his life choices? I hadn't really thought about it before that. I thought regulations were good because everyone told me so. I hadn't paid attention to the downsides. Forgive me, and let me prove to you I am sincere."

He cleared his throat as if getting ready to make a speech. "On the subject of teen labor: ideally, I hire as many teens as I can at my companies. You're cheap, you have no negotiating power—because no one else will hire you—and even though most of your work isn't terribly valuable, especially at first, it's not totally worthless."

Emily stared. "That's… um…"

"The first honest appraisal you've ever heard of teenage workers? Well, thank you. I try. But in all seriousness, government regulations on wages and working hours might be well-meant—"

Emily snorted. She covered it with her hand, but still.

"—uh, might have *originally* been well-meant," Kohn said, amending, "but what they mostly do now is stop enterprising youth from getting experience they're going to need if they're ever going to do *valuable* work. College is fine for some, and that sort of education can be very helpful in certain fields, but what we really need right now, as an economy, is a much larger group of entry-level workers who can learn experientially. Our laws are actually making that *harder*. I'd like to change that. You see, I really have learned my lesson."

Ethan applauded, rising from his chair.

Kohn waved his hand airily. "Thanks, I'll be here all week. I take it you two approve of that policy? Good. That will make our conversation so much more pleasant. What's your school situation?"

"We're homeschooled," Emily said. "So we kind of set our own hours. We have three or four hours of study, plus reading and practicing instruments, but we can decide when we're going to do those things."

The eyebrow went up again. "You really manage all that yourselves?"

Ethan was getting over his stage fright. Kohn was easy to talk to. "We have to. Mom helps, of course. But we do most of it ourselves."

"That's an important skill," Kohn said. The door opened, and Alannah came in with a can of soda and a bottle of water. She grabbed coasters from the rack in the middle of the table and set the drinks in front of the twins. She perched herself on a chair and fixed her eyes on Kohn.

"Thank you, Alannah. We've just been getting acquainted. I've been doing all the talking though. You know at least some of why I wanted you here, but I'm curious as to why you wanted to come and talk to a geezer like me."

"You nailed it before," Emily said. "I'm sixteen. I know *how* to drive, but I can't drive because I have no car."

"And no insurance," Ethan said.

"Thus, I need money so I can have those things, so then I can drive."

Kohn stared at her for a moment, then burst into laughter. "Well, that came right to the point. I think you might be under a mistaken impression about how much I pay my people though."

"I don't expect to get paid a lot," Emily said, "but I think I'll like the work, I think I'd like to work with Alannah, and I'm pretty sure you're going to pay me *something*, or the exposé on the news about indentured servitude will have a negative impact on your election chances."

Kohn went back to staring. "I am struggling to figure out how you can possibly be this intelligent and forthright at sixteen."

"It's his fault," she said, pointing to Ethan. "He doesn't understand what I'm talking about unless I'm pretty direct."

"It saves a lot of time, being dense," Ethan said. "Otherwise she'd talk in circles for months."

Kohn raised his hands in mock surrender. "Good grief. You're hired. I've been hiring people and putting them to work for decades now, and I have never been involved in a weirder interview. Fortunately, Senate races are very deeply weird, so you might have skills that translate quite well. In fact, after I show you around a little bit, I have a choice for you as to where you think your particular skills might be best used."

He stood up. "Bring your drinks, if you like," he said, and led them out into the hallway.

The operation was impressive. The front part of the office was plush, but the back part—ten times as large—was bare bones, without paint on the walls in some places. Cavernous spaces were laid out with desks, tables, phones, legal pads, envelopes, everything a staffer might need to be able to make contacts with voters.

"This is the heart of the operation," Kohn said. "What's out there," he waved his hand toward the front part of the office—"that's mostly just for show. What's back here is what wins elections."

On one massive wall, a hundred feet long, were maps of the entire state, broken into smaller parts, and buckets of pins sat at the feet of the maps waiting to be stuck into the paper at the appropriate points. Above each map were signs indicating what district they were showing, and beside those signs were names, email addresses, and phone numbers. "What do those names mean?" Ethan said.

"They're the captains for those districts," Alannah said.

"Wouldn't this be a lot more efficient if you did it electronically?" Emily said.

"We do it electronically also, but there's power in being able to see all of it at once. You can't really do that on a 15" screen unless you zoom out to the point that it becomes meaningless. You'll see when you're here," Kohn said.

One table was staffed by four people making phone calls, one after the other. They had laptops in front of them, and the calls were generated by the computer system.

"That's high-tech," Ethan said.

"We try," Kohn said, walking over to the table and reaching into his pocket. He pulled out a handful of brass coins and dumped them on the table. They chingled pleasantly, and the phone crew looked up and smiled.

"Is that a tip?" Emily said.

Alannah laughed. "No. Well, kinda. The coins are for the Cool Room."

"The what?" Ethan said.

"This sounds like something we ought to see," Emily said.

"The only thing you have left to decide is what part of the operation you want to be part of. I need people everywhere. You're the kinds of people I'd love to have anywhere in the organization, so I'll leave it up to you,"

Kohn said, snapping off a celery stick. He leaned back in his chair and considered the twins. "Alannah is part of the vote-hunting team, but we have a specialized group that does something else you might be interested in."

"You're not going to tell us what that is?" Emily said. She took an Oreo from the pile in the middle of the table.

"Not right now, no."

"We have to decide without knowing what both options are?"

"Sometimes that's how things work. Cool Room access is much better on the vote hunting team. That's all I'm going to tell you."

Emily could see Alannah wanted her on the same squad she was a part of. But the other thing, whatever it was, sounded like it might be interesting, too. Not a simple decision.

She looked over at Ethan. "Don't look at me," he said. "I'm good with whatever. You decide, and I'll go along with it."

If you think they should take the vote-hunting job, turn to page 63.

If you think they should take the other job, whatever it is, turn to page 142.

Angela came over and sat next to Ethan. "I love this kid's fire, Cathy. He's a good egg. He's going places."

"I know. I just hope one of them isn't prison. But he's a tough kid when he believes in something."

Ethan wasn't sure whether to be flattered or insulted. His mouth was dry.

Angela chuckled and said, "But we have to take this money. As long as we can do it without pledging our immortal souls, we need the infusion of cash—more, we need the credibility that comes from getting people like this on board the Harmon campaign train. Much as I hate to admit it, there's really no choice here."

"I was afraid you were going to say that," Cathy said. "But that's what my gut tells me, too."

Ethan fumed. Had nothing he said made any sense to them? Were they ignoring him? His friend Gary? Politics again. He felt like he needed a shower.

"You're not going to like this, Ethan," Cathy said, "but you need to listen to us. We know what we're talking about when we say this is money we need. Money is life in a campaign. If you have it, you keep breathing. You stay in the fight. You give yourself a chance to make things happen, reach your goals. If you run out of money, you suffocate. You accomplish nothing."

"What can you accomplish when you've sold your soul!" Ethan said. He knew how that sounded, saw the stricken look on Aunt Cathy's face, and knew he'd gone too far. In truth, that wasn't what he'd meant to say. Not exactly. But the words were out there now, and he couldn't take them back. Deep in his gut there was a place that didn't want to take them back.

"Do you know me so little?" Cathy said. She didn't seem angry, just hurt. "Do you really think I would do that?"

"I don't know how you can avoid it," Ethan said. "Those don't seem like the kind of people who are going to hand over money without getting something in return."

"What do you think they want?" Cathy said.

"What do most people who have money want? Power."

"And how does contributing to and raising money for my campaign give them that?"

Ethan stood up. His muscles clenched and wouldn't let go. He paced back and forth like a tiger, a bitter taste in his mouth. "I don't know. I'm sure you don't want to give it to them. I didn't mean that crack about selling your soul, but doesn't it create an obligation? What's a 'steering committee' if it's not going to be steering anything?"

Angela and Cathy looked at one another. It was Angela that spoke first. "Steering committees set overall campaign strategy. They work on the look of the campaign, how it positions itself in the community. They have a lot of visible power, but not much day-to-day impact. Even if they were particularly meddlesome, we'd have a lot of latitude for action. Cathy would probably have to genuflect in their direction every few days. But mostly, they'd contact rich people and tell them to give us money, and otherwise leave us alone."

It sounded to Ethan like she was trying to talk herself into something rather than telling the bald truth.

"But the bigger point is this: if we don't take this money and get into the kinds of circles that these people can get us into, we're not going to have a campaign at all. We can't get enough money in ones and twos to make a real fight of this, especially against a fellow like Louis Sulla. He's already in the paper every day, and he'll take money from anything that moves."

"I thought you got money from Posey Sandborn," Ethan said.

"Not yet. We probably will, at some point. Some. And she's not peanuts either. But enough to make a real game of it? No. There's rich, and then there's *rich*. Posey has a few dollars, but not the kind of money these people have."

He still didn't like it. Angela made sense, but Ethan couldn't help feeling that they were walking into a trap.

"Okay," he said. "Not that you need my support anyway. I think it's a bad idea, but I'll do whatever you need me to do."

They called the two executives back into the room and told them the campaign would be delighted to have their assistance. Ethan went back down the hall to his shabby office and tried not to think about how things would change.

For a long time, they didn't. Angela came in an hour or so later, and their fundraising work went on like before. Except not. There were more lunch meetings with bigwigs, more golf, and fewer calls to personal friends and smaller contributors. Some of the things Ethan was most excited about—small-donor fundraisers and online work, cutting-edge stuff—got put on the back burner. The little guy didn't matter anymore—this was all about bigwigs.

Angela herself was delightful to work with: calm, determined, direct. She was a wealth of information about people and things, a whiz at research. She knew more about how campaigns worked than anyone Ethan had ever met. She knew how to look into databases, dig up information, find the places where the campaign could make a solid pitch and get contributions.

But even she, Ethan thought, wasn't entirely engaged. The campaign, which had started as an edgy, nontraditional counter to the politics-as-usual Sulla machine, morphed into something a lot more like a standard "We will fight for you!"-type of political operation.

But there was money. And money was life.

Primary election day came in midsummer. The papers all said it was one of the tightest races the state had ever seen. Sulla hadn't been popular in his time in the SecState seat, and there were rumblings of dissatisfaction. Negative comparisons had been made between Sulla and Forde.

The money, now, became supremely important as the campaign battle moved from the phone lines and golf courses to the airwaves. Every TV commercial break was filled up with ads for one candidate or another. Ethan mentioned this to Angela one day as they furiously worked the email lists, looking for a few more dollars.

"Yeah. It's as bad as I've ever seen it," she said. "We spent a quarter of a million dollars buying air time just this month!" She did *not* say that if they hadn't enlisted the big corporate donors, they would never have had the bullets to shoot in the first place. Ethan was glad of that.

He and Emily weren't excited about the big party at the hotel, but they had jobs to do, so they went. The campaign put them up in a fancy suite for the night, just the two of them. Mom and Dad said that after all the work that had been put in by the twins, they deserved a little time to themselves. Plus room service on the house.

Initial vote results were slow to come in—more evidence, Ethan thought, of Louis Sulla's incompetence, since as Secretary of State he was the state's chief election officer—but it was too late to make much difference now. The crowd was thick: fancy suits and fine dresses competing with t-shirts and jeans on the dance floor, waiting for the numbers.

The polls closed at 8. By 10, only 20% of the votes had been counted, and everyone agreed the race was too close to call.

"I'm going upstairs," Ethan said. "I'm really tired. This looks like it's going to take all night."

"I'll be up in a minute," Emily said. She had her political crew to hang out with, whereas Ethan had Angela, and Angela was busy keeping the steering committee happy.

The ride up in the elevator was a long one.

But a hot pastrami sandwich and fries, delivered to his door, made him feel better, and after he licked the milkshake glass clean, he almost felt like himself again.

There was a knock on the door, and a beep as someone swiped their keycard. Emily poked her head in. "You decent?" she said.

"Fully," Ethan said. "Why? You've never asked before."

She pulled the door wide, and Ethan got his answer. Aunt Cathy had come with her.

That was relatively impressive, actually, because of course she was the belle of the ball downstairs. Ethan was touched. He hadn't even seen Aunt Cathy the last couple of weeks because the schedule was so packed.

"Hey, slugger," she said. "I heard you weren't doing so well."

"I'm okay. I think I was just hungry, and I'm really tired."

Cathy took a seat in one of the overstuffed chairs arranged around the coffee table. The TV was on in the background, set to the local news, which was wrapping up its regular coverage and getting ready to move to an election special. The hotel room smelled strongly of fries, Ethan realized, and he wondered offhand when the last time was that Cathy had eaten.

"Look, you've been terrific the last couple of months," Cathy said. "I mean it. Both of you worked very hard all through the campaign, and it's been...

Well, it's been great to have you. When I first hired you, the rest of the staff was a little worried that we were giving a lot of responsibility to some pretty young kids. But I told them they had nothing to worry about, and you proved I was right. I'm grateful. Win or lose, I'm grateful to both of you."

"Thank you, Aunt Cathy," Ethan said. "We've enjoyed it, too. You're a great candidate. I hope you win tonight." Emily stood by the lamp, beaming.

"I hope *we* win tonight," Cathy said. "I want a chance to do something important for this state and carry on the legacy of Dennis Forde. If the voters can see that, we'll get the chance in November to make real change." She reached out and ruffled his hair. "You going to be okay up here?"

"You bet," Ethan said. "I'll have my eye on the results."

"Glad to hear it. I'll see you in the morning." Cathy got up, gave Emily a brief hug, and went out into the hallway. The door snicked shut behind her.

"You're a liar," Emily said. "But you're getting pretty good at it. She couldn't even tell."

"I'm okay," Ethan said. "I really am tired. But you're not wrong. Things didn't turn out the way I expected. None of this did. How does anyone in this game ever get to feel like *himself*, even for a moment? Is the playacting and the greasing and the log-rolling ever over?"

Just then, a fanfare blared from the TV's speakers, and the election special began with a pair of short cuts from each of the campaigns. Louis Sulla, looking like a

Vegas prizefighter, came on with a stump speech. "In November, we're going to do something really big in this state. The voters are looking to us to carry on the memory of Dennis Forde. And that's the most important thing to me, today and every day."

Ethan wanted to be surprised, wanted to ask Emily if there was an echo in the room. But he didn't have to—Emily had mouthed the words right along with Sulla as if she'd written them herself. And she had, only for Cathy instead. In the end, both candidates had ended up so close to the same that they were using each other's speeches.

Ethan had at least been right about one thing. It was a very long night indeed.

He even took that shower. He stood in the spray until his fingers pruned and he felt like his skin would slough off down the drain. And still, he never felt any cleaner.

THE END

Mom's scoop bit into the crumble on top of the peaches, sending curlicues of steam into the dining room air. She leaned over the pan and inhaled. A beatific smile creased her face. "Perfection," she said, "if I do say so myself."

"Smelling it is wonderful," Dad said, "but I'm hoping for something a bit more nourishing."

Ethan and Emily returned from the kitchen with bowls and spoons and ice cream. Conversation around the long oval table, tamped down a bit by the debate between Cathy's friends, resumed with a will. Heaps of peachy, sugary, creamy goodness were served out. Spoons dipped, rose. Eyes rolled back in heads. Another success.

The pan was licked clean, almost literally. It sat there in the center of the table, surrounded by the shattered remnants of dinner, and one by one everyone round the table leaned back a bit, wiped their mouths with napkins, and sighed gratefully.

Cathy was antsy, though. "You heard the arguments. What do you think?"

The Tuttles looked back and forth at one another. Some unheard communication passed between them.

Mom's face took on a satisfied look. "It's pretty obvious what you should do," she said.

"It is?"

"Completely," Dad said. "Consider Gordon's argument that Dennis wanted you to take his place."

"You think I should run for SecState?"

"Listen to what the argument actually is, Cathy. Dennis wanted you to take his place. Before, when he was SecState, that meant taking the state job. But remember he had already decided to run for Senate, and he still wanted you to take his place. So do it. Run for Senate, the way he was going to before he got sick."

Mr. Soffits furrowed his brow. "I'm not sure..."

"That does make sense," Cathy said.

"But the real argument," Emily said, "is that the action is in Washington, D.C. Miss Finn was right that all the stuff that matters to us is going on at the national level. It's where things are getting done. That's where you should be."

"It's your call, Cath," Mom said, reaching across to take her sister's hand. "But if it were up to us, we'd have you run for the big time. Take a shot at being one of a hundred. You should run for Senate."

To her credit, Miss Finn didn't gloat. "The Senate job is not going to be easy to get," she said. "I know I'm advising something that's going to be hard to accomplish. You've never been elected before, and you're not rich. You'll have to do a terrific job of fundraising."

"And you'll have opposition," Mr. Soffits said. "Randall Kohn is going to run, almost certainly. The seat's open. Senator Entwhistle is retiring. That's going to attract anyone in this state with any ambition."

Dad stuck his spoon back in his mouth, in case he missed some peach crisp molecules invisible to the naked eye. "You think Monty Burns will run? From Springfield?"

Miss Finn made a face. "He's a hundred and sixty, and looks older. I don't think he'll have the stomach for it. Anyway, Cathy would clean his clock."

"You sound very sure of yourself," Mom said. "It's going to take millions to pull this off. That kind of cash isn't going to grow on trees."

"Money *does* grow on trees," Miss Finn said. "You just have to shake them."

"This is all fascinating," Cathy said, "but I've not quite made up my mind. I'm going to think and pray about it some more, and I'll let you all know this week. Whatever I'm going to do, I have to get moving on it."

Conversation ran down, and before long the three guests got up and began making noises about getting home.

"It's a big week," Cathy said. "We've been in those offices for years. There's a lot to pack up. You wouldn't have any boxes, would you?"

Mom said she thought they did and took Cathy to check. They tromped down the stairs to the storage room.

Miss Finn came around the table to shake the twins' hands. "Good to meet you," she said. "I think we'll probably be seeing a lot of each other."

"Depends on what Aunt Cathy decides," Ethan said.

"Oh, she's decided. She's going to go with your advice. She thinks her sister is the wisest person she knows. Your opinions carry a lot of weight. So we'll need to start putting a staff together, and you'll surely get phone calls."

Mr. Soffits shook hands with Dad. "Your family is terrific. You have quite the library as well. I have many of those books myself."

"You have excellent taste, then," Dad said.

Mr. Soffits came toward the door, and Ethan opened it for him. Mr. Soffits stood there for a minute, thinking. "I'll need to make some phone calls," he said. "We'll need more than money for this. We'll need experienced people. Senate races aren't for novices. Meaning no offense to you, Ethan and Emily. Novices are good for carrying things and making phone calls. Is that something that would bother you?"

"Not a bit," Ethan said. "Assuming that on the other end of things would be a paycheck."

Cathy came up the stairs, laden with broken-down cardboard boxes, which she dumped on the first available square of floor. She handed her keys to Miss Finn. "Get the trunk open, will you?" Cathy leaned over to kiss the twins and hug Mom, picked up the boxes, and went down the walk with her guests.

The Tuttles waved her down the street.

"She's going for the Senate job," Mom said. "Barring an angelic intervention."

"I don't think even that would be enough," Dad said.

Sure enough, Wednesday of the following week, Aunt Cathy called a press conference and, flanked by the entire outgoing staff of the Secretary of State's office, announced her intention to seek the Republican nomination for the United States Senate.

There was some tepid cheering and a couple of articles on the web examining who Aunt Cathy was and commenting that she had never sought public office before.

"There's a nice quote here from Dennis' wife, Anniele," Mom said at the kitchen table, scrolling on her laptop. She picked up a piece of toast, bit into it, and replaced it on the plate. "She says she's sure Dennis would have been happy to endorse his closest friend in the office, his good right hand. Says Dennis could never have been as effective if it hadn't been for Cathy."

"That's very nice," Emily said. "She hasn't called you about hiring two enterprising young people who might be in possession of incriminating and/or embarrassing facts about her, has she?"

"Not as far as I'm aware," Mom said. "But I promise to text her if I haven't heard anything by the weekend."

It was actually the following Tuesday before Cathy called up. "I need the twins, if you can get them down here. I know they don't have a car, and that's a pain for you."

"Not a problem," Mom said. "If they're busy, I don't have to worry about what trouble they're getting into."

"Mom!" Emily said.

"Tell me where to bring them, and I'll get them there."

But when Cathy told her, Mom's face showed mixed emotions. "Okay. Tomorrow morning bright and early."

"What is it, Mom?" Ethan said, coming into the kitchen in search of an apple.

"This is a pretty swanky address," Mom said. "Office space in this complex must cost around our annual mortgage payment. I wonder how she can afford it."

"She's a shoo-in for the Senate, Mom," Emily said. "She's probably got donors lined up around the block."

"I thought I had donors lined up around the block," Cathy said, shaking her head. Her laptop was open in front of her, glowing softly. Around the table were arrayed the campaign's top brass—Pearl Hancock, the campaign director; Martin Abaticio, the political director; Miss Finn, the field director in charge of volunteers and vote hunting; and so on. Gordon Soffits, in what Emily would have sworn was the same outfit he wore to dinner a month before, sat back from the table in a chair by the wall, doing something on a clipboard.

"What's the damage?" Hancock said. To Cathy's right, Nora Oporto, the campaign accountant/finance director, clacked on her own laptop.

"We have enough in the bank for another month if we don't run any TV ads," she said.

"We're not going to last long without TV ads," Abaticio said. He had a stapled bundle of papers in front of him and periodically made a mark on them in red pen.

It was a pretty great place for a meeting, Emily had to admit. The tall windows along one entire wall arched above them, letting in copious natural light. Two of the other three walls were glass, allowing a view of the open office with its deep green carpet and cherrywood trim.

Everything gleamed. It was the nicest office she'd ever been in. But was the rent killing them?

"There's not really anywhere we can cut costs," Cathy said. "We've been over it a dozen times. We have big players in this race, and we have to match them—or exceed them—if we're going to have any chance to get into a primary, let alone win the nomination."

Ethan wondered if that were true. Wouldn't the fancy office just tell everyone they were the same as the other guys? Would it make it harder to stick to principles if those principles cost them big donations? Was this just something all politicians had to do—or was it a sign that Aunt Cathy wasn't who they thought she was?

"We can't outspend Kohn. That's for sure," Oporto said. "He can write checks forever, any time he needs another infusion of cash."

"Voters are responding to your message," Miss Finn said. "We don't have any trouble getting pledges to vote for you. We've got a good army of volunteers. I feel pretty confident that if we can get your message out there a little more aggressively we have a solid chance."

That was Emily's thought as well. She'd been out with Miss Finn knocking on doors, learning the ropes for how to collect votes and finding places to put signs. People liked Cathy once they knew about her. They just didn't know much about her. And if they had to make that happen with volunteer door-knockers, there was no way they could do it. They could knock until their knuckles were raw, and they'd never get to even a decent fraction of the people in the state.

Phones could help—and she was making phone calls now too—but only so much. They needed mass communication, and that took money. Lots and lots and lots of money.

More than one person had by now suggested they downsize offices. But the PR people were adamant—the press would see that as a sign of a tanking campaign. And then everyone else would, too. "If the press weren't so powerful..." they said, but it was—or they thought it was, and in Cathy's campaign that amounted to the same thing.

"Our small donations are pretty robust," Oporto said. "But we can't onesie-twosie this thing. We need committee money, and we need PAC money. We need money from Washington."

"And we were going to get it," Cathy said. "I had solid commitments from when Pearl and I went back there in May. But when Kohn got into the race, those commitments wavered. They got put on hold. I understand it even though I don't like it. With both of us in the race, they have to hedge their bets."

"Can we go back there and ask again?" Oporto said. "Because I'm not going to dance around this thing—without a major cash infusion, we have at best a couple of weeks left before people don't have jobs anymore."

"Well, there are some big fundraisers planned. We have the dinner this weekend at the Ritz Hotel, where we expect a large group of donors at $200 a plate. Then we have a mailing to likely donors that went out..."

Cathy looked down the table at Pam Werth, the communications director.

"Yesterday," Werth said.

Just barely, Emily thought. Her tongue was still raw from licking envelopes. But they got it done in time to make the mail.

"Those should hit tomorrow, and we should start seeing replies the first of next week," Wertz said. "And there's the social media advertising campaigns that are just ramping up."

"Tell me more about that," Cathy said.

"Well, we're running ads on those platforms that allow it. We're tweeting and posting and commenting all over the place. Our street team—those are volunteers watching the social media channels—is engaged."

Cathy frowned. "But. I hear a 'but' in there someplace."

"We don't control the platforms. The social media companies do. They can—not saying they will—shut

down our channels if they want to. They own the medium, and everyone on it is there on their sufferance. They could decide we're 'disruptive' or even 'dangerous.' And if they did, we'd be cut off. There are precedents."

"With *presidents*, yes, I know," Cathy said. "That's a lot of power. Who's to say that 'disruptive' doesn't just mean 'telling the truth when we don't want to hear it'? Who's then to stop their simply pushing their own narrative and pretending it's 'fair'?"

Wertz started to say something, but Cathy waved her down. "No, no, I understand what you're saying. For now, though, you're telling me we're getting traction on social media?"

"Except that those channels are currently draining cash," Oporto said. "They might be spreading the message, but they aren't paying for themselves."

Cathy twisted her face this way and that, considering. "I could go back to D.C.," she said. "Maybe being there would shake loose the funds I was promised."

Hancock scribbled on a legal pad for a second and said, "Look, people, the truth is we've got to do everything we can, right now. All the angles. All the options. If we're going to succeed, we need to try anything that might work. I'd much rather go out with my boots on, calling and asking, rather than curling up into a ball and getting squeezed to death a little at a time. Everyone get me?"

Nods from up and down the table. Emily liked Hancock. She was a blood-and-guts battleaxe, at least sixty years old, with steel gray hair and a voice like a chainsaw. If anyone could get the campaign into the next gear, she could.

"Then get to work," she said. "Make these two sweat for their money." She winked at the twins. They smiled back. If you were on her good side, she was one of the coolest people in the world. Heaven help the ones who got on her bad side though. As bad sides went, it was Genghis Khan.

The office was a flurry of activity all the rest of that day. Emily was called on for everything from making a phone call to ordering lunch to carrying boxes of letterhead up to the communications office. When Dad arrived to take the twins home, Emily nearly collapsed into the front seat of the car. Ethan slumped into the back seat and lay down across the whole width of the car.

"That bad, huh?" Dad said.

"No, that good," Emily said. "We're busy. We're trying to save things."

Dad pulled smoothly away from the curb. "Is it going to work?"

"It has to," Ethan said. "We don't have enough saved up yet to pay the insurance for a car."

And it looked, for a good while, that it would.

The fundraising dinner wasn't a huge success, but it brought in tens of thousands to the campaign. The mailer was successful at nearly the same level. And the reports from Washington were encouraging, as Hancock and Aunt Cathy made what they called the "Hail Mary" trip.

But there was too much Randall Kohn. His campaign was all over the airwaves, social media, billboards, everywhere. The twins could hardly open their computers without seeing something from the opposition.

And then the phone calls came. Aunt Cathy spent half a day in her office, closeted with Hancock and Oporto, as it became clear that the Washington trip had failed to produce any significant money.

Back in the spacious and beautiful boardroom, Cathy gathered the staff and made her announcement.

"We're going to suspend the campaign," she said, her voice heavy with fatigue.

Shouts of dismay, denial, defiance. She waited for them to subside then continued in precisely the same voice. "We can't continue. Oh, we have a few thousand in the bank, enough to pay everyone for the rest of the month. But we're not gaining ground. Kohn is pulling away from us, and he will continue to do that."

"You are ten times the candidate he is," Miss Finn said. She pounded the glossy table with the flat of her hand, making the wood vibrate.

"Twenty," Cathy said, with a wry smile. "Unfortunately, he has fifty times the money we do, and that's not going to change. He leads us in every possible metric. He commands the airwaves, has the ground staff and connections to Washington bigwigs, and has donors coming out of his ears. And in a pinch, he just writes a check and boom, done."

The only sound for a long moment was the quiet whirring of the air conditioning vents.

"It isn't fair," Ethan said.

"Well, who said life is fair? Where is that written?" Cathy said. "I know what you mean, Ethan, but our political system isn't built on 'fair.' It's built on getting votes. There's a very popular myth—no, that's not fair—an almost-myth that given the right organization, unlimited hard work, and a little luck, a no-name campaign can break through and win. It has happened. I thought it would happen this time. This organization is top-notch. It's the best I've ever worked with. So it isn't that."

"Don't say it's the candidate," Hancock said. "Or I'll throw you out these lovely arched windows." She sat with her back to the glass wall, her arms folded and her face dark and thunderous.

"Okay, I'll skip that part of my speech. But we also need luck. We need a misstep from Kohn. A break. A big influx of cash or a broad movement in the state. We aren't going to get them. Kohn is a good candidate. He's smart, he's clean, and he's rich. Even if I were Eleanor Roosevelt, I couldn't do much against that." She sighed and took a long look around at the office. "Big risk, big expense, big weight to carry around. Maybe I listened too closely to the wrong advisers when it came to this place."

Miss Finn broke in again. "But the first round is in three weeks! We might pull a surprise. Then the money would come in for the primary. Campaign limits would be lifted."

"For him as well as for us." Cathy shook her head. "No, we've looked at it from every angle. We're not going to pull it off. Keeping everyone around for another few weeks, only to get beat 75-25 in the primary, isn't fair to anyone. So we're going to shut it down. I'll be announcing that in a press conference later today. It's a done deal, ladies and gentlemen."

She swallowed, took a deep breath.

"I can't thank you enough. We did good work here. I think we raised some issues that Kohn will have to deal with. He'll have to address government reform in ways he wouldn't have otherwise needed to. He will have to confront relations between the police and the black community—that's not an issue that's going away, and Dennis Forde would be proud we carried on his work on that, even brought some national attention to it. Kohn will have to bend on education and taxes and immigration and a whole host of other issues. We accomplished some things. And I think we represented the memory of Dennis Forde in the best way we could. I don't think he would have been disappointed at what we've done. You are all my favorite people on earth." She paused to let her eyes sweep across every face in the room, lingering for just a moment on each one.

"Enough of that. We have packing to do. There are people we need to talk to and prepare for what's coming. Please don't leak this beforehand. And I want you all to stand with me at the press conference, if you will."

"Try and stop me," Hancock said. She stood up, all 5' 2" of her, and wrapped Aunt Cathy in a rib-crushing hug.

Mom and Dad came down for the press conference and had a minute to wrap their arms around Cathy and whisper a few words in her ear.

The car was quiet as they drove home. Emily thought about the funeral trip that had touched the whole thing off. That had felt a lot like this, actually. It was the death of something beautiful, something people had wanted to have last a little longer. She found that she was exhausted physically and emotionally, and hadn't thought that it would affect her quite so much.

Good people should be able to make a difference. And they could—she was still sure they could—but it was much, much harder than she had thought. Over dinner, people would say things like "why don't they just..." and "all we need is..." and "I don't see why it's so hard to..." but they didn't know. They hadn't tried. Emily had now, and she realized that it was going to take a lot more than earnest intent and self-righteousness to move the process in a positive direction. Maybe instead of campaigning, she needed to work on the system itself, the one that had taken a good woman like Aunt Cathy, sucked her in and chewed her up. And spat her out. Emily wondered what kind of person could avoid having that happen. Politics was so *big*. Even figuring out where to start was beyond her.

There would be work to do, no doubt. She would figure it out and start again, somewhere else, with some new project. But not today.

It was going to be a long, hot summer, and all she wanted was to sleep.

THE END

Angela stood for a moment by the door, her lined face acquiring new creases. Then she said, "No, Cath, I can't do it. Heaven knows I want to get paid, and everyone else along with me. It's no secret that I love money and all the things it does. But I can't go along with this. Even if we're just using them to get what we want while they're trying to use us to get what they want, I can't do it. It feels dirty. I don't like them. And I can't believe we'll be able to appeal to the right people—the people Dennis appealed to—if we're in league with them. Sorry. That's my gut reaction here."

"Which is great. But I need a promise. Or are you telling me to give the whole thing up?"

For a long moment—a *long* moment—Angela and Ethan simply looked at one another, sharing another wordless conversation.

Finally Ethan couldn't stand it anymore. "We can do it." He was emphatic, fists on his knees, pounding. "We can. I promise you we can."

Cathy said, "It's not *your* promise I—"

"I promise you as well," Angela said. Her voice was quiet, but hard as an overcooked steak. "We can do it. You tell us how much we need, and we'll get it."

Cathy blew out a breath and sat back on her couch. She and Miss Finn exchanged a quick glance, and a slow smile broke out on Cathy's face. "I was hoping you'd say that. Ethan, will you go get our guests? Then I think you and Angela have work to do. I'll break the news to them. Yes, people, I'll be gentle."

Angela jerked her head toward the door, and the two of them went out. Ethan was on his best behavior, inviting the two guests back to the office and asking them if there was anything he could get them.

"You did that without a trace of irony," Angela said. "I'm going to need to watch you more carefully from now on, I believe."

"What do we do now?" Ethan said. "My gut says, 'Yeah, we did it!' and my head says, 'Crap, we sure did it this time!' And I'm not sure which one I should be listening to."

Angela opened the battered door to their little office and grabbed her keys out of her purse. "First thing we're going to do is go over to the park with whoever wants to join us. If we're going to do this, we need fresh air and sunshine."

They went through the office asking for people who needed a break and some park time. Surprisingly, there were half a dozen people—including Emily—who said they thought the park for an hour or two sounded perfect. One of them had a frisbee, too.

"Great," Angela said. "I do my best thinking by frisbee."

So the eight of them went to the park and chucked the frisbee around, kicking around ideas about ways to raise money and get awareness that would neither break the bank nor look just like what everyone else had done before them.

"Dennis didn't have to get too creative because he was the first person of color to run for high office in this state, and that all by itself earned him as much media as he could use. Cathy doesn't have that going for her," Angela said. She snagged the frisbee with one hand, pivoted, and threw a perfect underhand strike to Reggie at the far end of the circle.

"Whoa," Ethan said.

Angela winked. "I wasn't always fifty years old, son."

The rule was, if you caught the frisbee, it was your turn to talk. And you better have something interesting to say. So Reggie said, "Isn't Cathy the first woman to run for that office?"

"No, sadly," Angela said, "There was another one twenty years back. We can't use that."

Ethan raised an eyebrow at Emily. Her face was set in a hard line. Identity politics—was that always the first thing political hacks went for? First woman this, first person of color that? What about the candidate's *ideas*? What about whether they were good people who did the right thing?

"How good is Dennis Forde's name ID?" Emily said. She had to jog three paces to her left to catch the throw from Reggie. Angela waved for the disk. "Dennis? Good. Most people recognize his name. Not everyone, of course, but 70%, maybe. And he's got 100% name recognition among those people who are likely to actually cast votes for SecState in the primary."

"How many is that?" Beth from accounting said. She looked very funny out there in her blouse and skirt, but she had no trouble catching the frisbee when it came her way, and her throws were low and flat.

"Two hundred thousand, give or take." Angela snagged the disk left-handed this time and threw backhand over to Meg, another deadly accurate throw.

"We could just give each of those people five bucks and tell them to vote for us. That's pretty cheap for a campaign like this." Meg was terrible at throwing. Her tosses were high and angled, and almost came down back at her feet. Ethan sprinted after it and just missed.

"I don't think we'll be allowed to bribe people," he said. But he checked with Angela, just a glance.

"No, that's illegal," she said, "but while we're brainstorming, all ideas are good ideas."

Emily couldn't hold back. "Aren't we just talking about buying votes anyway, even though it's not with a check? Promise people this or that, talk about how we're going to 'fight for them' or something equally meaningless, and get them to stampede the polls? It's like a colonial election where you go to a tavern, buy the people drinks, then put them in a wagon and take them to the polls."

Meg stared. "People did that?"

"*Everybody* did that," Ethan said, jogging back to the group. "Well, not everyone. James Madison wouldn't, so he lost a lot."

"Also he was short," Angela said. "Never a good thing in politics."

Emily glared at her.

Angela put up her hands in mock surrender. "Hey, hey. I'm not defending it. The guy did go on to become president, so it's not insurmountable."

"Don't we want this to be different, though, our campaign? Isn't there some way to focus on the issues instead of tossing candy from the campaign float?" Emily said.

"Hey! Campaign float!" Beth said. "Except we don't have the budget."

"Ideas are great, but they need friends," Angela said. "And friends are made with visibility and effort. Cathy can be the second coming of, well, James Madison, but unless we can get that message to people, she will lose. That's just how it works."

They tossed the disk for another half hour before the sun got to be a bit warm, though it was obvious to Ethan that Angela could go on all day. Maybe they'd have to have their meetings at the park from now on.

The ideas had come thick and fast—phone banks, campaign chain letters, Rolodex letters, email lists, Travelocity ads, all kinds of things. Ethan couldn't keep track of even a small fraction of them, but there was one he liked, and he liked it a lot—the shark fin.

It started with Reggie, who wanted to order a pizza when he saw a Fat Jack's Pizza delivery car go by with its car-top sign.

Angela rejected the pizza idea—"We're on a budget, people" she said, with a nod to the approving Beth—but as they went back to the office, Ethan started thinking about what that would look like if there were a few thousand cars all over the state sporting not old and tired bumper stickers, but flashy car-tops. Like mobile yard signs. But it wouldn't be enough just to put the signs up. They could dress the shape of them to make a point. Aunt Cathy was tough. She was quiet, but she was deadly to government waste and corruption. A shark, cruising the state Capitol. Government greed beware.

"Ooh!" When the idea for that tagline hit him, Ethan couldn't keep from gasping.

"What?" Angela tossed her keys into her purse and rolled her shoulders.

"What's our campaign tagline?"

"Um. Something about 'The Right Woman for the Job.'"

"Does the fact that you can't remember it make you just a bit concerned that it might not be right for us?"

"How can you be opposed to the right woman for the job?" she said. "No, no. Don't answer that. I see what you mean. Spill. You're on to something."

Ethan laid out the whole idea as it sat in his head, fully-formed. Angela listened to every word, making an occasional note. When he was done, she sat back in her chair and lifted her eyes to the ceiling. "You're talking about interfering with every part of this campaign from the ground up. Total redesign. Color, messaging, everything. That's not *saving* us money."

"But think about it," Ethan said, leaning forward. He could hardly sit still. "If we keep going the way we are, we have to repeat our message fifty times to get it to stick, because, no offense, it's boring. Nobody can remember it. What does Aunt Cathy stand for? Nobody knows. No one remembers when she tells them because it's the same as everyone else. So to cut through that we need lots and lots of money. But we don't have lots and lots of money. So no one will remember and we'll lose. Or we can redesign right now to something people will be talking about for years. Something that grabs them, makes them pay attention. Something—"

"Sleek and dangerous. The kind of thing you need to keep a dirty ocean clean. That weeds out things that don't belong there. The woman with a purpose, and teeth enough to make it happen."

"Quiet, but always there. Fearless. The perfect watchdog. Never sleeps. And true to the legacy of Dennis Forde—the reason Cathy started this whole thing."

"The hair on my arms is standing up!" Angela stood, feeling resolute. "This is above my pay grade. But we need to do this. We need to do it right now." Her phone buzzed. "See if Cathy's free for ten minutes. I have to take this call."

Ethan slipped into the hall, but not before he heard Angela say, "Posey. Glad you called. We just told the biggest money in the state to go jump in a lake. You need to send us a check. Right now."

The signs, a deep sea-green and black, like the stripes on a tiger shark, began appearing a week later. At first, they cost a lot of money—almost fifty dollars apiece—so they couldn't manufacture very many of them. But Meg came up with a way to cut the price to $5 of cheap corrugated plastic and a couple of bungee cords. Almost overnight they were everywhere.

"Chumming," they started calling the process of finding people to put signs on their cars. It took very little persuading, as it happened. Because these things were *cool.*

"Harmon" in white. "Greed beware" in lemon yellow underneath, on a deep green background shot through with lighter stripes, the filtering of sunlight through water. The sign itself was in the shape of a shark fin. Once you saw it, you couldn't stop seeing it.

The hashtag #greedbeware trended on social media at one point, the campaign was so popular. Cathy ran another promotion where she rented out all the municipal pools in the state and invited people to come and watch *Jaws* while sitting in tubes on the water. The show started with a two-minute message from Cathy and ended with so much media coverage Cathy couldn't get out from in front of a camera for three days.

A week before the election, they finally shot an ad. It ran for only one day. The message was this: I'm not just frugal. I'm ruthless. When I was on Dennis Forde's staff, I learned to see *any* instance of waste as a betrayal of the taxpayer. It's a waste of your money. I don't waste money, and I don't let other people waste it. This is the only ad I'm going to run. You're welcome.

Meg came dancing down the hall the day after the ad ran. "Donations are up," she said.

"Good," Angela said. "That's very nice."

"No, you don't get it. People were so refreshed by not being bombarded by ads that they sent us money *because we didn't ask them to*. We're seeing donations from everywhere. Someone posted the ad on VidNow backed by a soundalike *Jaws* theme. It exploded! 250,000 views just in the last 24 hours. We have money, people. Real money!"

Street sharks—as Ethan called them—cruised back and forth on the city streets, giving each other a beep of solidarity when they passed. The *Washington Times* ran a piece on innovative marketing, talking about the cutting-edge tactics of the Harmon campaign, finishing with "Louis Sulla's yard signs cower, staying rooted to land while Harmon's sharks cruise by just offshore, looking for something to gnaw. Probably best they don't get in the water. It wouldn't be safe. Greed beware."

But it wasn't until some joker made a car-top out of a Sulla campaign sign, with half of it missing from a shark bite, that they knew they were going to win. That piece of tomfoolery went viral in two ways: one on the web, and the other on cars, where people put the two car-toppers together, the shark chasing Sulla.

The primary had record turnout, and most of it went to Aunt Cathy. She held her victory press conference at the local aquarium. In front of the shark tank, of course. They donated all the money from the event to the aquarium. "I feel pretty safe doing that. After all, my friends here behind me can keep an eye on the books." The press ate that up.

The other political party had a nominee as well, but nobody paid any attention to him. Except to put his yard signs on their cars. With big bites out of them.

Cathy came to Sunday dinner the week before her inauguration to the Secretary of State position. She brought Mr. Soffits and Miss Finn again. Plus Angela, because Ethan insisted.

"It's not every boss that would put trust in a crackpot idea from some teenager and decide to totally revamp their entire operation around it. Angela is like a minor goddess as far as I'm concerned," Ethan said, peeling potatoes for the roast.

"A minor goddess?" Mom said, bedecking the huge pork shoulder with rosemary.

"Yeah, like the Greek goddess *Ate*. Nobody knows her, but she's the goddess of mischief and delusion. You better take care of her, or things could get ugly."

The dinner was a festival of conviviality. Toward the end, Cathy rose and proposed a toast to Angela and Ethan, "The architects of the weirdest political campaign since Warren G. Harding campaigned from his front porch."

Blank looks. "Come on, people," Cathy said. "Don't nobody learn no history no more?" Exasperated, she waved a hand at Emily.

Who smiled and said, "Warren G. Harding, twenty-ninth president of the US, elected in 1920 in a campaign during which he refused to make any speeches except

from his front porch. Won the largest share of the popular vote since the two-party system came about."

Ethan couldn't let Emily show off by herself. "And chose Calvin Coolidge for Veep, which gave us the only president in history to ever make the government budget *shrink* during his administration."

Lots of looking about and eyebrow-raising. Mr. Soffits shrugged, looking disappointed. Maybe not the time for a history lesson, then.

Cathy sighed and raised her glass. "Angela and all the rest are better than steak and eggs."

Cheers and laughter this time. After a suitable interval, Angela waved them away. "We had a promise to keep. That's all it was."

Mr. Soffits said, "Don't underestimate the power of a promise. It's what started this whole thing. And I personally think Dennis would be pleased it's worked out this well."

"I've been thinking about my office decor," Cathy said, sipping at her juice. "I think aquariums are nice, don't you?"

THE END

The Author

Connor Boyack is founder and president of Libertas Institute, a free market think tank in Utah. In that capacity he has changed dozens of laws in favor of personal freedom and free markets, and has launched a variety of educational projects, including The Tuttle Twins children's book series. Connor is the author of over two dozen books.

A California native and Brigham Young University graduate, Connor currently resides in Lehi, Utah, with his wife and two children.

The Illustrator

Elijah Stanfield is owner of Red House Motion Imaging, a media production company in Washington.

A longtime student of Austrian economics, history, and the classical liberal philosophy, Elijah has dedicated much of his time and energy to promoting the ideas of free markets and individual liberty. Some of his more notable works include producing eight videos in support of Ron Paul's 2012 presidential candidacy. He currently resides in Richland, Washington, with his wife April and their six children.